FAE Core

# Corporate and Individual Tax Planning (RoI)

## 2016–2017

Chartered
Accountants
Ireland

Published in 2016 by
Chartered Accountants Ireland
Chartered Accountants House
47–49 Pearse Street
Dublin 2
www.charteredaccountants.ie

ISBN  978-1-910374-58-0

Typeset by Deanta Global Publishing Services
Printed by CPI Group (UK) Ltd, Croydon, CR0 4YY

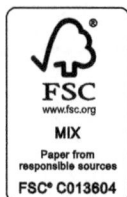

FSC
www.fsc.org
MIX
Paper from
responsible sources
FSC® C013604

# Contents

# Trading as a Sole Trader

**Learning Objectives**

By the end of this chapter you will be able to:

■ Analyse the potential tax implications for a business trading as an unincorporated entity, with particular reference to the following:

● definition of a trade;
● commencement rules;
● optimum use of losses in the start-up years;
● advantages and disadvantages of operating as a sole trader;
● understanding the issues to be considered before incorporation.

■ Understand the restriction on tax reliefs for "high earner" individuals.

## 1.1 Life Cycle of a Business

A business will always have a life cycle. This cycle may last for many generations of owners, and in other cases may be significantly shorter. The typical life cycle of a business can be separated into the following phases:

■ start-up of the business;
■ growth of the business;
■ maturity of the business; and
■ decline/sale/handover of the business.

The challenges faced by the owners and management of a business during the varying stages of the life cycle are different, as are the tax issues which can arise. It is unlikely that a well-established business will be faced with tax commencement and assessment issues. Thus, the advice required by the owners/management depends on what stage of the life cycle their business is at.

While a company may be built on a solid foundation, the tax advice given in its early years is crucial to the efficient management of its tax affairs. A business can be operated by means of either a limited liability company or a sole trader. The tax implications of operating under either structure must be considered separately.

## 1.2    What is a "Trade"?

In most cases, Irish businesses operate either through limited liability companies or as sole traders. Sole trade businesses are typically small business operations, primarily because, as a trade grows and expands, the likelihood that a trade would be transferred to a limited company becomes more probable. This is generally for commercial reasons, and not just tax reasons. Often in the early years, however, there are no particular commercial or tax requirements to operate a trade through a limited company and, in such cases, traders will operate as sole traders. While this chapter focuses on the tax issues for sole traders only, students should be aware that the commentary in **Sections 1.3**, **1.5**, **1.6** and **1.7** are equally applicable to companies.

The question "Does a trade exist?" may often arise. The answer can often impact significantly on the subsequent tax implications. You will have already addressed this in your earlier studies and should revise the key points. A brief outline of the issues to be considered is set out below.

Over the years, this "trade" question has given rise to a significant body of case law. In general, the rate of income tax is much higher than, for example, the rate of capital gains tax (CGT). Consider the following questions:

- Is an isolated transaction that gives rise to a profit to the vendor a "trade" for tax purposes, or indeed liable to tax at all?
- Is the disposal of a refurbished house by a part-time builder liable to income tax or capital gains tax?

The Taxes Consolidation Act 1997 (TCA 1997) contains all relevant tax legislation in respect of income tax, corporation tax and CGT. Section 3(1) TCA 1997 describes a trade as including "every trade, manufacture, adventure or concern in the nature of a trade". It can often be difficult to establish if a particular activity constitutes trading, taking into account the above legislative definition of a trade. Guidance as to what constitutes a trade must also therefore be taken from case law. A trade will typically take on the generally accepted meaning. More specific and practical guidance can be found in the UK Royal Commission *Badges of Trade Rules*. The badges of trade concept has been covered as part of your CA Proficiency 1 studies and students should be familiar with these trading criteria.

---

**Key Issue**

Students should revise the **badges of trade rules**. These rules can be critical in understanding whether or not a trade exists for tax purposes. In summary, the badges of trade factors to be taken into account in determining if a trade exists consist of the following:

- subject matter realised;
- length of the period of ownership;
- frequency of the number of transactions;
- supplementary work on or in conjunction with the property realised;
- circumstances giving rise to the realisation of property; and
- motive for the transaction.

---

If a taxpayer were to operate on the mistaken basis that a trade did *not* exist, the implications of such a position being challenged could lead to significant tax liabilities.

Students will not be expected to know all relevant case law. A review of applicable case law could, however, assist your understanding of what a "trade" is for tax purposes.

## 1.3    When does the Trade Commence?

The date on which a trade commences is a question of fact, being the set of circumstances applicable to that particular trade/activity. There is a significant body of case law in this area that can be used as the basis for establishing when a trade commences. For example, in the UK case *Birmingham and District Cattle By Products Ltd v. IRC* (1919), it was held that the trade commenced when the company first received raw materials for processing. The activities undertaken by the company prior to receipt of its stock, in this case being a significant outlay in respect of machinery/infrastructure, was held not to constitute the commencement of a trade.

It is worth noting that sales do not have to have been made for a trade to have commenced. In certain cases, therefore, the date on which the trade commences is not always clear and will require consideration.

## 1.4    Commencement Rules: Basis of Assessment for Income Tax Purposes

The commencement rules will determine the income tax liability of profits in the first three years of a new trade. It is assumed that the student is familiar with the commencement rules, but in summary, they are as follows:

- **Year 1 (First Year)**
  In the first year of trading, the Case I profits liable to income tax will be those taken from the date of commencement to 31 December of that year.
- **Year 2 (Second Year)**
  In the second year of trading, the Case I profits liable to income tax will be computed by reference to the following criteria:

  - if there is a 12-month period of accounts ending in the second year, which is the only accounting period in that year, the profits liable to income tax will be the profits of that 12-month accounting period; **or**
  - if there is an accounting period ending in the second year of trading, and the period is **less** than 12 months and is the only accounting period ending in that second year, the profits liable to income tax will be for a 12-month period ending on that accounting date; **or**
  - if there are two or more accounting periods ending in the second year of trading, the profits liable to income tax will be for the 12-month period ending on the latest accounting date; **or**
  - where none of the above apply, the taxable accounting period in the second year of trading will be from 1 January to 31 December.
- **Year 3 (Third Year)**
  In the third year of trading, the profits liable to income tax will be the profits of the 12-month accounting period ending in that third year. The third-year profits liable to income tax may be reduced if a second-year "excess" arises. This excess is the amount of profits liable to income tax in the second year less the actual profits that arose. Put simply, actual profits are profits that arise between January and December.

---

**Example 1.1: Commencement rules**

John Ryan commenced his sole trade printing business on 1 May 2015. He has prepared his first set of accounts up to 30 April 2016, being his first 12 months of trading.

John's taxable profit in his first year is €120,000 and he plans to change his accounting date to November, and confidently predicts profits of €200,000 in the short period ending 30 November 2016. Year 3 profits for the 12-month period up to 30 November 2017 are projected to be €220,000.

John's accountant has told him that his commencement profits liable to tax will be computed as follows (using the projected figures provided):

*First Year* – 2015

Period 1 May 2015 to 31 December 2015
€120,000 × 8/12                                  €80,000

*Second Year* – 2016

There are two accounting period ends in 2016. The Year 2 rules state that, where there are two accounting periods ending in the year, the taxable profits will be based on the 12-month period ending on the later accounting period end.

|  | € |
|---|---|
| April 2016 y/e €120,000 × 5/12 | 50,000 |
| 1 May 2016 to 30 November 2016 | 200,000 |
| Total profits liable to tax in 2016 | 250,000 |

*Third Year* – 2017

The profits liable to income tax in the third year of commencement will be the profits arising in the 12-month period up to 30 November 2017.

1 December 2016 to 30 November 2017          €220,000*

*There is, however, provision that the third-year assessable profits can be reduced by the second-year excess.

The second year excess is computed as follows:

| Profits assessed in second year | € | € |
|---|---|---|
| vs actual profit (Jan to Dec) |  | 250,000 |
| 1 January 2016 to 30 April 2016 | 40,000 |  |
| 1 May 2016 to 30 Nov 2016 | 200,000 |  |
| 1 December 2016 to 31 December 2016 |  |  |
| €220,000 × 1/12 | 18,333 | 258,333 |
| Year 2 excess |  | n/a |

As the actual profits in the second year are higher than the profits assessed, there is no second-year excess and therefore no adjustment. If the actual profits arising in 2016 were less than €250,000, then the excess would be deducted from the 2017 taxable profits in Year 3.

---

In the vast majority of cases, a sole trader will not have a high expectation of profits in the early years of trading, the likehood being trading losses occurring. The commencement rules will therefore compute the Case I losses arising from the trade. The critical issue is that, if the individual has any other income, the losses arising in the trade can be utilised to reduce the individual's total taxable income. This issue will be discussed in **Section 1.8**.

## 1.5    Pre-trading Expenditure

As mentioned above (**Section 1.3**) the actual date on which a trade commences is not always clear. The basis of assessment for the commencement rules also needs to be considered.

> **Key Issue**
> Students should ensure that they are familiar with all computational rules and, if required, be in a position to prepare a tax computation.

Expenditure incurred in the period prior to commencement may not always be considered deductible for tax purposes. Section 82 TCA 1997 considers the possible tax deductions for pre-trading expenditure incurred by a trader. Expenditure that is revenue in nature (i.e. not capital such as buildings, plant, etc.) incurred within three years prior to commencement of trading may be deductible for tax purposes (despite the fact that the expenditure may not be reflected in the profit and loss account of the period).

The following are the necessary conditions in order for pre-trading expenditure relief to apply:

- The expense is allowable as a deductible expense, and would not be otherwise considered as not being deductible. It must also be related to that trade/activity.
- The expense can only be set-off against the income of that trade or profession, and not be set-off against any other income of the trader.

> **Example 1.2: Pre-trading expenditure**
> On further examination of John Ryan's records, you find that he incurred some costs prior to setting up his business. He informs you that the following costs were incurred before trading commenced on 1 May 2015:
>
> - He spent €5,000 on a feasibility study carried out by a printing industry expert in March 2012.
> - He spent €3,000 in total on attending the printing industry conference. It is held every June in Killarney, so he attended in June 2012, 2013 and 2014.
> - He spent €2,000 on a laptop in September 2013. Before trading commenced, he only used it for material in relation to his printing business. He still uses it.
>
> You point out to him that he can claim additional relief as follows:
>
> - He can't claim for the feasibility study – the expenditure was incurred more than three years before he started to trade.
> - The conference costs are all allowable under the wholly and exclusively test.
> - The cost of the laptop is not allowable as a Case I deduction as it is capital expenditure.
>   He can, however, claim normal wear and tear allowances on this item of plant and machinery.
>
> In summary, he can claim an additional €3,000 as a trading deduction for the period ended 30 April 2016, as well as additional capital allowances of €250.

## 1.6 Start-up Relief for Long-term Unemployed

Section 6 Finance (No. 2) Act 2013 introduced a relief from income tax for long-term unemployed individuals who start a new business. The relief provides an exemption from income tax on profits up to a maximum of €40,000 per annum for a period of two years to individuals who set up a qualifying business. Immediately prior to the commencement of the business, the individual must have been unemployed for 12 months or more and have been in receipt of an unemployment payment from the Department of Social Protection or have been on a Government training course.

The business must be set up between 25 October 2013 and 31 December 2016 and must be a new unincorporated business (trade or profession) and not an existing business that is acquired. The relief does not extend to USC or PRSI.

The amount of relief in Year 1 depends on when the new business started. If the new business starts on 1 January, the cap is the maximum of €40,000 (i.e. basis period for first-year commencement is 1 January to 31 December and therefore covers 12 months). If the new business starts later in the year, the cap is reduced proportionately according to the month of commencement. For example, if the commencement date is 1 April, the cap is €30,000 (i.e. €40,000 × 9/12). The relief therefore operates as follows:

- Year 1 – profits are relieved from income tax where they are less than the cap (€40,000 or less as adjusted where required).
- Year 2 – profits are relieved from income tax where they are less than the €40,000 cap.
- Year 3 – profits for any part of this year that fall within the first 24 months of business are relieved if they are less than the cap.

Where a business starts on 1 January, then the two years' (24 months') relief is utilised in Year 1 and Year 2 and there is no relief available for Year 3. Where a business starts later in the year, then there is still some relief available for Year 3.

---

**Example 1.3:**

Kieran Murphy commences a new business as a frozen foods distributor on 1 March 2016. His accounts are prepared to 31 December each year. His adjusted profits are:

| | |
|---|---|
| For the 10 months up to 31 December 2016 | €40,000 |
| For the year to 31 December 2017 | €55,000 |
| For the year to 31 December 2018 | €45,000 |

*Year 1 Relief*

The business commenced on 1 March, therefore relief is €33,333 (€40,000 x 10/12).

*Year 2 Relief*

The first €40,000 is relieved, leaving €15,000 taxable.

*Year 3 Relief*

Since there are two months left within the first 24 months, then the cap for those two months that can be relieved is €40,000 x 2/12 = €6,667.

The total amount relieved from income tax is therefore:

| | |
|---|---|
| 2016 | €33,333 |
| 2017 | €40,000 |
| 2018 | €6,667 |
| Total | €80,000 |

A charge to PRSI and USC will arise as normal on the above profits.

---

## 1.7 Expenditure not Deductible for Income Tax Purposes

The following expenditure, while often included in the profit and loss for accounting purposes, is specifically not deductible for the purposes of the tax computation (i.e. it is added back):

- any expenses not incurred wholly and exclusively for the purposes of the trade;
- any expenses laid out for non-business use (e.g. for domestic or personal use);
- any drawings from the trade;
- capital expenditure (but capital allowances may be available on plant and equipment, etc.);
- entertainment expenditure;
- political donations;
- non-specific provisions in respect of bad debts;

- donations below a specific threshold amount;
- certain motor expenses (e.g. the cost of leasing a high-value passenger vehicle may be restricted for tax purposes);
- amounts otherwise to be considered as charges (e.g. certain interest or annual payments); and
- depreciation of assets.

The above expenditure must be identified and excluded when computing profits that are liable to tax for an accounting period. The sole trader will be required to make the required adjustments to the reported accounting net profit/loss for amounts not deductible for tax purposes. (Once again, it is important that students are familiar with all key tax computational rules.)

---

**Example 1.4: Non-deductible expenditure**

In preparing his accounts for the period ended 30 April 2016, John advised you of the following:

- He claimed a deduction for a €300 donation to Trócaire, as well as €250 he gave to the local county councillor.
- He has also claimed a deduction for the costs of a trip to Manchester with his son to see a Champions League game on the basis that it was only an add-on to the real reason for going – to look at a second-hand printing machine he wanted to buy. The total cost of the trip was €1,000.
- He made a provision for bad debts of €5,000 on the basis that "some customers are bound not to pay me". He also claimed a deduction for this.

You point out to him that he needs to adjust his profit for tax purposes as follows:

- The €550 in donations needs to be added back. Political donations are not allowable. While charitable donations were allowable as a tax credit up to 2012, from 2013 onwards an individual donor may not claim tax relief.
- Unless he can clearly show that the cost of the trip to Manchester (for himself only) was wholly and exclusively for the purposes of his printing trade, this amount needs to be added back.
- The bad debt provision is a general provision and needs to be added back.

---

## 1.8 Revenue versus Capital: Receivables Liable to Income Tax or CGT?

A sole trader is liable to income tax on the full amount of "profits or gains" in their trade or profession. Income tax, however, will not be assessed on the **capital** profits of a trader. Typically, an item is regarded as revenue in nature if it is an item of stock for resale, whereas capital items would be more permanent in nature and held for use in the trade (as opposed to being for immediate resale). In certain circumstances, however, it may be difficult to establish whether a receipt is to be regarded as capital or revenue.

A capital receipt of a trader would be taxed under the CGT regime, whereas a revenue receipt would be subject to income tax as a trading receipt. The difference in tax rates between the two regimes is significant (i.e. a CGT rate of 33% versus an income tax rate of up to 40% plus PRSI/USC). A taxpayer may seek to argue that the consideration received is in respect of a capital disposal. However, that may not be the case.

The following issues are relevant to the revenue versus capital argument:

- A conclusion has to be determined from the relevant circumstances of the case.
- A receipt that relates to an asset forming part of the capital business assets (e.g. sale of goodwill) of a business should, on general principles, be considered to be a capital receipt.

- A receipt that relates to a permanent capital asset used as a means of producing goods/services for resale (i.e. used to produce goods for sale) is considered a capital receipt.
- An asset acquired in the normal course of the trade and subsequently sold, or combined into goods, should most likely be considered as revenue in nature.
- Compensation payments received in respect of a trader's capital assets are considered as capital receipts.
- Payments in respect of a trader's stock are revenue in nature.

The above should assist in establishing the level of a trader's liability for either income tax or CGT on their "profits or gains".

---

**Example 1.5**

In preparing his accounts for the period ended 30 April 2016, John also advised you of the following:

- In March 2016, he sold a second-hand machine that the business had been using for €10,000 and "put it through the P&L". He had bought it for €8,000 in June 2015, so he had included the €2,000 profit in the accounts.
- He also sold three large rolls of paper for €5,000 each. He had bought the three of them for €10,000 in total. He had meant to use them over the next two years or so, but got an offer he couldn't refuse and took the money. He had included the €5,000 profit in the accounts.

You point out to him that he needs to adjust his profit for tax purposes as follows:

- The profit on the sale of the machine is liable to CGT, not income tax. As he bought and sold it within the same accounting period, neither depreciation nor capital allowance issues arise.
- This is a "bulk" disposal of trading stock, so income tax treatment is correct.

---

**Example 1.6**

John has surplus space in his business premises. He has been approached by another trader who says he is willing to pay him a lump sum in addition to whatever annual rent amount is agreed between them. They agree to a 21-year lease with a lump sum payment of €20,000 and a rent of €30,000 per annum. John knows he has to pay income tax on the rents but does not know the tax treatment of the lump sum.

John is advised that the lump sum is a premium receivable under a short lease, i.e. a term not greater than 50 years. Part of the premium is revenue in nature and liable to income tax with the balance liable to CGT. To determine the amount liable to income tax, the formula: $P \times (N - 1)/50$ is applied, where P is the premium and N is the number of complete years of the term of the lease. €20,000 $(21-1)/50 = $ €8,000

Therefore, €8,000 is liable to income tax under Case V with the balance of €12,000 liable to CGT.

---

## 1.9 Case I Losses: Sole Trader

Often a sole trader may be operating at a loss, for both accounting and tax purposes. This could either be due to a decline in market demand/conditions, or merely losses incurred in starting up or expanding the trade.

Sections 381–390 TCA 1997 legislate for the utilisation of current-year trading losses generated by a sole trader. Below is a summary of the key sections and the relief available for such trading losses:

| Loss relief | Use | Claim or automatic? | Effect on tax liability |
|---|---|---|---|
| Section 381 TCA 1997 | Set against statutory total income for year of loss. | Claim must be made to Revenue not later than two years after the end of the tax year in which the loss occurs. | Reduces current-year tax liability. All or nothing claim – cannot make a partial claim. If income is too low, it could waste tax credits and/or only benefit at the lower tax rate. |
| Section 382 TCA 1997 | Losses may be carried forward and set against future profits of same trade. Unrelieved trading charges are added to the loss to carry forward (section 390). | Automatic relief – no claim is necessary. Applies to losses remaining after a section 381 claim, or if no section 381 claim is made. | Only shelters future trading income, loss relief is delayed. |
| Section 385 TCA 1997 | Terminal loss relief – carry back to the three preceding years prior to the last 12 months of trading; claim against latest period first and against trading income. | No time limit for the claim. | Only shelters past trading income and there may be a tax refund. |

Under section 381, tax relief can be available for a Case I trading loss against that sole trader's other gross taxable income. For example, a taxable person may have other income such as salary or rental income against which a Case I loss can be utilised. To the extent that the Case I tax loss is not available for utilisation against other current-year income (e.g. salary, rental income, dividend income, etc.), that Case I tax loss may be carried forward against future profits of the trade (but not against other income).

---

**Example 1.7**

Take a situation whereby a person has Schedule E employment income (i.e. a salary) of €100,000, but also conducts a trade as a sole trader. If that person generates a loss of €20,000 during the operation of the sole trade for the accounting period ending in the tax year, the tax loss will have the effect of reducing that person's gross income liable to income tax as follows:

|  | € |
|---|---|
| Schedule E income | 100,000 |
| Case I loss relief claim | (20,000) |
| Taxable income after loss relief | 80,000 |

Therefore, assuming that that person has no other taxable income, a refund of tax deducted through their PAYE employment should arise.

- The tax refund will be at the taxpayer's marginal tax rate (i.e. 40% in this case), which will be €20,000 × 40% = €8,000. The taxpayer has obtained tax relief at an effective tax rate of 40%.
- A claim for relief must be made by the individual in their annual tax return (known as a "Form 11", see also **Section 1.14**).

---

It is important for a sole trader to consider the utilisation of loss relief in the early years of their business. If the sole trader has other income, and the trade is likely to be loss-making for a number of years, there may be merit in continuing to operate as a sole trader (rather than as a company), and obtain the benefit of loss relief. The tax relief could in turn help fund the trading activity.

The decision to incorporate a company will arise at some point in a sole trader's business. The question of loss relief may be a key issue in deciding whether or not to incorporate a company and the best time to incorporate. One of the main benefits of operating through a company is the low rate of corporation tax that will attach to trading profits. If profits do not exist, then income tax loss relief could be beneficial to a sole trader.

---

**Key Issue**

The decision to operate as a sole trader or as a company should be weighed against the maximisation of loss relief. Always take into account the likelihood of profits arising and the extent to which loss relief can be utilised against the **higher rate of income tax (i.e. 40%)**.

There is no obligation on the taxpayer to claim loss relief against other personal income in the current year. If the sole trade profits are expected to arise in the next year (and are due to be liable at the higher rate of tax), there may be merit in carrying the loss forward to the next year to maximise the tax advantage.

---

### 1.9.1 Planning Points for Loss Relief

- The decision to incorporate a company should be weighed against the benefits of utilising loss relief. Personal tax refunds could help fund a start-up sole trade operation.
- Loss relief must be claimed by the taxpayer in their annual tax return.
- There may be circumstances where the taxpayer might decide not to claim relief in a particular tax year, especially if there is no income taxable at the higher rate of tax.

---

**Example 1.8**

| 2015 Tax Year | € |
|---|---|
| Trading loss Case I | (10,000) |
| Other income | 25,000 |

| 2016 Tax Year | |
|---|---|
| Anticipated Case I trade profits | 100,000 |
| Other income | 25,000 |

It is obvious that the taxpayer will be liable to the 40% rate of income tax on 2016 taxable income. He has told you that the 2015 income is liable to the 20% rate of income tax. If the taxpayer does not claim loss relief in 2015 against the 2015 "€25,000 other income", he can carry forward that trade loss to offset against the anticipated 2016 €100,000 trading income (liable at the 40% rate). This is more beneficial.

---

- The level of income that will be liable to the higher rate of income tax should be determined. This will assist in determining the relief available at the higher rate of income tax: gross income of taxpayer **less** standard rate band in tax year (e.g. €33,800 in 2016 for a single person).
- Where a taxpayer has a trading loss, they should consider any means of **increasing their income** in that applicable tax year to maximise the level of relief at the 40% rate (e.g. pay a dividend/extra salary from a controlled company). **This could be a key tax-planning step to maximise personal loss relief**.
- If a business ceases, or is due to be sold/transferred to a company (i.e. there is a change in ownership), terminal loss relief may be claimed but the timing of the cessation of trade will be important for the purposes of the relief. (This relief is discussed in **Section 1.12**.)

## 1.10   Personal Tax: Loss Relief and Computation of Loss

Students will be familiar with the basis of assessment rules applying to the first three years of a trade. These rules determine the taxable profits or losses arising from the operation of a sole trade. As critical as the commencement rules are for the computation of profits, the basis of assessment rules are equally important in computing the losses of a sole trade.

Technically, the Case I trading loss that may be set-off against any other income of the individual for a tax year is the loss actually arising in the year of assessment (i.e. January to December). However, it is understood that Revenue practice allows a set-off of the loss arising in the 12-month accounting period ending in the year of assessment of **a continuing business**. However, the strict technical basis for claiming loss relief will apply for:

- the first three years of assessment on commencement of a trade;
- for any year of assessment following a year in which a claim for loss relief has been made on a strict statutory basis; and
- for the year in which a trade ceases.

---

**Example 1.9: Application of the strict legal basis of loss relief**

| Profit/(Loss) | Scenario 1 | Scenario 2 | Scenario 3 |
|---|---|---|---|
| | € | € | € |
| A/C y/e 30/09/15 | (24,000) | (36,000) | (12,000) |
| A/C y/e 30/09/16 | (3,000) | 24,000 | 60,000 |

*Scenario 1*

In scenario 1, a section 381 claim for loss relief in 2015 would be based on the following:

| | € |
|---|---|
| 9/12 × (24,000) | (18,000) |
| 3/12 × (3,000) | (750) |
| Total loss available for utilisation | (18,750) |

*Scenario 2*

In scenario 2, a section 381 claim for loss relief in 2015 would be based on the following:

| | € |
|---|---|
| 9/12 × (36,000) | (27,000) |
| 3/12 × 24,000 | 6,000 |
| Total loss available for utilisation | (21,000) |

*Scenario 3*

In scenario 3, a section 381 claim for loss relief in 2015 would be based on the following:

| | € |
|---|---|
| 9/12 × (12,000) | (9,000) |
| 3/12 × 60,000 | 15,000 |
| Total loss available for utilisation | Nil (i.e. overall actual profit) |

However, as noted above, in practice Revenue will accept the losses computed by reference to the trader's accounting period when processing a claim for loss relief (for a continuing business).

---

## 1.11   Utilisation of Loss Relief

### 1.11.1   Key Legislative References in Respect of Loss Relief

The following technical points should be noted in respect of loss relief:

- Section 381 TCA 1997 contains the relevant legislative provisions in respect of Case I trading losses and surrender against the taxpayer's other income.

▨  A section 381 loss is deductible from an individual's gross income in arriving at their total income.

▨  If a section 381 claim is made, it is important that the full amount of loss can be claimed, as it is not possible to claim only part of the loss **unless** there is insufficient other income.

Finance Act 2014 introduced a new section 381B, the purpose of which is to limit the use of loss relief where the business owner is not actively involved in the business. An individual is deemed to be carrying on a trade in a non-active capacity if they do not work for the greater part of their time on the day-to-day management of the trade. The individual must spend an average of at least 10 hours per week personally engaged in the activities of the trade. In addition, those activities must be carried out on a commercial basis. Where the individual is deemed to be carrying on a trade in a non-active capacity, the loss relief available is limited to €31,750 or, if lower, the actual amount of the loss sustained.

Section 382 TCA 1997 contains the relevant legislative provisions in respect of the carrying forward of unutilised Case I tax losses. The key issue to note in respect of losses carried forward is that the loss can only be used against future profits of that same trade. Losses carried forward cannot be set-off against any other income, other than the profits of the trade itself. Relief under section 382 is given, as much as possible, against the **next profitable year of assessment** (i.e. the taxpayer cannot be selective about the year of the next claim for loss relief). Therefore, if the trader does not generate a future profit, then the benefit of loss relief carried forward will be lost.

### 1.11.2  Utilisation of a Case I Loss

A sole trader's taxable profit/loss is computed by reference to the standard computational rules (i.e. after add-backs, deductions and other tax adjustments, etc.). As such, there may be a difference between a trader's accounting loss and their tax loss.

Section 381 TCA 1997 legislates for the utilisation of current-year Case I trading losses generated by a sole trader. Relief under section 381 is obtained by reducing a taxpayer's gross income for that applicable tax year by the amount of the tax loss incurred in operating that person's trade.

If, for example, an individual had a loss from their sole trade operation but did not make a claim for section 381 loss relief, a back claim for loss relief will be limited to two years following the year of assessment.

> **Example 1.10: Two-year rule for claiming loss relief**
> Assume a sole trader generated a trading loss in the year ended 31 December 2016. A claim for section 381 loss relief must be made by 31 December 2018 in order to meet the relevant time limit to ensure the loss is available against other income in 2016.

On making a section 381 loss relief claim, the full amount of the loss must be claimed against the trader's gross income. This provision avoids a situation whereby a trader uses losses to such an extent that the balance of their gross income would be covered by their tax credit entitlements.

Where a sole trader carrying on a trade generates a tax loss that cannot be fully utilised for section 381 purposes due to the insufficiency of their other income, then the balance of that unutilised loss will be carried forward for use against future trading profits (i.e. a section 382 loss carried forward).

Note: trading losses carried forward cannot be offset against income other than that of the actual trade. The provisions relating to the carrying forward of losses are found in section 382 TCA 1997.

Note: the difference when a limited company generates a tax loss. A company's trading loss cannot be set-off against the income of the shareholder. The loss remains within the corporate regime.

> **Key Issue**
> When claiming loss relief, it is very important to check that the loss relief is not restricted by the tax rules on "specified" reliefs for high earners. For example, trading losses derived from accelerated capital allowances or double rent relief are impacted by these rules. (This topic is discussed at **Section 1.13**.)

---

**Example 1.11: Section 382 loss relief for losses brought forward**

Jim's only source of income is his travel agency business, which he has carried on for many years. He prepares his annual accounts up to 30 June each year. Recent tax-adjusted results are as follows:

| | |
|---|---|
| 2014 tax-adjusted loss | (€50,000) |
| 2015 tax-adjusted profits | €60,000 |
| 2016 tax-adjusted profits | €130,000 |

Jim is single. His personal tax credit entitlement is assumed to be €2,500 per annum. Jim's tax assessment (ignoring PRSI/USC) will be as follows:

| | 2014 | 2015 | 2016 |
|---|---|---|---|
| | € | € | € |
| Case I | 0 | 60,000 | 130,000 |
| Less: Case I loss b/f | 0 | (50,000) | 0 |
| Assessable Case I | 0 | 10,000 | 130,000 |
| Less: relief | 0 | 0 | 0 |
| | 0 | 10,000 | 130,000 |
| | | | |
| Taxed as follows: | | | |
| €10,000/€33,800 @ 20% | 0 | 2,000 | 6,760 |
| Balance @ 40% | | | 38,480 |
| | 0 | 2,000 | 45,240 |
| Less: credits | (2,500) | (2,500) | (2,500) |
| Tax due | 0 | 0 | 42,740 |

Jim is obliged to use the loss relief brought forward to the first year in which Case I profits are generated. This occurs in 2015, and in this example it means a loss of personal tax credits of €500. It would be much more beneficial for Jim to defer claiming loss relief until 2016 (since €96,200 of his income is liable to the 40% higher rate of tax), but the deferral of losses is not allowed in such circumstances.

---

**Key Issue**

Losses carried forward must be used against the next available profits generated in a sole trader's business.

---

### 1.11.3 Loss Relief and Interaction with Capital Allowances

Capital allowances and trading losses carried forward from previous years cannot be used to directly create or enhance a section 381 loss relief claim. However, the losses brought forward may be used to shelter any current year balancing charges and to reduce current year profits.

---

**Example 1.12**

John has been in business for many years and prepares his annual accounts to 30 September. His tax-adjusted profit for the year ended 30 September 2016 is €28,000.

Unutilised capital allowances brought forward from 2015 are €30,000.

The capital allowance position for 2016 is as follows:

| | € |
|---|---|
| Wear and tear allowances | (21,000) |
| Balancing allowances on sale of assets | (1,500) |
| Balancing charges | 2,400 |

*continued overleaf*

| The 2016 tax-adjusted profits will be computed as follows: | |
|---|---|
| | € |
| Case I tax-adjusted profit | 28,000 |
| Less: 2015 capital allowances b/f | (28,000) |
| 2016 taxable profit | Nil |
| Add 2016 balancing charge | 2,400 |
| Less: balance of 2015 capital allowances b/f | (2,000) |
| Less: 2016 capital allowances | (22,500) |
| Current year Case I loss | (22,100)* |
| *Available for utilisation against other income as a section 381 loss relief claim. | |

*Note:* from **Example 1.12**, the benefit of prior year capital allowances is that the current year balancing charges and profits can be eliminated, with the result that the current year capital allowances generate a Case I loss available for current year section 381 utilisation (or carry forward if there is insufficient current-year other income).

### 1.11.4  Maximise Utilisation of Tax Losses and the Timing of Incorporation

If a decision to incorporate has been taken, it is key that the actual timing of the cessation of the sole trade and its transfer to the company is such that it maximises the tax benefit of any losses.

---

**Example 1.13**

Take the following projections prepared by Thomas O'Leary, a sole trader, who has been developing a new software-assisted design process since 2008. Given the nature of his business, he will have to incur significant costs and time before the product is capable of going to market. At best, he does not see profits arising until 2018.

Thomas is a single individual. He is wondering whether he should set up a company to carry out his trade and, if so, when. He wishes to maximise any tax relief associated with trading losses and to efficiently manage his tax liabilities once he is profitable.

**Income Projections**

| Gross Income/Loss Position | 2015 | 2016 | 2017 | 2018 | 2019 |
|---|---|---|---|---|---|
| | € | € | € | € | € |
| Salary | 90,000 | 95,000 | 30,000 | 30,000 | 0 |
| Property income | 10,000 | 16,000 | 16,000 | 16,000 | 16,000 |
| Sole trader (loss)/profits | (15,000) | (22,000) | (40,000) | 50,000 | 350,000 |
| Taxable income after loss relief | 85,000 | 89,000 | see below | see below | 356,000 |

Thomas is planning to leave his job in 2017 to dedicate himself to his business full time. He will, however, do some part-time work to fund day-to-day living expenses.

*2015 and 2016*

For 2015 and 2016, Thomas will be liable to the 40% rate of income tax on his salary and rental income above the standard rate band of €33,800. As he has incurred sole trader Case I losses, he can offset these losses against his other income. This will give Thomas tax relief at the 40% rate, which is a favourable tax result (i.e. tax relief at the highest rate of tax).

*continued overleaf*

*2017 and 2018*

In 2017, Thomas has only worked part time. In the absence of a section 381 loss relief claim, he has income liable to income tax at the 40% rate. Assuming a single person standard rate band of €33,800, Thomas's total income liable to the higher rate of tax is €12,200.

Thomas should therefore continue to trade as sole trader because:

1. he is not generating profits in his sole trade; and
2. he should use the loss relief against any other income liable at the higher rate of income tax (subject to the timing of the loss relief claim, i.e. whether to use it in 2017 or 2018 – see below for the computations showing the tax impact of a claim in either 2017 or deferral until 2018).

Thomas should seek to achieve the lowest possible effective tax rate on his total income, and the timing of the loss relief claim is critical to achieving maximum tax benefit. Thomas should only use loss relief to the extent that he can offset the loss against income liable to the 40% rate. Thomas can claim loss relief in 2017, or alternatively, not make a claim for loss relief in 2017 and carry forward the €40,000 losses against future Case I trading profits (i.e. 2018 taxable Case I profits of €50,000).

**2017 tax computation** *without loss relief*

|                        | €        |
| ---------------------- | -------- |
|                        | €        |
| Schedule E salary      | 30,000   |
| Case V rental income   | <u>16,000</u> |
| Total income           | 46,000   |
| €33,800 @ 20%          | 6,760    |
| €12,200 @ 40%          | <u>4,880</u> |
| Income tax             | 11,640   |

**2017 tax computation** *with loss relief*

|                        | €        |
| ---------------------- | -------- |
| Schedule E salary      | 30,000   |
| Case V rental income   | <u>16,000</u> |
|                        | <u>46,000</u> |
| Less: section 381 loss | (<u>40,000</u>) |
| Total income           | 6,000    |
| €6,000 @ 20%           | 1,200    |

The tax saving in 2017 using loss relief is €10,440 (i.e. €11,640 − €1,200).

**2018 tax computation** *without loss relief*

|                        | €        |
| ---------------------- | -------- |
| Schedule E salary      | 30,000   |
| Case V rental income   | 16,000   |
| Case I trade income    | <u>50,000</u> |
| Total income           | 96,000   |
| €33,800 @ 20%          | 6,760    |
| €62,200 @ 40%          | <u>24,880</u> |
| Income tax             | 31,640   |

*continued overleaf*

**2018 tax computation *with loss relief***

|  | € | € |
|---|---|---|
| Schedule E salary | | 30,000 |
| Case V rental income | | 16,000 |
| Case I trade income | 50,000 | |
| Less: section 382 loss b/f | (40,000) | |
| | | 10,000 |
| Total income | | 56,000 |
| €33,800 @ 20% | | 6,760 |
| €22,200 @ 40% | | 8,880 |
| Income tax | | 15,640 |

Thomas should not make a section 381 loss claim in 2017. Instead, he should carry forward the loss to 2018 under section 382. As has been demonstrated above, the tax saving in 2017 on the €40,000 loss is:

€26,800 × 20% = €5,360

€13,200 × 40% = €5,280

Total          €10,640

Whereas in 2018 the tax saving on the €40,000 loss is €40,000 × 40% = €16,000, leaving him better off by €5,560 (i.e. €16,000 − €10,440).

(Remember: the loss carried forward can only be used against the income of the same trade. It is therefore important that there are future Case I profits to set this loss against.)

**2019**

The trade is expected to be very profitable in 2019. At this point, all Case I income tax losses have been exhausted. Thomas should consider the transfer of his trade to a limited company on 1 January 2019.

As the final year of trading (i.e. 2018) will be profitable, the question of terminal loss relief does not arise. Terminal loss relief arises on cessation of a trade, which includes a situation whereby a trade is transferred to a company. The timing of a transfer of a trade to a limited company, and the associated loss relief issues, is discussed in **Section 1.12**. The tax saving in 2018 using loss relief is €16,000 (i.e. €31,640 − €15,640).

---

**Example 1.14: Maximising loss relief**

|  | 2015 | 2016 |
|---|---|---|
| | € | € |
| Gross income of a single person | 20,000 | 70,000 |
| Assume a Case I loss for 2015 | (19,000) | |
| | | |
| **Assumption 1: Claim for loss relief in 2015** | | |
| *2015 Tax Computation* | | |
| Gross income | 20,000 | |
| Less: section 381 current year loss relief | (19,000) | |
| Taxable income | 1,000 | |

*continued overleaf*

| | |
|---|---:|
| Taxed @ 20% | 200 |
| Less: Single person credit (non-refundable) | (1,650) |
| Tax payable/repayable | Nil |

*2016 Tax Computation*

| | |
|---|---:|
| Gross income | 70,000 |
| Less: Loss relief | 0 |
| Taxable income | 70,000 |
| Taxed @ 20% standard rate band | 6,760 |
| Taxed @ 40% | 14,480 |
| Less: single person credit (non-refundable) | (1,650) |
| Tax payable/repayable | 19,590 |

**Assumption 2: No claim for loss relief in 2015 and a carry forward of losses to 2016**

*2015 Tax Computation*

| | |
|---|---:|
| Gross income | 20,000 |
| Less: section 381 current year loss relief | 0 |
| Taxable income | 20,000 |
| Taxed @ 20% | 4,000 |
| Less: Single person credit (non-refundable) | (1,650) |
| Tax payable/repayable | 2,350 |

The tax saving in 2015 using section 381 loss relief is €2,350.

*2016 Tax Computation*

| | € |
|---|---:|
| Gross income | 70,000 |
| Less: section 382 loss relief brought forward | (19,000) |
| Taxable income | 51,000 |
| Taxed @ 20% standard rate band | 6,760 |
| Taxed @ 40% | 6,880 |
| Less: single person credit (non-refundable)* | (1,650) |
| Tax payable/repayable | 11,990 |

The tax saving in 2016 using section 382 loss relief is €7,600.

Therefore, in this case, the maximum tax benefit achieved is with a carry forward of tax loss to 2015.

*FA 2015 introduced the earned income tax credit of €550, which is ignored for the purposes of this illustration.

## 1.12  Cessation of a Sole Trade

The date of cessation of a sole trade will be established by virtue of the facts surrounding the trade/activity. For example, the cessation point could be when all of the trade's stock has been sold. A subsequent sale of the business's capital assets at a later date would not extend the cessation date. The existence of sales would also indicate that a trade has not yet ceased.

If the ownership of a business changes, the date of sale/transfer is the date of cessation of that business for tax purposes. The sole trader who is selling his business will be deemed to cease for income tax purposes. A sole trade will also be deemed to have ceased in circumstances where a business is transferred to a company. A trade is also deemed to cease on the death of the sole trader (unless the surviving spouse/civil partner continues the same trade after the death).

Receipts collected by the sole trader, following cessation to trade, will be liable to income tax as Case IV income (i.e. not as Case I trading income).

### 1.12.1 Tax Assessment Rules on a Cessation

On the cessation of a trade, the profits liable to tax will be those profits from 1 January to the date of cessation. An adjustment to taxable income in the year prior to cessation may also be required. The prior year's profits will be revised to an actual basis (i.e. January to December in the year prior to cessation). If those profits on an actual basis are higher than the profits originally assessed, the sole trader's assessment will be revised in line with the higher actual Case I profits.

---

**Example 1.15: Cessation**

John Jones ceased to trade on 31 July 2016. His sole trade profits over the last three years were as follows:

|                  | €      |
|------------------|--------|
| 31 July 2016     | 20,000 |
| 31 January 2016  | 90,000 |
| 31 January 2015  | 50,000 |
| 31 January 2014  | 60,000 |

*Final Year – 2016*

John's profits liable to income tax in the year of cessation will be those profits arising between 1 January 2016 and 31 July 2016:

|                          | €      |
|--------------------------|--------|
| €90,000 × 1/12           | 7,500  |
| €20,000                  | <u>20,000</u> |
| Total 2016 taxable profits | 27,500 |

*Prior Year – 2015*

The 2015 tax year profits, under an ongoing trading basis, liable to tax were €50,000 (i.e. Case I year ended 31 January 2015). However, as the trade has ceased, an adjustment of 2015 to an actual basis is required, if it gives a higher taxable profit:

|                           | €      |
|---------------------------|--------|
| €50,000 × 1/12            | 4,167  |
| €90,000 × 11/12           | <u>82,500</u> |
| Revised 2015 taxable profits | 86,667 |

Under self-assessment, John must advise Revenue of the "prior year adjustment", i.e. the uplift in profits assessable.

---

**Short-lived Businesses**

The profits liable to income tax for a business that commences and ceases within the first three years will be the actual profits (i.e. on a January to December basis).

## 1.13   Cessation of a Sole Trade and Loss Relief: Terminal Loss Relief

The interaction of loss relief and the cessation of a trade will often arise in practice. This can occur where:

- a trade ceases; and
- there are losses in the final 12 months prior to cessation.

When this occurs, those losses in the final 12 months up to the date of cessation may be carried back against the trading profits in the three years prior to cessation. This carry back relief is subject to relief for these losses not being claimed under any other section (e.g. section 381, etc.). This is known as **terminal loss relief.**

The amount of the terminal loss is the sum of the following:

- the adjusted loss generated in the final 12 months of trading (which may include a portion of the prior year of assessment figures); and
- capital allowances available in that final 12-month period (which may include a *pro rata* proportion of capital allowances for the period in the prior year of assessment).

If the period prior to cessation was a profitable period, the issue of terminal loss relief will not arise. The profits eligible for the relief in the preceding three-year period are defined as the full amount of profits arising in the relevant period less any capital allowances in that period and less any annual payments or losses deductible in arriving at taxable profits in that period (section 387 TCA 1997).

### 1.13.1   Timing of Cessation

A trade is deemed to be permanently discontinued or to have ceased when there has been a change of ownership. The **transfer of a trade to a company** will constitute a cessation of trade (and hence terminal loss relief could be available). In this regard, the timing of a transfer of a trade should be considered in the context of terminal loss relief. A review of current losses and profits within the prior three-year period should be undertaken.

A planning point would be to ensure that there are profits within the prior three years to avail of terminal loss relief. The timing of the transfer should be considered to ensure maximum benefit of terminal loss relief (i.e. attract profits that were taxed at the 40% rate of income tax).

The timing of the incorporation and transfer of a business to a limited company is discussed in detail in **Section 2.3.4**, and the issue of terminal loss relief (and timing of same) should be considered in conjunction with the CGT transfer of a business relief.

---

**Example 1.16: Timing of transfer of a business**
Stephen Byrne carries on a sole trade. His accounting year-ends to date have been 31 December. He plans to transfer his business to a limited company on 30 September 2016.

The profits, losses and capital allowances of his trade are as follows:

| Year | Capital Allowance | Profit/Loss |
|---|---|---|
| | € | € |
| 2012 | (3,000) | 5,000 |
| 2013 | (2,500) | 6,500 |
| 2014 | (3,500) | 2,000 |
| 2015 | (2,500) | 6,000 |
| 9 months to 30/09/2016 | (2,500) | (7,000) |

*continued overleaf*

---

| Prior Tax Assessments | 2012 | 2013 | 2014 | 2015 |
|---|---|---|---|---|
| | € | € | € | € |
| Profit/loss | 5,000 | 6,500 | 2,000 | 6,000 |
| Less: capital allowances | (3,000) | (2,500) | (3,500) | (2,500) |
| Taxable profit/loss | 2,000 | 4,000 | (1,500) | 3,500 |
| Loss relief b/f claim | | | | (1,500) |
| Taxable profits | 2,000 | 4,000 | 0 * | 2,000 |

\* Assume section 381 loss relief not claimed in 2014.

Since Stephen plans to transfer his business to a limited company on 30 September 2016, the trade will therefore cease and terminal loss relief can be claimed. The terminal loss in the final 12 months is computed as follows:

| | € |
|---|---|
| Loss up to 30 September 2016 | (7,000) |
| Add: capital allowances | (2,500) |
| Total loss for nine months | (9,500) |

*Three months of prior year (i.e. 2015 period)*

As there was no loss in this three-month period, the terminal loss for the 12-month period is €9,500.

Terminal loss relief will be taken as follows to the preceding three years of assessment:

| Year | Profits Assessed | Terminal Loss | Revised Assessment |
|---|---|---|---|
| | € | € | € |
| 2015 | 2,000 | (2,000) | Nil |
| 2014 | Nil | Nil | Nil |
| 2013 | 4,000 | (4,000) | Nil |

**Key Issue**
If Stephen decided to defer the transfer of the business to a limited company until 2017, he would only be able to claim terminal loss relief for the three preceding taxable periods prior to 2017 (being 2016, 2015 and 2014). This would result in losing the benefit of terminal loss relief in 2013 (being the last tax year with substantial profits). As such, it is more beneficial from a tax perspective for Stephen to cease trading in 2016.

## 1.14   Restrictions on Tax Reliefs for High Income Individuals

Finance Act 2006 introduced provisions limiting the use of certain tax reliefs, including exemptions, by certain high income individuals effective from 1 January 2007. A summary of the main restricted reliefs is as follows:

- Capital allowances incentive schemes (e.g. property capital allowance relief schemes).
- All property schemes qualifying for accelerated allowances (e.g. hotels, nursing homes, etc.).
- Trading losses derived from capital allowances incentive schemes and property schemes (as mentioned above) or derived from double rent relief. This category also extends to losses forward and to terminal loss relief where the loss is derived from such restricted reliefs.

- Film relief.
- Exempt royalty income (from patents).
- Artists' exemption.
- Donations to sports bodies.
- Any amount carried forward to a later period as a result of the operation of the above restriction in an earlier period.

The above are known as "specified reliefs". For 2007, 2008 and 2009, broadly speaking, the restrictions only applied to those individuals whose adjusted income was greater than or equal to €250,000 per annum. The objective of the provision was to ensure that "high earners" paid a minimum amount of tax (i.e. approximately 20%). Finance Act 2010 amended the legislation by lowering the level of "adjusted income", etc. The income entry level was reduced from €250,000 to €125,000 and the specified relief limit of €250,000 was reduced to €80,000. Tapering relief applies to income between €125,000 and €400,000. Therefore, full restriction applies where income is greater than €400,000 (previously €500,000).

### 1.14.1 Computation of the Restriction of Relief

The restriction applies to an individual where all of the following three criteria apply:

1. the "Adjusted Income" of an individual for the tax year is equal to or greater than an "income threshold amount" which is, in general, €125,000 but is less if the individual had ring-fenced income (e.g. deposit interest);
2. the aggregate of specified reliefs that are used by the individual for the tax year is equal to or greater than a "relief threshold amount" which is set at €80,000; and
3. the aggregate of specified reliefs used by an individual for the tax year is greater than 20% of the individual's adjusted income.

The restriction is calculated by using the formula:

$$T + (S - Y)$$

where:

$T$ = is the individual's taxable income (before the restriction);
$S$ = is the aggregate amount of specified reliefs used in the year; and
$Y$ = is either €80,000 (the relief threshold amount) or, if greater, 20% of the individual's adjusted income for the year.

---

**Example 1.17: No ring-fenced income**
Bert Howley's Case I income for 2016 is €300,000, he has "section 23-type" relief in that year amounting to €200,000 (S). His taxable income is therefore €100,000 (T). He has no ring-fenced income (R). His adjusted income (T + S) – R is €300,000.

The restriction applies to Bert since his adjusted income is greater than €125,000 and his specified relief is greater than €80,000. His recalculated taxable income for 2016, using the formula T + (S – Y), is €220,000 as follows:

T (€100,000) + S (€200,000) – Y (€80,000 – this is greater than 20% of his adjusted income).

The unused relief of €120,000 is carried forward as excess relief to the year 2017.

---

To compute the specified relief restriction, the following must be adhered to:

1. Total all specified tax reliefs for the tax year (this could be a mix of various reliefs or alternatively a single relief from the listing at the start of this section).
2. Add back the total amount of specified reliefs to the taxable income.
3. From the taxable income at step 2, deduct Irish/European bank interest income to give the "adjusted income". For 2010 and onwards, if this adjusted income amount is in excess of €125,000 and the specified reliefs are above the limit set out below, the high earners' restriction will apply.

The restriction is computed by way of capping the person's specified reliefs to the greater of:

- €80,000, or
- 20% of the individual's "adjusted income".

Any unused relief can be carried forward for future use.

### 1.14.2 €125,000 Threshold Adjustment: Adjusted Income below €400,000

In deciding whether the restriction is applicable for the year 2016, the income threshold amount for 2016 is in general, €125,000 but is less if the individual had ring-fenced income (e.g. deposit interest) and the adjusted income is less than €400,000. In that situation, the income threshold amount is calculated by using the formula:

$$€125,000 \times A/B$$

where:

A = is the individual's adjusted income (i.e. less the ring-fenced income), and
B = is the individual's adjusted income + the ring-fenced income.

---

**Example 1.18: With ring-fenced income**
Rose Healy's Case I income for 2016 is €120,000, she has bank deposit interest of €70,000 (R) (ring-fenced income) and she has "section 23-type" relief in that year amounting to €100,000 (S). Her taxable income figure is €90,000 (T). Her adjusted income (T + S) – R is €120,000. Because Rose's adjusted income is less than €400,000, her income threshold amount is:

$$€125,000 \times \frac{120,000}{190,000} = €78,947$$

The restriction applies to Rose for the year 2016 as her adjusted income of €120,000 is greater than her income threshold amount of €78,947 and her use of specified reliefs of €100,000 are greater than €80,000. Her recalculated taxable income for 2016, using the formula T + (S − Y), is:

€110,000 (€90,000 + (€100,000 − 80,000)) – this is greater than 20% of her adjusted income (€120,000 × 20% = €24,000).

The unused relief of €20,000 is carried forward as excess relief to the year 2017.

---

**Example 1.19: Restriction of specified reliefs – 2016**
John Ryan has specified reliefs of €140,000 in 2016, and has the following income:

|  | € |
|---|---|
| Property income | 120,000 |
| Salary | 180,000 |
| Total income | 300,000 |

In taking into account the specified reliefs (SR) restriction, John's "adjusted income" would be computed as follows:

*continued overleaf*

**Step 1**

|  | € |
|---|---|
| Gross income |  |
| Property income | 120,000 |
| Salary | 180,000 |
|  | 300,000 |
| Less: specified reliefs | (140,000) |
| Taxable income before restriction | 160,000 |

**Step 2**

|  | € |
|---|---|
| Net taxable income | 160,000 |
| Add back specified reliefs | 140,000 |
| Adjusted income | 300,000 |

The specified relief is restricted to the greater of €80,000 or 20% of the adjusted income.

The specified relief available to John in 2016 will be the greater of €80,000 or 20% of the adjusted income (i.e. €300,000 @ 20% = €60,000).

John will claim €80,000 relief in 2016, and carry the balance of €60,000 forward to the 2017 tax year.

---

**Example 1.20**

Emily and James O'Fallon have the following income for 2016:

|  | Emily | James | Total |
|---|---|---|---|
|  | € | € | € |
| Dividends from their company | 94,000 | 96,000 | 190,000 |
| Rental income from properties | 250,000 | 250,000 | 500,000 |
| Salary from their company | 100,000 | 180,000 | 280,000 |
| Consultancy income | 200,000 | 0 | 200,000 |
| Total income | 644,000 | 526,000 | 1,170,000 |

Emily has specified reliefs of €260,000 in 2016. James has specified reliefs of €50,000 in 2016.

Emily and James are jointly assessed. The couple's total income (before the restriction is applied) is:

|  | € |
|---|---|
| Total income | 1,170,000 |
| Specified reliefs (Emily) | (260,000) |
| Specified reliefs (James) | (50,000) |
| Taxable income before restriction | 860,000 |

The high earners' restriction is applied to each spouse separately. The restriction will be the greater of €80,000 or 20% of the person's adjusted income.

*continued overleaf*

| Adjusted Income | Emily | James |
|---|---|---|
| | € | € |
| Taxable income | 384,000 | 476,000 |
| Deduct Irish or European bank interest | 0 | 0 |
| Add back specified relief | 260,000 | 50,000 |
| Adjusted income | 644,000 | 526,000 |
| @ 20% | 128,800 | 105,200 |

Emily will be entitled to a tax deduction up to a maximum of €128,800 in respect of specified reliefs. There is a restriction on the relief she can claim and the unused balance of €131,200 is carried forward to 2017. James may claim the full amount as the amount of relief is less than the limits.

| | € |
|---|---|
| Total income | 1,170,000 |
| Restricted deductions: | |
| Specified relief (James) | (50,000) |
| Specified relief (Emily) | (128,800) |
| Taxable income | 991,200 |

---

**Key Issue**
If an individual is obtaining the benefit of tax relief in any form, students should consider whether there is a requirement to restrict the level of tax relief. Students should recognise this as a fundamental change to the Irish tax system and it must be considered when advising clients contemplating expenditure that is a specified relief.

---

## 1.15 Compliance Obligations of a Sole Trader

A sole trader will be considered a **chargeable person** for income tax purposes. By contrast, individuals who do not have income other than Schedule E employment income (i.e. salary on which payroll is operated) would not be considered chargeable persons. Proprietary directors are an exception to this as they are regarded as chargeable persons and hence must file tax returns under the self-assessment system. A proprietary director is one who can control directly or indirectly 15% of the ordinary share capital of the company.

---

**Key Issue**
It is important that students are familiar with the key differences between chargeable and non-chargeable persons (and the filing requirements).

---

All chargeable persons are required to:

- Make a return of income to the Collector General for each year that they are chargeable persons. The current prescribed return form is the Form 11 return and must be filed electronically. In exceptional cases a paper Form 11 will be accepted.

- The return, if permitted to be filed in paper format, should include a declaration by the taxpayer regarding the income and gains earned in the period, along with any deductions claimed by the taxpayer during that period.
- File a 'self-assessment' (i.e. calculation of the tax liability for the year).

Failure to file a return will lead to the imposition of penalties and interest by the Revenue Commissioners. The Revenue Commissioners also reserve the right to impose more serious penalties, including imprisonment.

## Chapter 1 Summary

| Does a trade exist? | • Badges of trade<br>• Deductibility of expenditure<br>• Capital versus revenue |
|---|---|
| Operating as a sole trader | • Consider appropriate accounting date taking into consideration anticipated profits/losses<br>• Special rules apply for allocating profits/losses to tax years on commencement<br>• Loss reliefs available to a sole trader – how to maximise tax relief and cash flow<br>• Implications if trade ceases |
| Other | • Restrictions on tax reliefs for high income individuals |

# Questions

## Review Question
(See Suggested Solutions to Review Questions at the end of this textbook.)

### Question 1.1

Joe Smyth, a sole trader trading as Lemon Fresh, a manufacturer of toilet cleaning products, ceased to trade on 30 June 2017 due to a decline in a demand for its product. Joe Smyth prepared his accounts to 31 December. He had the following results for the periods below:

| Period to 30 June 2017 Trading loss | (€55,000) |
|---|---|
| Y/E 31 December 2016 Trading loss | (€5,000) |
| Y/E 31 December 2015 Trading profit | €25,000 |
| Y/E 31 December 2014 Trading profit | €22,000 |
| Y/E 31 December 2013 Trading profit | €15,000 |

**Requirement**

Calculate the terminal loss claim, ensuring that loss relief claimed is maximised and assuming that Joe Smyth had no income other than his trade income.

## Challenging Question

(Suggested Solutions to Challenging Questions are available through your lecturer.)

### Question 1.1

You had a recent meeting with a potential new client, Ted Hickey. Ted is married, and his wife works on a part-time basis. Her annual salary is €25,000. While Ted has been working as an employee, his annual salary is normally in the region of €70,000. He also has an active interest in horticulture and garden design.

He has been dabbling in this area a lot more recently and, in the last year, he won a competition to design a garden for the Bloom Garden Festival in 2016. In 2016, his employer asked him to work a four-day week and has recently asked him to work a three-day week until things pick up again. With this extra time on his hands, Ted wants to try to start a garden design business to capitalise on his appearance at the Bloom Garden Festival. He has incurred a loss of some €70,000 to date on this activity as he has acquired lots of tools and equipment. He has also attended courses costing €5,000 and wants to claim these as business expenses. Ted thinks his initial commissions in 2016 may end up costing him about €10,000 as he wants to build his reputation and create some good examples of his work, but he cannot afford to charge the clients enough to pay for his time. Ted is unsure of the future prospects but, if things go well, he may perhaps break even in 2017.

Ted's wife inherited a substantial sum from her aunt and this was invested in different types of investment properties. She has Case V income of €260,000 each year and is entitled to a section 23 type relief of €50,000 in each of the years 2016 to 2019 with a carry forward of the relief of €10,000 from 2015.

**Requirement**

Ted asks for a letter to set out their expected income tax position for 2016 and advice on the best use of all initial trading losses in his business. As he is not great with tax things, he would like any "technical parts" explained with simple calculations.

# Taking Stock of Your Business – The Incorporation Decision

**Learning Objectives**

By the end of this chapter you will be able to:

- Analyse the potential tax implications for a business trading through a company, with particular reference to:
    - consideration of reasons to incorporate a business;
    - comparison of sole trade profits to incorporated profits;
    - cessation issues for a sole trader;
    - optimum use of incorporation relief.

## 2.1 Benefits and Disadvantages of Operating as a Sole Trader

In almost every business, the question will arise as to how to **structure** that business. In some cases, a business may commence as a sole trade and either remain this way or at some point may be transferred to a limited company. In some cases, a trade can be transferred out of a limited company. In practice, however, this is not common. A company can also be incorporated so as to conduct the trading activities from the date of commencement.

There are benefits and disadvantages to operating as a sole trader. Often it will come down to an individual's business and their particular circumstances. Some general **benefits and disadvantages** of operating as a sole trader can be summarised as follows:

| Benefits of Operating as a Sole Trader | Disadvantages of Operating as a Sole Trader |
|---|---|
| Offers a degree of flexibility to the trader. | No limited liability protection. |
| Low professional costs in respect of annual filings. | Could be difficult to introduce outside investors into a non-corporate structure. |

*continued overleaf*

| Benefits of Operating as a Sole Trader | Disadvantages of Operating as a Sole Trader |
|---|---|
| Loss relief can be utilised against other income. This can help finance the ongoing trading activities and expansion. | Limited scope for pension planning. Tax benefits are limited by reference to earnings and the person's age. |
| Cash is received directly from trading activities, therefore no cash extraction issues compared to a company. | Profits liable to the higher rate of income tax (compared to a 12.5% rate for companies). |
| Direct ownership of trading assets. Proceeds of a future sale will be received directly. | May be difficult to raise finance to fund trade expansion. |

(Students should be able to identify the critical issues associated with each business model presented.)

## 2.2 Incorporation of a Company: Critical Issues

### 2.2.1 Incorporation Decision Matrix

The key issues/conditions that could prompt the incorporation of a limited liability company are as follows:

- Anticipation of significant profits and the benefit of the 12.5% rate of corporation tax (as opposed to income tax rates).
- Tax exemption for start-up companies (this topic is covered in **Section 3.2**).
- Is the trader incorporating an existing business? If so and there are losses carried forward, these will effectively be lost. Consideration must also be given to Case I cessation rules and their implications. Note that these "historical" issues have no relevance for the individual who has never operated as a sole trader and commences trading through a company from the beginning.
- Availability of R&D credit (covered in **Section 3.9**).
- Need for limited liability protection.
- Vehicle for raising capital/borrowings.
- Borrowings could be repaid out of post-12.5% income, which should facilitate a quicker repayment of borrowings.
- Multiple owners of the business and a means to facilitate shared ownership of a business.
- Creation of clear ownership structure to a business.
- Means to formalise a business structure.
- Introduction of new investors into a business and the requirement to have a limited company.
- Banking requirements (trade expansion, audit and security issues).
- Plans for future disposal of a business (share sale requirement).
- Pension planning opportunities are limited for sole traders/individuals.
- Funding the business – Employment and Investment Incentive Scheme (EIIS) and Seed Capital Relief.
- Staff schemes such as share options, etc.

Some issues that may influence the decision **not** to incorporate a company are as follows:

- Complexity and administration.
- Case I losses not available for offset against an individual's other income if the business is incorporated.
- Significant close company legislation.
- Cash extraction issues on an ongoing basis. How can funds be extracted from a company tax efficiently?
- A company is a separate legal entity and valuable assets would not be directly held by shareholders. This is often a key issue and generally arises where a valuable property asset is held by individuals.
- Additional costs, such as legal costs.

- Lifestyle funding requirements of the individual – cash extraction issues.
- Potential for double CGT charge if the business/assets are sold by the company (and cash is extracted by way of a liquidation/capital distribution to shareholders).

The individual(s) behind the business will have to take account of their business and personal requirements. The decision to incorporate will be evaluated on the basis of these requirements and also will have taken into account its impact for income tax and CGT purposes.

The decision to incorporate a company can also link in with other more long-term strategies. For example, an individual wishing to build up a business for a future sale may wish to incorporate a company if it is likely that the purchaser of the business will want to purchase shares in a company rather than a sole trade operation.

---

**Key Issue**

Consider all of the other tax charges and reliefs (including CGT and SD) when considering the structure of a new or existing business. It is likely that there will be many issues to consider, and it is important that consideration is always given to future events rather than short-term plans.

---

### 2.2.2  Start-up Business: Key Issues Arising

---

**Example 2.1: Start-up business and key issues arising**

Joe Ryan is giving up his current job. He works for a multinational film production company and became CEO of the Irish operation. Joe has a great relationship with his clients and effectively built up the Irish customer base from zero. The multinational is leaving Ireland, so he has decided to set up his own business.

Joe expects his new business to be very profitable. He would like to build it up with a view to a potential sale as a going concern within the next 10 years, all going to plan. At that stage, Joe will be 60 years of age and due for retirement.

To establish his new business, Joe will have to:

- Recruit 10 members of staff to manage the expected workload.
- Purchase a new office, which Joe has already found and is negotiating to purchase for €1 million.
- Purchase all equipment, insurance, etc. necessary to run the business.

Joe is relatively wealthy, but he will require circa €60,000 to cover his general costs of living.

In principle, Joe has two options:

- Commence the new business as a sole trader.
- Commence the new business through a limited company.

As the business is likely to be very profitable, setting up a limited company to run the business is most probably the better option. Also, as the trade is set to grow very quickly, the limited company is likely to offer Joe the desired limited liability protection if commercial problems arise. However, Joe must consider further issues given his long-term plan for the company:

**Will Joe take out a bank loan personally to fund the new business or will the company draw down the loan?**

Interest as a charge relief is no longer available to Joe for new loans taken out after 7/12/2010. He would have to fund repayments of the loan and interest. If he does not have those funds, he would have to extract them from the company and pay tax on the extracted funds.

*continued overleaf*

---

If the company takes out a loan, Joe's company may be able to repay the loan faster, as the company's trading income is liable to the 12.5% rate of tax (unless the three-year start-up exemption applies), so in theory the company should be capable of generating higher excess post-tax funds. The bank may require security, and the new company may not yet have assets for collateral purposes. Commercial issues such as these may arise.

Joe may wish to bring in outside investors, which will most likely mean investment into a company by way of a share issue or loan note. If Joe introduces funds by way of subscription for shares, the subscription cost will be Joe's base cost on a future disposal of those shares. Seed capital and EIIS relief (covered in **Section 3.8**) are tax-efficient means of raising equity funds. Unfortunately, one of the conditions for both reliefs is that the business activity must be that of a "relevant" trade. Since film production is an excluded trade, Joe's company will therefore not qualify for either seed capital or EIIS relief.

If Joe introduces funds to the company by way of a shareholder's loan, he may charge interest on the loan to the company. There is, however, close company legislation that would deem excessive interest paid to Joe to be a distribution (and not deductible in the company's tax computation).

If Joe lends the money to the company, those loans can be repaid to Joe tax free.

Joe may fund the company through a mixture of loan and share capital.

### *Will Joe buy the property himself and rent to the company?*

If Joe purchases the property personally, then it will give Joe a rental income. Joe may separately decide to not draw a salary from the company if he wishes it to remain as profitable as possible (with a view to a future sale).

The rental income earned by Joe will be tax deductible in the company's tax computation, subject to it not being excessive and incurred wholly and exclusively for the purposes of the trade. Joe will also personally hold a valuable asset, which can be sold and will be liable to CGT rates if a gain arises on a future sale.

The rental charge to the company may be sufficient to repay Joe's loan, if Joe decides to purchase the property personally. However, he will only be entitled to a deduction for interest, so he will have a tax liability on the net rent, most likely at 40%. Alternatively, the company can purchase the property. If the company draws down bank funding, it can finance the loan from after-tax profits (rather than Joe having to pay income tax on rental income and then discharge the bank liabilities).

The financing on the property purchase is likely to influence this property acquisition decision.

This property issue frequently arises in practice and, in general, it can often be very beneficial from a tax perspective to hold the property outside of the company. The property can be a source of income for the individuals, while the rental expense should be tax deductible in the company. Any future gain on disposal will be taxed at the CGT rate and the consideration will be received personally by the individual. If, by contrast, the company has to sell the property first, the after-tax proceeds then need to be extracted from the company, which will give rise to a personal tax charge. This is often referred to as the double charge to tax that usually arises if a valuable property is owned by a company. (This is covered in more detail in **Chapter 4**.)

If Joe purchases the property and rents it to the company, on a future sale of the company and the attaching property, Joe may be entitled to claim retirement relief in respect of both asset sales provided the sales happen together and to the same person.

### *Will Joe require a pension?*

A director's pension scheme can be set up to maximise pension funding, especially if Joe is no longer a young man. The tax relief restrictions for income tax purposes for personal pension contributions are much stricter than those where the company pays into a corporate pension scheme. A company scheme may facilitate lump sum payments by the company to the scheme, which are tax deductible.

*continued overleaf*

---

***Future sale of the company?***

Joe may wish to keep profits at a high level in the company. These profits will be liable to the relatively low rate of 12.5% corporation tax. The high profits should increase the value of the company on a future sale.

Joe should be entitled to claim retirement relief on the sale of the trading company in future years (subject to all conditions being met at that time).

The interaction of retirement relief and the property should also be considered. If Joe is to hold the property personally, he will have to sell it with the company in order to claim retirement relief. If he sells it separately, retirement relief cannot be claimed even though it was used for business purposes throughout its period of ownership.

If Joe wishes to incorporate a holding company structure (i.e. the trading entity is 100% held by a "Hold Co"), the future sale of its trading subsidiary can be made tax free. This exemption is known as the section 626B TCA 1997 participation exemption and is a key tax relief that all students should be very familiar with. This relief has been covered in CA Proficiency 2.

If a holding company structure is not initially put in place, it can be implemented at a later date. Reorganisation reliefs are available, which can facilitate a tax-free implementation of a holding company structure.

---

It is clear from the above example that there are many corporate tax, personal tax and commercial issues to consider when incorporating a company. Students should bear in mind all forms of tax relief and charges when considering the taxpayer's intentions.

## 2.3   Transfer of a Sole Trade Business to a Company

### 2.3.1   *Transfer of a Business Relief: Transfer of a Trade as a Going Concern*

On making the decision to incorporate a company, a sole trader will be required to transfer the existing business to their new company. The question will arise as to how this can be done and what the tax implications are. A limited company is a distinct legal entity, legally separated from its shareholders. The transfer of the trade will involve a disposal of the trade by the trader to the company.

The trade will most likely contain at least one capital asset, namely the goodwill of the trade. The goodwill is the value of the trade over and above the value of the underlying assets.

---

***Example 2.2: Transfer of a business relief***
Stephen O'Brien, t/a Irish Boilers Ltd, held the following at 31 July 2016:

|  | € |
|---|---|
| Business premises (open market value) | 2,000,000 |
| Goodwill | 1,800,000 |
| Stock | 200,000 |
| Debtors | 150,000 |
| Creditors | (150,000) |
| Total assets and liabilities | 4,000,000 |

The trade has been valued at €4 million. If Stephen O'Brien is to transfer his trade to a company, he will effectively be disposing of two chargeable assets, namely the property and the goodwill of Irish Boilers.

---

Where there is a disposal/transfer of chargeable assets between connected persons, a charge to CGT may arise based on the market value of those assets (disregarding the fact that money is not changing hands in the transaction). Specific relief from CGT will be available to the extent that the deemed sales proceeds (i.e. the value of assets) are exchanged for shares in the new company. This is known as the "transfer of business relief" (section 600 TCA 1997). This relief is not an exemption, but is more a deferral of the CGT arising on the transaction. The deferred CGT will be taken into account on a future disposal of the shares in the new trading company by reducing the base cost of the shares by the amount of the deferred gain.

In order for the **full** transfer of a business relief to apply:

- there must be a transfer of a business by a person to a company;
- the transfer must occur for bona fide commercial reasons;
- the business must be transferred as a going concern;
- **all the assets of the business** must be transferred to the new company (though there is provision for the retention of some cash, which is a notable provision and worth bearing in mind); and
- the transferor must receive shares in the new company in return for the business (see note below regarding creditors and liabilities).\*

\* Where the company agrees to take over the liabilities of the sole trade (as part of the transfer of the business to the company), the value of the liabilities taken over is considered as "consideration other than shares" for the purpose of this relief. Concessionally, Revenue treats the transfer of bona fide trade liabilities (e.g. creditors, etc.) as not being consideration other than shares for the purpose of this relief, if the only consideration is the shares and the takeover of trade liabilities.

---

**Example 2.3: Transfer of a business relief**

Taking Example 2.2 again, Stephen O'Brien Ltd, t/a Irish Boilers, held the following at 31 July 2016:

|  | € |  |
| --- | --- | --- |
| Business premises | 2,000,000 | (cost €1 million in 2005) |
| Goodwill | 1,800,000 | |
| Stock | 200,000 | |
| Debtors | 150,000 | |
| Creditors | (150,000) | |
| **Total assets and liabilities** | **4,000,000** | |

Stephen transferred the entire business to Irish Boilers Ltd in exchange for 100 shares on 31 July 2016. The value of the whole business was €4 million, so the 100 shares are therefore worth €4 million. The company agreed to take the debts owing by Stephen (i.e. the €150,000 creditors).

On 31 July 2016, Stephen was deemed to have transferred his business and a disposal for CGT purposes occurred. The values of the assets transferred were as follows:

|  | € |  |
| --- | --- | --- |
| Premises | 2,000,000 | chargeable asset |
| Goodwill | 1,800,000 | chargeable asset |
| Stock | 200,000 | non-chargeable asset |
| Debtors | 150,000 | non-chargeable asset |
| Total assets | 4,150,000 | |

The company agrees to take over the creditors of €150,000 as part of the transfer of the business. This is concessionally treated by the Revenue Commissioners not to be consideration other than shares for the purposes of this relief. Obviously, there is a benefit to Stephen by the company taking over the value of the business creditors.

*continued overleaf*

The premises and the goodwill are the only chargeable assets and, as such, the following will apply for CGT purposes on their transfer to the company:

|  | € |
|---|---|
| Deemed disposal of premises | 2,000,000 |
| Less: base cost | (1,000,000) |
| Chargeable gain | 1,000,000 |
| Deemed disposal of goodwill | 1,800,000 |
| Less: base cost | Nil |
| Chargeable gain | 1,800,000 |
| **Total chargeable gains** | **2,800,000** |

The base cost of the shares in the new company in the event of a future disposal will be reduced as follows:

|  | € |
|---|---|
| Share value on 31 July 2016 | 4,000,000 |
| Less: deferred gain | (2,800,000) |
| Future "base cost" of shares | 1,200,000 |

In summary, the following has occurred:

- Based on the above structure, Stephen has no chargeable gains in 2016 on the transfer (i.e. disposal) of his business to a new company. The chargeable gains of €2.8 million are fully deferred.
- Stephen's share base cost is reduced by reference to the amount of the current gain deferred.

---

**Example 2.4: Transfer of a business relief**

Consider again the case of Stephen O'Brien, except in this example he transferred all the **assets** to Irish Boilers Ltd in exchange for 100 shares **and a director's loan account in his favour of €150,000**. The tax implication of the loan is as follows:

The value of the assets was €4.15 million. As there is a loan account in his favour of €150,000, the 100 shares are worth €4 million.

On 31 July 2016, Stephen was deemed to have transferred his business and a disposal for CGT purposes occurred. The values of the assets transferred were as follows:

|  | € |  |
|---|---|---|
| Premises | 2,000,000 | chargeable asset |
| Goodwill | 1,800,000 | chargeable asset |
| Stock | 200,000 | non-chargeable asset |
| Debtors | 150,000 | non-chargeable asset |
| Total assets | 4,150,000 |  |

The premises and the goodwill are the only chargeable assets and, as such, the following will apply for CGT purposes on their transfer to the limited company:

|  | € |
|---|---|
| Deemed disposal of premises | 2,000,000 |
| Less: base cost | (1,000,000) |
| Chargeable gain | 1,000,000 |
| Deemed disposal of goodwill | 1,800,000 |
| Less: base costs | Nil |
| Chargeable gain | 1,800,000 |
| **Total chargeable gain** | **2,800,000** |

The deferred chargeable gain is computed as follows:

Chargeable gain × Value of shares/Value of total assets

*continued overleaf*

---

€2.8 million × €4 million/€4.15 million = €2.7 million

The total chargeable gain is €2.8 million and the deferred gain is €2.7 million. Therefore, the gain arising on the transfer of the business is €100,000, which is taxable in the normal manner at the 33% rate of CGT.

The base cost of the shares in the new company, in the event of a future disposal, will be reduced as follows:

|                               | €           |
| ----------------------------- | ----------- |
| Share value on 31 July 2016   | 4,000,000   |
| Less: Deferred gain           | (2,700,000) |
| Future "base cost" of shares  | 1,300,000   |

By way of summary, the following has occurred:

- Stephen has a current chargeable gain of €100,000 on the transfer (i.e. disposal) of his business assets to a new company. He is immediately liable to CGT at the 33% rate on this gain.
- Stephen's share base cost is reduced by reference to the amount of the current gain deferred.

---

**Planning – Revenue Concession**

In the examples above, Stephen should have structured the transfer so that he benefited from the Revenue concession. He could have transferred the whole business, including trade creditors of €150,000, and not had any loan in his favour. From a **cash perspective**, this would have left him in the same situation. However, from a **tax perspective**, the transfer of the trade is concessionally treated by the Revenue Commissioners as "not for consideration other than shares". This would mean that he would have no gains in 2016 and the base cost of his shares would be €4 million less €2.8 million = €1.2 million.

---

**Key Issue**
A sole trader should consider whether it would be of benefit to retain some assets (e.g. property) and transfer the balance of the trade to a new company. This could remove an entitlement to the transfer of a business relief, but it may be beneficial to hold certain assets personally. For example, a property could increase significantly in value and be available for immediate sale (by the taxpayer). The proceeds of a property sale would be liable to CGT. A sale by a company would also be liable to effective CGT rates, but cash would then have to be extracted from the company leading to an additional tax charge.

It might be more advantageous not to claim transfer of a business relief. This could involve an immediate tax charge in favour of the avoidance of a future greater gain and avoidance of stamp duty – see **Section 2.3.3**.

---

### 2.3.2 VAT Issues on the Transfer of a Trade

A VAT exemption is provided for by section 20(2)(c) and section 26 Value-Added Tax Consolidation Act 2010 when a business, or part of an undertaking, is transferred from one VAT-registered person to another. For the exemption to apply, all of the following conditions must be met:

- the purchaser is VAT registered; and
- the purchaser is entitled to full input credit; and
- the transfer must constitute an undertaking or part of an undertaking capable of being operated on an independent basis.

### 2.3.3 Stamp Duty Issues on the Transfer of a Trade

Where the change in ownership is documented, stamp duty may arise unless the assets can pass by delivery (e.g. plant, equipment, etc.). Normally, property or goodwill would attract stamp duty at a rate of 2%.

No relief from stamp duty is available on the transfer of such assets from an individual to a company. The cost of this tax charge when transferring land or buildings should be weighed up against the potential benefits of the CGT relief for the transfer of all assets to the company.

In **Example 2.4** above, the stamp duty on the property is 2% of €2 million, which is €40,000. While this is a significant cost, it is outweighed by the CGT on the disposal of the goodwill (€1.8 million at 33% or €594,000), and, as a cash flow or cost decision, it would appear advisable to claim the CGT relief. However, if the goodwill was only €100,000, the CGT on this would be €33,000 and, based on immediate tax charges, it would be advisable to hold the property outside the company.

When advising on making such decisions, it is necessary to consider:

- the immediate cash flow impact;
- the age of the individual and if a future sale could qualify for CGT retirement relief (see **Appendix 2.1** at the end of this chapter); and
- whether they wish to hold the property in their own name, earn an income from the property and any future gain accrues to them individually, etc.

Then, on the balance of all these factors, a decision can be reached that best suits the individual.

### 2.3.4 Loss Relief Issues on the Transfer of a Trade

If a sole trader has Case I losses and wishes to transfer that trade to a company, the timing of the transfer should be carefully considered. The transfer of a trade will constitute a cessation of trade for tax purposes.

Losses carried forward cannot be transferred to the company and must be used by the individual to shelter other income of that year or used as a terminal loss claim. Carrying forward the losses will not be beneficial when the trade is moved to a separate legal entity. The potential for the individual to make use of any losses incurred should be examined and then the cessation date chosen.

---

**Example 2.5**

Ann is a sole trader who plans to transfer her business to a company in December 2016. It is now 1 December 2016. Ann has unutilised Case I sole trade losses of €50,000 and €25,000 for the 2015 and 2016 (predicted) trading periods respectively. Ann has no other income.

*Tax Implications*

If Ann transfers the trade in December 2016 to a new company, she cannot transfer the right to carry forward pre-incorporation losses and the relief will therefore be lost.

Ann may be able to make a terminal loss claim in respect of the €25,000 trading loss forecast for the 2016 period. Terminal loss relief is applied in respect of the final year's loss being available for carry back against profits in the three previous tax years (i.e. 2015, 2014 and 2013).

If, however, Ann transfers the business to a new company in 2017, terminal loss relief will be available for the 2016, 2015 and 2014 tax years. However, since she sustained a loss in both 2016 and 2015, she may only benefit from terminal loss relief in 2014, assuming she has sufficient profits in that year. If taxable profits existed in 2013, the benefit of terminal loss relief would be lost. Therefore the timing of the transfer of the business should be considered carefully if loss relief is an issue. (This topic has been discussed in detail in **Section 1.13**.)

---

### 2.3.5 Balancing Charges/Allowances on the Transfer of a Trade

Under section 289 TCA 1997, on the cessation of the sole trade, a balancing allowance or charge will be triggered as the assets are deemed to be sold at their market value. There is a subsection in section 289 under which the parties to the transaction may elect to transfer such assets at their tax written-down value.

However, this election is not available where the transfer is to a company and the transferor (i.e. the sole trader) is not a company.

For example, one key area could involve the transfer of assets that have qualified for capital allowances. Here, there is the potential to create a gain or a loss for the individual and the company can benefit from either an artificially high or low 'cost'.

Anti-avoidance provisions exist (section 312 TCA 1997) that prevent artificial transactions between connected persons (whether or not incorporated) or persons who are not connected. The latter refers to parties who have agreed to enter into a transaction, the main purpose of which is to secure a tax benefit.

These provisions are for transactions in general and are not exclusive to a cessation of a trade. These anti-avoidance provisions were introduced to counter abuses where assets are transferred/sold at such a price as to artificially increase a balancing allowance or reduce/eliminate a balancing charge. In such cases, the assets are deemed to be disposed of at their market value. However, where the parties to the transaction are deemed to be under common control and both are tax-resident in Ireland, section 312 TCA 1997 allows for the transfer of the assets at their tax written-down value rather than at the deemed market value. This can prove useful, depending on the circumstances of the parties. A formal election by both parties is required for this section to apply. Control in relation to a body corporate is measured through share ownership, voting power or powers conferred on that person so that the affairs of that body corporate are conducted in accordance with that person's wishes. A person controls a partnership if the person has a right to more than 50% of the income or assets of the partnership.

### 2.3.6 Cessation Rules Implication on the Transfer of a Trade

Where the profits of a trade have been increasing up to the date of cessation, the "prior year" cessation rules will apply. As demonstrated at **Section 1.12.1**, the profits of the year prior to the year of cessation are revised to an actual basis. Any uplift in profits resulting from the revision is liable to income tax. Timing can be a key consideration as to when to incorporate.

---

**Example 2.6**
In Example 1.15 at Section 1.12.1, we saw the impact of John Jones ceasing to trade on 31 July 2016 using the following profits:

|  | € |
|---|---|
| 31 July 2016 | 20,000 |
| 31 January 2016 | 90,000 |
| 31 January 2015 | 50,000 |
| 31 January 2014 | 60,000 |

His prior year (i.e. 2015) assessment was increased from €50,000 to €86,667, an uplift of €36,667 assessable profits.

In this example, the profits for the six months ended 31 July 2016 were €20,000. Assume anticipated profits for the 12 months to 31 January 2017 are €40,000. What is the implication of John deferring his decision to cease until 31 January 2017?

His "prior year" is 2016. His original assessment is based on profits of €90,000. Applying the actual basis to the 2016 year:

|  | € |
|---|---|
| 90,000 × 1/12 | 7,500 |
| 40,000 × 11/12 | 36,667 |
| Total | 44,167 |

Since there is no uplift in profits based on the actual basis, the original assessment does not require adjustment.

---

## Appendix 2.1: Whether or Not to Incorporate a Company

The following questions should be addressed before commencing to trade:

**Is the business likely to be profitable?**
- If not, it may be more tax efficient to operate as a sole trader and obtain section 381 loss relief until such point as profits are anticipated. The business can be transferred to a company at a future stage. Transfer of a business relief may be available on this transfer.
- If the trade is to be operated as a sole trade, the first three years' profits/losses will be computed by reference to the commencement basis of assessment rules.
- If significant profits are anticipated, the incorporation of a company to carry out the trade may be beneficial if it is done before commencing as a sole trader, as there is the exemption for new start-up companies – see **Section 3.2**. If the business has been carried on as a sole trader, then there is the benefit of the lower corporate rate of tax of 12.5% on trading profits.

**How will the business be funded?**
- Interest as a deduction can be a valuable relief. This will involve the individual drawing down a bank loan for investment in a trading activity as a sole trader. The individual will be entitled to tax relief on the interest payments as a Case I deduction if operating as a sole trader.
- Alternatively, if a company is to be incorporated, the company can draw down the bank loan and can repay the bank debt easily from after-tax funds (as its profits are either exempt for the first three years or liable to the 12.5% rate of tax).
- The Employment and Investment Incentive scheme could provide a means of introducing funding to a qualifying company. The Seed Capital Relief scheme could be used to assist the funding of a qualifying new trading company.
- Other tax reliefs, such as research and development (R&D) tax credit, could help fund the business of a company. Changes in recent Finance Acts allow for a tax refund of the R&D tax credit even where a corporation tax liability does not exist. The refund is computed by reference to the company's payroll costs when the company's corporation tax liability is nil.
- If the shareholders fund a company by way of subscription for share capital, the amount paid for the shares will be their CGT base cost on a future disposal of those shares.

Often you may see a mixture of share capital subscription and an element of loans from the shareholders to the company. These loans can be repaid tax free to the shareholders. Please note, however, that any interest charged on these loans could be treated as a distribution for tax purposes (please reference the close company rules as covered in CA Proficiency 2).

**Is the business likely to be subject to significant commercial risks?**
- If yes, it is perhaps best to establish a company as soon as possible to protect the personal assets of the individual if business failure is possible (i.e. limited liability protection).

**What is the spouse's level of involvement in the business?**
- Does the spouse have their own source of income? If no, can they legitimately draw a salary from the business that can utilise personal income tax bands and tax credits?

▓ Drawing a salary could create a pensionable employment and allow for the funding of a private pension scheme for the spouse. Also, PRSI contributions would be payable on the salary, which may entitle the spouse to a State contributory pension (assuming sufficient PRSI contributions are paid).

▓ If the spouse is to be a shareholder and the shares are to be subsequently disposed of, consider appointing the spouse as a director (for the required time on either a part-time or full-time basis) to allow access to CGT retirement relief in the future.

### Does the taxpayer intend to sell the business?

▓ If yes, it may be beneficial to conduct the business through a company to maximise business growth/development (i.e. with the 12.5% tax rate applying to profits generated). Also, a purchaser may prefer to purchase a business by way of share purchase since stamp duty on shares is only 1% (as opposed to 2% on a trade/asset purchase).

▓ Retirement relief may be available on the future disposal of shares in a trading company. Consider transferring shares to a spouse before the transferor is aged 55 years, and then, if all other conditions are met, claims for retirement relief can be maximised.

▓ A holding company structure could be put in place. This could facilitate the exempt sale of the shares in a trading subsidiary by the holding company. The tax-free funds could then be used for either further investment, or be extracted out of the holding company by way of liquidation.

### Does the taxpayer intend to gift the business to their family/children?

▓ Tax relief such as retirement relief (for CGT) and business asset relief (for CAT) will have to be considered. These reliefs can facilitate a tax-efficient transfer of assets to the next generation.

### Property issues

▓ Factors such as a purchase of the property by a company could lead to issues if the company ceases trading and the property is subsequently sold. If a third-party purchaser wishes to purchase the property only (as opposed to buying the shares in the company from the shareholders), a double charge to tax could arise on extracting cash from the company. This will arise as follows:

  ● CGT at 33% (from 6 December 2012) on a disposal by the company of the property.
  ● CGT at 33% (from 6 December 2012) on a liquidation of the company and distribution of cash to the shareholders.

▓ It may be a planning point to consider whether to purchase the property personally and rent it to the company. This will generate rental income for the shareholders personally and also keep the property out of the corporate regime. The rental income could be used to finance bank borrowings taken out to purchase the property. A Case V tax deduction should be available in respect of interest repayments on bank loans. However, the shareholder may not have sufficient income after tax to pay back the loan and therefore will need another source of funds to repay some of the loan.

▓ One incentive to purchase property in a company is that it may be easier to fund bank borrowings for a property in a company (as the company profits will be liable to 12.5% tax, as opposed to higher income tax rates).

## Chapter 2 Summary

| Incorporation decision | • Consider how well the sole trade is performing before incorporating<br>• Compare tax savings to be made on incorporating<br>• Consider the tax implications of incorporation – cessation of trade, balancing adjustments, VAT<br>• Consider the non-tax implications of incorporating<br>• Consider future plans for exiting the business – sale, retirement, etc. |
| --- | --- |
| How to incorporate | • Consider assets to be transferred<br>• Consider if any assets should be retained personally |
| Changes on incorporation | • Separate legal entity<br>• Corporation tax regime applies to profits<br>• No longer self-employed<br>• Whether or not to incorporate |

# Questions

## Challenging Questions

(Solutions to Challenging Questions are available through your lecturer.)

### Question 2.1

Mr Bear is a long-established client of your firm. Mr Bear is 53 years old and the sole proprietor of his trading business, Bear Toys ("Bear"), which manufactures cuddly toys, and which was set up over 10 years ago. He is married and his wife works at home to mind their children.

Bear trades from a property owned by Mr Bear. The current market value of the property is €450,000 and was purchased for €150,000 when Mr Bear commenced trading.

The business was slow to take off, with losses incurred in the opening years. However, over recent years the trade has excelled and Mr Bear has recently undertaken a programme of restructuring to allow the trade to progress further. This, together with capital allowances claimed on the capital investment, has resulted in current year losses.

Mr Bear currently takes drawings of €40,000 from the business and has no other sources of income.

Mr Bear has provided you with projections in respect of the next two trading years. He has estimated that profits will be in the region of €230,000 per annum and will continue at this level for the foreseeable future.

Mr Bear wishes to talk to you about how best to progress his business in the future, and is keen on the idea of incorporating the trade. You have reviewed the projections, together with the current market position of the business, and have estimated that the goodwill on incorporation would be €200,000, however Mr Bear is of the view it would be €1 million (both figures to be considered).

**Requirement**

Prepare a report on the potential incorporation to cover the following areas:

1.  A broad outline of the potential tax savings on incorporating the trade against trading as a sole trader.
2.  The potential CGT liability arising on the incorporation.
3.  Any reliefs that may be available to reduce the CGT liability.
4.  Advice on whether the property should be transferred to the new limited company or held outside in personal ownership and the implications of the goodwill.
5.  Any tax relief available on the pre-incorporation tax losses.

# Trading Through a Limited Company and Funding the Business

**Learning Objectives**

By the end of this chapter you will be able to:

- Analyse the potential tax implications for a business trading through a company, with particular reference to:

  - differing rates of corporation tax;
  - tax exemption for start-up companies;
  - special tax treatment for investment companies;
  - use of corporate losses;
  - Employment and Investment Incentive Scheme and seed capital relief;
  - Research and Development tax credit; and
  - Entrepreneur relief.

## 3.1 Company Residence Rules – Finance Act 2014 Changes

From previous studies students will be aware of the definition of company residence rules as provided for in section 23A TCA 1997. Changes to these rules have been provided for in section 43 FA 2014, which bring Ireland's rules into line with the rest of the OECD.

A company that is incorporated in Ireland will be regarded as tax resident in Ireland for the purposes of the Taxes Consolidation Act 1997 unless "the treaty exception" applies. The relevant double taxation agreement (DTA) must provide that the company is resident in another territory and not in Ireland. This could be achieved by the application of the residence 'tie-breaker' clause or otherwise as a result of the rules in the DTA for determining residence. These changes will ensure that a foreign incorporated company that is centrally managed and controlled in Ireland will be resident in Ireland for tax purposes. FA 2014 provisions apply with effect from 1 January 2015 for any company incorporated in Ireland on or after 1 January 2015; and from 1 January 2021 for companies incorporated on or before 31 December 2014.

To combat any possible abuses of the new provisions, where, after 1 January 2015, there is both a change in ownership of a company and a major change in the nature or conduct of the company's business either a year before or five years after the change in ownership, the company will instead be regarded as Irish resident from the date of change of ownership and not from 1 January 2021.

## 3.2 Rates of Corporation Tax

A sole trader's profits are liable to tax according to the income tax rules. The profits earned by a limited company will be taxed according to the corporation tax rules and applicable rates. These rules are contained in the Taxes Consolidation Act 1997 (TCA 1997). In general, the rates of corporation tax are much lower when compared to the income tax regime.

Trading income of a company is liable to corporation tax at a rate of 12.5%.

### 3.2.1 Non-trading Income

For tax purposes, non-trading income is commonly known as "passive income". Passive income is typically income earned from investments, for example:

**Case III income:**
Irish bank interest income
foreign interest income
foreign dividend income (see **Section 3.6** – some taxable at 12.5%)
foreign rental income
income of a foreign trade
any other foreign income

**Case IV miscellaneous income:**
royalty income
all other miscellaneous income (not taxed under Cases I, II, III, or V)

**Case V rental income:**
Irish rental income

The above classifications of income are liable to the 25% rate of corporation tax. It is therefore important to be aware that any income other than trading income is liable to a higher rate of corporation tax.

In some instances, non-trading income can be liable to an additional 20% tax known as a "close company surcharge". In this regard, students should bear in mind that, if a close company has passive income, due consideration will have to be given to any exposure to a close company surcharge (see **Section 3.4**).

### 3.2.2 Other Income and Corporation Tax Rates

Other types of income and applicable rates of corporation tax are as follows:

| | | |
|---|---|---|
| Franked investment income | Exempt | |
| Income from minerals | 25% | (excepted trade) |
| Petroleum activities | 25% | (excepted trade) |
| Land-dealing income | 25% | (excepted trade) |

## 3.3 Tax Exemption for Start-up Companies

Finance (No. 2) Act 2008 introduced a relief from corporation tax for new 'start-up' companies. The relevant legislation is contained in section 486C TCA 1997. The purpose of the relief is to encourage new business activity in recessionary times.

The relief applies to the profits of "qualifying trades" and to the disposal of assets used for the purposes of the qualifying trade. It operates by reducing the corporation tax attributable to such profits to nil, but it only applies where the total amount of corporation tax payable by the company for an accounting period is not greater than €40,000. Marginal relief applies where the total corporation tax payable by the new company is between €40,000 and €60,000. The relief applies for three years from the commencement of the trade, subject to conditions. Unused relief in the first three years can be carried forward (see **Section 3.3.3** below).

Although the concept seems straightforward, the legislation is quite restrictive and complex.

### 3.3.1 What is a "Qualifying Trade"?

Originally a "qualifying trade" was defined as a trade that was set up and commenced by a new company between 2009 and 2015. Section 30 Finance Act 2015 extended the set-up and commencement date to 31 December 2018. A qualifying trade does not include any trade:

- that was carried on previously by another person and to which the company has succeeded (which would rule out the incorporation of a business by a sole trader/partnership), including trades transferred between connected companies;
- the activities of which were previously carried on as part of another person's trade or profession;
- that is an excepted trade (e.g. land developers, mining and petroleum activities), which are typically trades taxed at the 25% rate; or
- the activities of which, if carried on by a close company with no other income, would result in that company being considered a service company for the purposes of the close company surcharge (which rules out newly incorporated professional services practices).

The corporation tax attributable to income from a qualifying trade is computed by reference to what is known as "relevant corporation tax". Relevant corporation tax is the total corporation tax exclusive of:

- close company surcharges under section 440 and section 441 TCA 1997;
- profits attributable to dealing in residential development land under section 644B TCA 1997;
- the corporation tax chargeable on the profits of the company attributable to chargeable gains for the period; and
- the corporation tax chargeable on profits charged at the 25% rate.

Finance Act 2011 introduced a link between the amount of relief and the amount of employer PRSI contributions paid. To avail of the maximum relief of €40,000, the company needs to have paid at least €40,000 in employer PRSI contributions. In quantifying the amount of employer PRSI contributions, the maximum allowed per employee is €5,000.

---

**Example 3.1**

James Mead decides to set up a new manufacturing company, James Mead Ltd, in 2016. He owns 100% of the shares. The tax-adjusted trading profits for the year ending 31 December 2016 are €200,000 and the company also has investment income of €20,000. The company paid €30,000 in employer's PRSI in 2016. He understands the company has no corporation tax to pay.

(a) Is he correct?

No. Assuming James Mead Ltd meets all the conditions of the relief as set out above, it will not have to pay the €25,000 corporation tax (€200,000 × 12.5%) that would otherwise be due on the trading profits. However, the company is liable to €5,000 corporation tax (€20,000 × 25%) on the investment income (plus potentially a close company surcharge if the after-tax investment income is not distributed).

(b) Would your answer be different if James were an engineer and, instead of manufacturing, James Mead Ltd will provide engineering services?

Yes. Engineering is a professional service (as distinct from carrying on a trade), so the relief would not apply. James Mead Ltd would therefore be liable to the €25,000 corporation tax on the "trading profits" in addition to the €5,000 corporation tax on the investment income (plus potentially a close company surcharge if the after-tax income is not distributed).

### 3.3.2   Marginal Relief

Marginal relief applies where the total corporation tax is between €40,000 and €60,000. In this instance, the sum of corporation tax on income from the qualifying trade and the corporation tax on chargeable gains from the disposal of qualifying assets is reduced by reference to the formula:

$$3 \times (T-M) \times \frac{(A+B)}{T}$$

where:

- T is the total corporation tax payable by the company for the accounting period;
- M is the lower limit, i.e. €40,000;
- A is the corporation tax payable by the company on income from the qualifying trade for the accounting period; and
- B is the corporation tax payable by the company for that accounting period so far as is referable to chargeable gains on the disposal of qualifying assets of the qualifying trade.

---

**Example 3.2**

Referring to Example 3.1 again, except this time the trading profits are €400,000 and the employer's PRSI paid was €50,000. The tax due for the year ended 31/12/2016 is calculated as follows:

T = €55,000 (12.5% × €400,000 plus €5,000 tax on the investment income)

M = €40,000

A = €50,000

B = nil

Applying the formula gives us:

$$3 \times (55,000 - 40,000) \times \frac{(50,000 + 0)}{55,000} = €40,909$$

Therefore, the total corporation tax bill for the company will be €45,909, being €5,000 tax on investment income plus €40,909 maximum tax on trading income, using marginal relief.

---

### 3.3.3   Unused Relief Carried Forward

Section 34 Finance Act 2013, which amends section 486C TCA 1997, provides for the carrying forward of unused reliefs from the first three years of trading. Unused reliefs occur where the company's corporation tax liability in the first three years of trading does not exceed €40,000 per accounting period and the employer's qualifying PRSI liability exceeds the corporation tax liability for those years. This part of employer's PRSI liability that exceeds the corporation tax liability for the first three years of trading is known as the "specified aggregate". The application of this provision is best illustrated using the example below:

**Example 3.3**

|  | Year 1 | Year 2 | Year 3 | Total |
|---|---|---|---|---|
|  | € | € | € | € |
| Case I | 20,000 | 150,000 | 80,000 | |
| Corporation tax @ 12.5% | 2,500 | 18,750 | 10,000 | |
| Total employer PRSI | 15,000 | 15,000 | 15,000 | |
| Corporation tax after section 486C relief | 0 | 3,750 | 0 | |
| Specified aggregate | 12,500 | 0 | 5,000 | 17,500 |

*continued overleaf*

|  | Year 4 |
|---|---|
|  | € |
| Case I | 150,000 |
| Corporation tax @ 12.5% | 18,750 |
| Total PRSI | 18,000 |
| Specified aggregate b/f | 17,500* |
| Corporation tax after section 486C relief | 1,250 |

* If the employer's PRSI in Year 4 was, say, €16,000, the specified aggregate brought forward would be limited to €16,000 in Year 4 with the unused balance of €1,500 carried forward to Year 5.

Some points to bear in mind:

- As we have seen, not all types of profit qualify (e.g. non-trading gains or income) and not all types of trading companies apply (e.g. professional services).
- If the company is exempt from tax on the profits, the traditional advantage that salary had over dividends (i.e. no tax deduction for dividends as paid out of after-tax income) has narrowed somewhat.
- A combination of a corporate relief like this plus personal reliefs, e.g. EIIS or seed capital relief could give a very good tax result to a start-up entrepreneur. For example, if the EIIS or seed capital relief (see **Section 3.8.3**) refund could sustain an entrepreneur while the company is exempt from corporation tax on profits, it may make sense to defer drawing a salary until the company can claim a tax deduction for it at the 12.5% corporation tax rate.

> **Key Issue**
> This new exemption has the potential to assist a lot of start-up companies by reducing their overall effective tax liabilities. It is not effective, however, for sole traders wishing to incorporate an existing business.

## 3.4 Overview of Trading Loss Relief for a Company

The loss relief rules for companies are broadly similar to those for sole traders. However, the rules differ in certain key respects. As group relief is covered in **Chapter 6**, students will need to be aware of these rules and should take time to review them, particularly the order of use of the losses and the restrictions on charges. A brief recap of the key points is set out below:

| Legislative reference | Use of the loss | Claim required |
|---|---|---|
| Section 396(2) TCA 1997 – Case I (25% rate) | Set-off against other profits in the same or preceding accounting period of same length. | Within two years of the end of the accounting period. |
| Section 396(1) TCA 1997 – Case I | Carry forward against future profits of the same trade. | Automatic. |

| Section 396A TCA 1997 – Case I (12.5%) | Set-off against other relevant trading income in the same or preceding accounting period of same length. | Within two years of the end of the accounting period. |
|---|---|---|
| Section 396B TCA 1997 – Case I (12.5%) | Set-off on value basis against corporation tax on profits of the same or preceding accounting period of same length. | Within two years of the end of the accounting period. |
| Section 396(1) TCA 1997 – Case III trade | Carry forward against future Case III profits. | Automatic. |
| Section 397 TCA 1997 – terminal loss | A loss in the last 12 months of trading can be set back against trading income of the preceding three years. | Must be made after all other possible claims are made. |

## 3.5    Close Company Surcharge

A close company is one that is controlled by five or fewer participators or by any number of directors who are also participators or where, on a full distribution of its income, more than half of it would fall to be paid to five or fewer participators or to participators who are directors. Several tax disadvantages attach to close companies, such as the surcharge outlined below, limitations on deductible interest, the withholding tax in respect of loans by the company to participators, etc. As most Irish companies are close companies, students should be aware of how to identify a close company and, in particular, those companies under foreign ownership.

A close company surcharge of 20% is levied on a close company that does not distribute its after-tax estate and investment income. In general, estate and investment income will include rental income, interest income and dividend income. Generally, there is no surcharge levied on trading income. However, the close company surcharge applies to trading income of a "service company". Students will be aware of the definition of a service company from their CA Proficiency 2 studies. It is essentially a company deriving its income from professional services. The surcharge levied, however, is confined to half of its distributable Case I/II income and the rate is 15% (and not 20%). The surcharge does not apply to the after-tax income of all companies where such income is €2,000 or less. Previously this *de minimis* amount was €635. The increase to €2,000 applies to accounting periods ending on or after 1 January 2013. The surcharge is designed as a disincentive to retaining investment/professional earnings within the close company.

Finance Act 2008 introduced a provision whereby dividends paid between Irish companies can be elected as being not surchargeable (section 434 TCA 1997). This is a key development in close company legislation. It can effectively facilitate wholly tax-free dividends to be paid between Irish companies (i.e. as franked investment income and is also now non-surchargeable on making the appropriate election in the **Form CT1**). The critical issue associated with the election, however, is that the non-surchargeable dividend paid by the payer company is deemed not to be a distribution for the purposes of its own close company surcharge computation. As such, if the payer company has significant investment and estate income of its own, it may find itself liable to a close company surcharge even though it has made a distribution to another Irish company. However, if it does not, an election can save tax.

| Example 3.4: Section 434(3A) TCA 1997 election | | | |
|---|---|---|---|
| **ABC group** | **A Ltd** | **B Ltd** | **C Ltd** |
| | € | € | € |
| Dividend – B Ltd/C Ltd | 100,000 | | |
| Investment income | | 50,000 | 0 |
| Trading income | | 0 | 80,000 |
| Corporation tax @ 12.5%/25% | | (12,500) | (10,000) |
| Dividend paid | | (30,000) | (70,000) |
| Election? | | No | Yes |
| Distributable estate and inv. income | 30,000 | 7,500 | 0 |
| Surcharge if election made by C Ltd and not B Ltd | 6,000 | 1,500 | 0 |
| Surcharge if elections made by both | 0 | 7,500 | |
| Surcharge if elections not made | 20,000 | 1,500 | 0 |
| Surcharge savings by making the election | 14,000 | | |

**Key Issue**

When you see passive income included in a company's income, always consider if there is a close company surcharge issue.

## 3.6 Other Close Company Issues

The main disadvantages associated with close companies are briefly summarised as follows:

- Certain expenses for participators and their associates are treated as distributions out of the company.
- Interest paid to certain directors and their associates that exceeds a prescribed limit is treated as a distribution.
- No corporation tax deduction for loans to participators (or their associates) which are subsequently written off.
- There is a tax penalty for close companies making loans to participators or their associates.

A significant amount of close company legislation is designed to make any monies or value passing from a company to its shareholders liable to income tax (as opposed to being either exempt or liable to lower CGT rates of tax).

---

**Example 3.5**

Mike and Mary are the shareholders and directors of Double M Ltd. Their 20-year-old son Marty is in college and wants to work in Boston for the summer. The return flight is €600, which is paid for by Double M Ltd. Marty doesn't work for Double M Ltd.

The tax impact of this payment is as follows:

- This is a non-deductible expense for Double M Ltd.
- Double M Ltd is obliged to apply dividend withholding tax (DWT) to the deemed distribution to Marty of €600.
- Depending on his personal circumstances, Marty may be able to reclaim a refund of the DWT if his taxable income for the year is below the income tax exemption limits.

## 3.7   Distributions of Trading Income from EU/Treaty Companies

Finance Act 2008 introduced a provision whereby dividends received from an EU (or country with which Ireland has a double taxation treaty) trading entity can now attract the 12.5% rate of Irish corporation tax (section 21B TCA 1997). Section 53 Finance Act 2012 extended such foreign entities to include non-EU, non-tax treaty partners that have ratified the OECD Convention on Mutual Administrative Assistance in Tax Matters. Prior to FA 2008, all foreign dividend income was liable to Irish corporation tax at the 25% rate.

For example, if the dividend is paid out of a foreign subsidiary's trading profits, the 12.5% rate of tax can be applied in the recipient's hands in Ireland (i.e. the parent company). The 12.5% rate will also apply where the dividend is paid through the tiers of foreign trading subsidiaries.

This 12.5% rate will not apply to dividends paid out of excepted trades, typically being the trade of dealing in development property or minerals.

---

**Example 3.6**

Holdings Ltd, an Irish company, intends to receive a dividend of €90,000 from its trading subsidiary in another EU Member State where the rate of corporation tax is 10%. The finance director of Holdings Ltd has been told they can elect to have the dividend taxable at 12.5%. Should he make the election?

Yes, he should. If he does, the total tax cost is as set out in column 1; if he does not, the total tax cost is set out in column 2:

|  | With election – 12.5% | Without election – 25% |
| --- | --- | --- |
|  | € | € |
| Gross dividend | 90,000 | 90,000 |
| Foreign effective tax rate | 10% | 10% |
| Regross @ lower effective rate | 100,000 | 100,000 |
| Irish tax before credit | 12,500 | 25,000 |
| Foreign tax credit | (10,000) | (10,000) |
| Irish tax after credit | 2,500 | 15,000 |
| Total tax paid | 12,500 | 25,000 |

A similar dividend is proposed from another trading subsidiary in another EU Member State where the rate of corporation tax is 15%. Should he make the 12.5% election?

Yes, he should. The total tax here will be €15,000, which is more favourable than the €25,000 if the election is not made.

---

## 3.8   Land-dealing Provisions: Special Tax Rates

Students will note from **Section 3.1.2** that there are specific rates for the profits of a **land-dealing trade**. This was an important area of Irish tax law in recent years, given the high levels of property development in Ireland (and profits arising thereon).

A land-dealing company will hold land as an item of stock for resale in the course of its trade. The company will compute its profits or losses from that trade in the normal manner. The company will be entitled to a deduction in respect of its trading stock and also all other revenue expenditure incurred wholly and exclusively for the purposes of its trade. The land will therefore be considered a revenue item for tax purposes (i.e. an item of stock acquired for the purposes of sale/development as part of the trade). **The CGT rules will not apply to development land held as stock**.

The profits from the sale of development land will be liable to the 25% rate of corporation tax (**and not CGT as noted above**). Prior to Finance Act 2009, a lower corporation tax rate of 20% applied to land zoned for residential development by the appropriate local authority. However, this was increased to the 25% rate in line with non-residential development land.

It is important to note that the 12.5% rate will apply to profits from the development of land, typically being the construction, demolition, alteration or reconstruction of a building on land. The disposal of fully developed land will also attract the 12.5% rate. Fully developed land will be land on which a building has been constructed by or for the company, and there is no expectation of further development for a period of 20 years.

**Typical charge to corporation tax on property-related profits:**

| | |
|---|---|
| Profit from the sale of commercial land | 25% |
| Profits from construction contract | 12.5% |
| Profit from sale of site and building agreement | Apportion profit between 12.5% and 25% rate on just and fair basis. |
| Profit from sale of finished property | 12.5% |

---

**Key Issue**

When a company derives income from land dealings or property development activity, the rate of tax which the profits are liable to will have to be carefully considered.

---

## 3.9 Employment and Investment Incentive Scheme (EIIS) and Seed Capital Relief: Tax Reliefs and Benefits Associated with Business Funding

### 3.9.1 EIIS and Seed Capital Relief: Overview

Raising capital is a key objective for companies seeking growth and the ability to raise it tax-efficiently is worthy of consideration. The above reliefs are incentive schemes that provide tax relief for investment in certain corporate trades. A decision to trade as a sole trader means these types of tax incentives are not available. Finance Act 2011 introduced a new investment incentive, the Employment and Investment Incentive Scheme (EIIS), which replaced the Business Expansion Scheme (BES) relief that was around for many years. The purpose of the EIIS is to promote job creation and encourage companies to carry out research and development (R&D) activities. Seed capital relief continues to be effective, with some Finance Act 2011 amendments.

While these reliefs are attractive in principle, the qualifying criteria for both can be complex, which may act as a disincentive to potential investors. Furthermore, both reliefs are included in the "specified reliefs" restriction for "high earners" (discussed at **Section 1.13**); this has not enhanced their attractiveness. Note, however, that EIIS is no longer a specified relief for investments on or after 15 October 2013.

### 3.9.2 Main Issues for Companies Using the Reliefs for Funding

The main rules that currently apply to a company seeking to raise either/both EIIS and seed capital funding are included in Part 16 of the TCA 1997 and are broadly as follows:

- A company can raise both seed capital and EIIS funding up to a total of €15 million, subject to a maximum of €5 million in any one 12-month period.
- The shares issued in respect of an individual's investment must not carry any preferential rights to dividends, assets or redemption.
- The investor must not dispose of the shares for at least four years, and there must be no attempt to pass the investment back to the investor during that period. Furthermore, the investor must not enter into any agreement, arrangement or understanding that would eliminate the risk from the investment.
- The company must be an unquoted company resident in Ireland or the EEA.

▨ The company must be a micro (less than 10 employees and an annual turnover and/or annual balance sheet total not exceeding €2 million), small (less than 50 employees and an annual turnover and/or annual balance sheet not exceeding €10 million) or medium-sized (less than 250 employees and an annual turnover not exceeding €50 million or an annual balance sheet total not exceeding €43 million) enterprise. If the company is a medium-sized enterprise it must be in an "assisted" area of Ireland. If the company is in a "non-assisted" area (i.e. Dublin, Meath, Kildare, Wicklow or Cork, other than the Cork Docklands), it can only qualify if it is in its "seed" or start-up stage of development, as defined.

▨ Section 27 Finance Act 2014 has expanded the scheme to include the management and operation of nursing homes; and internationally traded financial services (as defined), subject to conditions (see **Section 3.8.4**).

▨ The company must use the amounts invested for the purposes of job creation or increase in R&D.

▨ Both schemes are currently available until 31 December 2020.

Further analysis of both reliefs is set out below.

### 3.9.3   Seed Capital Relief

Seed capital relief is designed to provide an incentive for individuals who intend to start up their own business. The relief is available to a specified individual who makes a relevant investment in a company. The individual must also be employed by that company.

The relief is granted in respect of that person's investment in the share capital of a new Irish resident company. This new company must typically be engaged in manufacturing, although certain service trades can also qualify.

The method for granting seed capital relief allows that person to elect to have the amount invested in the new company claimed as a deduction and thereby receive a refund of tax paid in any of the six years immediately prior to that investment. The relief is effectively designed as a refund of PAYE paid by the individual in prior years.

With effect from 1 January 2007, a sum of up to €600,000 invested in the share capital is available for tax relief. A maximum annual relief of €100,000 (being a deduction against gross income) is available in any one year (section 490 TCA 1997). Where any part of an investment cannot be relieved in a tax year because of insufficient income, it can be carried forward to a later tax year.

The rules applicable to seed capital relief as detailed in Part 16 of TCA 1997 are as follows:

▨ The person must become a full-time employee of the company in the tax year in which the investment is made in the share capital. The person must also remain employed for a minimum of one year.

▨ The qualifying investment may be made in two investments, the second investment being made within two years of the end of the tax year in which the first investment was made.

▨ The individual must own at least 15% of the ordinary share capital of the company for a period of one year from the date of issue or date from which trade commences, whichever is later.

▨ The individual must not have had a beneficial interest of more than 15% in any other company within 12 months prior to commencing employment in the new company.

▨ The seed capital relief is designed for those who were previously in PAYE employment (and more specifically have been in PAYE employment for the three years prior to making the investment in the company). Excluding the year prior to that of the investment year, if the individual's non-employment income is in excess of €50,000, then the relief will not be available. The relief is essentially designed for former employees who wish to start their own business.

▨ The company must be carrying on a trade that would qualify for EIIS relief (see **Section 3.9.4**).

▨ If any of the relief conditions are breached, there will be a clawback of the relief.

The relief is designed to generate income tax refunds for the investor. To qualify for the relief, the company must be carrying on a new business. For example, the business could not have been operated by the individual as a sole trader and subsequently transferred to a limited company.

The relief is achieved by deeming the investment to have been made in each of the six years prior to the issue of the new share capital. For each of the six years, the refund is limited to the total tax paid with an upper limit relief claim of €100,000 per tax year. The seed capital relief is a very attractive source of funds to an individual who is embarking on a new venture. The actual tax paid by the investor will be a critical issue to establish. The relief should be targeted for the years in which the most income tax was paid by the investor.

Where any part of the investment cannot be relieved in a tax year due to insufficiency of income in that year, the balance unused can be carried forward to a later year.

---

**Example 3.7**

John, a qualifying individual, invested €150,000 in a qualifying investment on 1 March 2017. His taxable salary income for the previous six tax years was as follows:

|      | €       |
|------|---------|
| 2011 | 45,000  |
| 2012 | 40,000  |
| 2013 | 45,000  |
| 2014 | 92,000  |
| 2015 | 80,000  |
| 2016 | 125,000 |

John will be entitled to make a claim for tax relief subject to the maximum claim in any one year of €100,000. The refund due to John will depend on the rate of tax applicable to his income in each of the relevant tax years.

To maximise the relief, John should select the tax year within the last six years (in which the investment is deemed to occur) in order to maximise tax relief. As John's earnings have been higher in recent years, the tax paid will also be higher in those years. John should target those years to maximise the tax refund due.

The nominated tax year for the claim will be 2015, as 2015 and 2016 would appear to be the years in which, taken together, the highest amount of tax has been paid:

|                          | 2011   | 2012   | 2013   | 2014   | 2015     | 2016     |
|--------------------------|--------|--------|--------|--------|----------|----------|
|                          | €      | €      | €      | €      | €        | €        |
| Taxable income           | 45,000 | 40,000 | 45,000 | 92,000 | 80,000   | 125,000  |
| Less : seed capital relief | 0    | 0      | 0      | 0      | (80,000) | (70,000) |
| Revised taxable income   | 45,000 | 40,000 | 45,000 | 92,000 | 0        | 55,000   |

If John had selected 2011 as his nominated year, tax relief would not be maximised, as a significant portion of his income in 2011, 2012 and 2013 was taxed only at the standard rate of tax (i.e. 20%). The tax relief should target years in which the 41%/40% rate of tax applied. If John's income for 2015 had been €200,000, then all of the €150,000 investment would have been relieved at 40%.

---

### 3.9.4 EIIS Relief

The EIIS provides income tax relief to an individual by reference to his or her investment in the share capital of certain qualifying companies. The scheme is designed to attract investors to Irish businesses. The company benefits from funding and the investor benefits from the income tax relief by reference to the amount invested in a qualifying company. This scheme was designed to encourage investment in relevant companies and to stimulate and encourage further employment of staff.

**Qualifying Company**

A qualifying EIIS company must:

- be incorporated in Ireland or another EEA state;
- be unquoted;
- be resident in Ireland (or else be a resident of an EEA state and carry on a business in Ireland through a branch or agency);
- be a trading company carrying on relevant trading activities;
- have all issued shares paid up;
- not be connected with a non-qualifying company;
- not be under the control of another company; and
- not control another company, other than a company that is a qualifying subsidiary. A qualifying subsidiary can usually be described as a company that carries on relevant trading activities and must be a 51% subsidiary of a qualifying company.

**Relevant Trading Activities**

The definition of trades that qualified for the former BES relief was quite restrictive (it only applied to primarily manufacturing-type activities). For EIIS purposes, a company will qualify if it is carrying on a relevant trading activity, i.e. an activity that is assessed to tax under Schedule D Case I. Therefore all trades will qualify, with the exception of the following:

- adventures or concerns in the nature of trade;
- dealing in commodities or futures in shares, securities or other financial assets;
- financing activities;
- professional service companies;
- dealing in or developing land;
- forestry;
- operations carried on in the coal industry or in the steel and shipbuilding sectors; and
- film production.

Under the former BES, companies were required to obtain prior approval of their trading activities from the various certifying agencies or authorities. This requirement has been removed for the EIIS in respect of all trading activities, except tourist traffic undertakings. A company carrying on tourist traffic undertakings must have prior approval from Fáilte Ireland before making any application to the Revenue Commissioners.

Section 27 Finance Act 2014 also provided that a company whose relevant trading activities includes international trading services will not be a qualifying company unless it receives a certificate from Enterprise Ireland to the effect that its activities are of a kind specified in the Schedule to the Industrial Development (Service Industries) Order 2010.

**Qualifying Investor**

Relief for the investor is granted by way of deduction against their total income. Relief is granted at the individual's marginal rate of tax. If an investment is to be made, it will be important to ensure that tax relief is obtained, to the furthest extent possible, against income liable to the 40% rate of income tax. If a taxpayer is in a position to increase their income in a particular tax year (e.g. pay extra salary or special dividends), this could be a useful planning point in maximising tax relief.

An individual must be a **qualifying individual** for the purposes of the relief. This means that the person must not be connected with the company in the two years prior to the purchase of shares and for a period of three years following acquisition of the shares. "Connected to the company" means the individual or an associate of the individual is:

▦ a partner of the company; or

▦ a director or employee of the company, or of another company which is the partner of that company, and who is in receipt of excessive remuneration.

An associate means any partner of the individual making the investment.

An individual is also regarded as connected with the company if he or she controls the company, or directly or indirectly is entitled to acquire an interest of 30% or more in the company. The conditions relating to connected parties as qualifying investors do not apply to an investor investing in their own company where the amounts subscribed for the issued share capital and the loan capital do not, in aggregate, exceed €500,000. Therefore, an individual can obtain relief if he owns 100% of the share capital provided that, when the shares are issued, the aggregate of share and loan capital does not exceed €500,000.

## Eligible Shares

EIIS relief is available only for an investment in "eligible shares", which are new ordinary shares that for a period of three years from the date of issue do not carry any present or future preferential rights to dividends, or assets on a winding up or redemption.

## Withdrawal of the Relief

The relief will be withdrawn from the individual if the shares are disposed of within four (previously three) years of issue or if the individual ceases to qualify within the four-year period. The relief will also be withdrawn if the individual receives any value from the company within a three-year period (e.g. a redemption of a portion of shares).

The relief will also be withdrawn if the company ceases to qualify within a period of four years. This could arise by virtue of the trade becoming a non-qualifying trade, or perhaps the company becoming a quoted company.

If the company goes into liquidation for bona fide commercial reasons, any value received by the qualifying investors will be deemed to be value received from the company, and the level of relief previously claimed will be reduced by virtue of any amounts received.

## Other Conditions

Other more particular conditions in respect of the relief are as follows:

▦ The company must use the funds raised for the purposes of carrying on relevant trading activities or, if the company has not yet commenced to trade, in incurring expenditure on R&D. In addition, the use of the funds must contribute directly to the maintenance or creation of employment in the company.

▦ Relief is available in a full tax year subject to a maximum amount of €150,000.

▦ If more than €150,000 is invested by an investor, the excess over that amount is deemed to have been invested in the following tax year and tax relief may be claimed in that next year.

▦ If full relief is not possible in the year of investment (due to the investor not having sufficient income), the unutilised amount can be carried forward to the next tax year.

▦ EIIS is deducted from total income before the investor's tax liability is calculated. This can have the effect of wasting annual tax credits and the 20% standard rate band if the investor does not have sufficient taxable income. A feature of the EIIS relief is that, initially, an individual may only claim relief at 30/40 times the amount invested. This means that if the investor's marginal rate is 40%, the investment is only relieved at 30%. The remaining 10/40 relief (i.e. relief at 10%) will be available where it has been proven that employment levels have increased by the company at the end of the holding period of three years, or where evidence is provided that the company used the funds for expenditure on R&D.

▓ If the shares are disposed of within four years of issue, the relief will be withdrawn.

▓ The individual cannot obtain relief if, at the date of share issue, they own more than 30% of the share capital of the company. The percentage ownership of the investor's close relatives is not taken into account when computing this 30%.

▓ Both a husband and wife and civil partners can obtain relief for up to €150,000 each in a tax year. The investment by the husband and wife or civil partners must be separate, however, and each party should have sufficient personal income (i.e. the EIIS relief is non-transferable between spouses/civil partners).

▓ An individual cannot claim any other tax relief in respect of borrowings drawn down to make an EIIS investment.

An individual may obtain EIIS relief by investing in an EIIS designated fund (as opposed to a direct single investment). Such EIIS funds are subject to the same conditions as those of a single investment as outlined above. While a single investment is subject to a €250 minimum investment, no such minimum applies for a designated fund.

A claim for tax relief must be made within two years of the end of the tax year in which the shares were issued. There will be a clawback of the EIIS relief if the shares are sold within four years of acquisition.

If the shares are disposed of in the future and a gain is realised, the full cost of acquisition is allowable as a base cost for CGT purposes. If the disposal results in a loss, the full cost of acquisition is reduced by the amount of the EIIS relief which restricts the amount of loss relief available.

A key point to note is that, if a company requires funding, it may be able to avail of the EIIS as a means of raising the required funds.

---

**Key Issue**
Always consider an EIIS scheme if the company is a qualifying company and funding is required.

---

## 3.10 Research and Development (R&D) Tax Credit

There is a 25% tax credit for companies for qualifying expenditure on R&D.

### 3.10.1 Expenditure on Research and Development

Section 766 TCA 1997 provides for a credit on expenditure on R&D. Section 766A TCA 1997 provides for a credit on capital expenditure on buildings or structures used for an R&D activity.

The credit is given in addition to the normal tax deduction as a trading expense (therefore, tax saving of 12.5% + 25% = 37.5%). For many years expenditure on R&D in the base year (2003) was compared to the expenditure on the R&D in a "relevant period" (accounting period) to determine the level of incremental expenditure qualifying for relief. Recent Finance Acts introduced a certain level of expenditure allowable on a volume basis with the balance allowed on an incremental basis. For example, Finance (No. 2) Act 2013 provided that the first €300,000 for group R&D expenditure be removed from the incremental basis of calculations. Section 26 FA 2014 has now provided for the complete removal of the incremental basis of calculating the R&D credit for relevant periods commencing on or after 1 January 2015.

**Qualifying Expenditure**
Normal revenue-type expenditure (such as consumables, salaries, overheads, etc.) and expenditure on plant and machinery qualify for the credit, provided proper records are kept. There is no minimum spend and there is no upper limit. The expenditure on R&D that qualifies for the credit must be net of grants.

Non-qualifying expenditure includes:

- royalty payments if paid to a connected person who is exempt from tax on the royalty income or to the extent that the royalty payment exceeds an arm's length payment;
- interest payments;
- payments to sub-contractors or outsourcing do not qualify for the tax credit, except:
    - an amount that is the greater of 5% of total R&D expenditure and €100,000, which is paid to a university or institute of higher education to carry on R&D activity, may qualify; and
    - the greater of 15% (10% up to 31 December 2013) of R&D spend and €100,000 to third parties.

### Qualifying Company

A qualifying company, while carrying out R&D activities, must carry on a trade in the State throughout the relevant period. It must maintain a record of expenditure incurred by it. If a member of a group, it must be a 51% member of a trading group. In a group situation, it is necessary to look at the group expenditure on R&D and then the group may decide how to allocate the credit between the companies in the 51% group. Companies claiming the R&D tax credit are not required to hold the intellectual property rights and the R&D does not have to be successful.

### How the Credit Operates

The corporation tax of an accounting period can be reduced by 25% of the qualifying expenditure on R&D. If the credit exceeds the corporation tax against which it can be offset, the excess may be carried back to an accounting period of equal length or carried forward for offset against corporation tax payable in the following accounting period. Unused credits can be carried forward indefinitely. There is a refund mechanism for tax already paid, if the company so wishes to make a claim.

### Offset of Credit

Offsetting credit is best illustrated by an example.

---

**Example 3.8**

A company incurs qualifying R&D expenditure in the year ended 31/12/2016. Assuming that there is sufficient credit, the company may make all of the following claims for the year ended 31/12/2016:

- Offset against corporation tax of current year 2016.
- Offset against corporation tax of prior year 2015.
- Remaining excess paid over 33 months.
- First payment of 33% of that excess payable no earlier than 23/09/2017.
- Remaining balance used to offset against corporation tax of following year – 2017.
- If excess still exists, 50% of that excess is paid to the company as a second instalment – no earlier than 21/09/2018.
- Remaining balance used to pay corporation tax of following year again – 2018.
- If excess still exists, that excess is paid to the company as a third instalment – no earlier than 23/09/2019.

---

Claims must be made within 12 months of the end of the accounting period in which the expenditure was incurred.

---

**Example 3.9: R&D credit**

Company Inventions Ltd incurs qualifying R&D spend in 2016 of €400,000. The tax credit is therefore €400,000 × 25% = €100,000. The corporation tax liability is as follows:

|  | € |
| --- | --- |
| Y/E 31/12/2015 | 30,000 |
| Y/E 31/12/2016 | 10,000 |
| Y/E 31/12/2017 | 15,000 |
| Y/E 31/12/2018 | <u>10,000</u> |
| Total | 65,000 |

Credit due is €400,000 × 25% = €100,000:

- Offset in 2016 = €10,000
- Offset in 2015 = €30,000

Balance forward = €60,000:

- 33% × €60,000 = €19,800 claimed as first instalment and payable no earlier than 23/09/2017.
- Balance €40,200 not yet claimed. Carry forward and claim against corporation tax for 2017 of €15,000.
- Balance €25,200 not yet claimed. 50% of remaining balance will be paid as a second instalment i.e. €12,600 will be paid no earlier than 23/09/2018.
- Balance €12,600 not yet claimed. Carry forward and claim against corporation tax for 2018 of €10,000.
- Balance €2,600 not yet claimed. Balance will be paid as a third instalment, i.e. €2,600 will be paid no earlier than 23/09/2019.

---

Finance Act 2012 extended the use of R&D credits by allowing companies to use a portion of the credit to reward key employees who have been involved in the R&D process. In order to qualify as a "key employee", the employee must not be a director of the company or a connected company; they cannot have a material interest in the company (i.e. own more than 5% of the share capital); and they must perform 50% or more of their duties in the conception or creation of new knowledge, products, processes, methods or systems. At least 50% of the cost of their emoluments must qualify as R&D expenditure.

### 3.10.2 R&D Tax Credit: Capital Expenditure

Expenditure on buildings by a qualifying company qualifies for a credit at 25% of the expenditure. It is not incremental, i.e. the actual spend on a building for R&D qualifies for the credit. It is given in addition to capital allowances. At least 35% of the building must be used for R&D activities. If it is partly used for another activity, only part of the building qualifies for the credit.

Corporation tax of the company may be reduced by 25% of the expenditure (net of grant). The corporation tax reduction is given in the year in which the expenditure is incurred. As with the credit for revenue expenditure, any excess credit can be carried forward, back or repaid in instalments.

---

**Example 3.10**

A building cost €1,000,000 net of grant in 2016. In addition to capital allowances, the company may reduce its corporation tax for 2016 by €250,000 (€1,000,000 × 25%).

---

**Clawback**

If the building or structure is sold or ceases to be used within 10 years, any credit already given is withdrawn. There is a Case IV assessment of four times the credit granted. This amount is then taxed at 25%, i.e. the credit given is clawed back.

## 3.11  Other Reliefs

### 3.11.1  Intangible Assets Scheme

Section 291A TCA 1997 provides for a special capital allowances scheme for capital expenditure by companies on the provision of specified intangible assets for the purposes of a trade – whether acquired or developed by the company. It applies to a broad range of intangible assets (e.g. patents, copyright, trademarks, know-how) and is recognised as such under generally accepted accounting practice.

Capital allowances are based on either:

- the amount charged to a company's income statement; or
- the amount of allowances and related interest expense granted per annum for a relevant trade. A relevant trade is the trade of managing, developing or exploiting of the specified intangible asset, i.e. the trade that exploits the intangible asset is treated as a separate trade and the capital allowances are ring-fenced against this source of income. For accounting periods up to 31 December 2014, the amount of allowances and related interest expense were capped at 80% of the trading income from the relevant trade. However, section 40 FA 2014 removed the 80% restriction, allowing 100% to be claimed for accounting periods commencing on or after 1 January 2015.

Pre-trading expenditure qualifies for relief. In the first year a company can opt for a fixed write-down period of 15 years, i.e. at an annual rate of 7% of qualifying expenditure for first 14 years and 2% in the final year. There was a clawback of capital allowances on a disposal of the intangible asset within 10 years after the beginning of the accounting period in which the asset was first provided for the trade. The 10-year holding period was reduced to five years by Finance Act 2013 for expenditure incurred after 13 February 2013. There is no clawback of capital allowances if transferred to a connected company.

### 3.11.2  Relief for Certain Disposals of Land and Buildings

Finance Act 2012 introduced a relief from CGT for both individuals and companies. For properties acquired between 7 December 2011 and 31 December 2014 (amended by Finance (No. 2) Act 2013), no CGT will arise on the gain provided the property is held for at least seven years. The first seven years of ownership is effectively tax exempt, and any remaining years are liable to CGT as normal. For example, if the property is held for nine years, 7/9 of the gain is exempt.

Property can be residential or commercial, and may be situated in Ireland or in the EU, Norway, Iceland or Liechtenstein.

### 3.11.3  Entrepreneur Relief – CGT

Section 45 Finance (No. 2) Act 2013, originally introduced a relief for individual entrepreneurs (section 597A TCA 1997). Section 35 Finance Act 2015 introduced a revised version of the relief, which is included in section 597AA TCA 1997. The 'old' relief has not been abolished. Section 597AA, the new relief, provides that if the CGT payable under this section is higher than that calculated under the rules set out in section 597A, then the CGT payable will be calculated by reference to section 597A. For this reason the relief under both sections are set out below.

**'Old Rules' – Section 597A**

Section 597A TCA 1997 provides for individual entrepreneurs who, in the period 1 January 2014 to 31 December 2018, reinvest the proceeds of disposals of assets made on or after 1 January 2010 in chargeable business assets in new business ventures. The relief is granted in the form of a tax credit against any capital gains tax liability arising on the ultimate disposal of the chargeable business assets more than three years after they were acquired. The relief is effectively a reintroduction of rollover relief, a valuable capital gains tax relief that was abolished a few years ago. That relief allowed a business to roll over a chargeable capital gain once the proceeds were invested in replacement assets. The current relief is much more restrictive than the former relief.

Chargeable business assets include assets used wholly for the purposes of a new business carried on by an individual; or new ordinary shares issued on or after 1 January 2014 in a qualifying company over which the shareholder has control and in which the shareholder is a full-time working director. There is a minimum investment requirement of €10,000. Original legislation provided that the individual had to own not less than 50% of the ordinary share capital. Section 52 FA 2014 reduced this 50% requirement to 15%. The definition excludes assets that are held as passive investments.

A "new business" refers to relevant trading activities carried on by an individual or by a qualifying company that were not previously carried on by that individual or qualifying company, or by any person connected with that individual or qualifying company. A "qualifying company" is defined as a company that is a micro-, small or medium-sized enterprise and "relevant trading activities" are the same as those for EIIS and seed capital relief and include farming.

The relief takes the form of a tax credit equal to the lower of:

- the capital gains tax paid on or after 1 January 2010; or
- 50% of the capital gains tax that would otherwise be payable on the disposal of the chargeable business assets of the new business.

Where less than the full proceeds of a disposal on which capital gains tax has been paid are reinvested, only that proportion of the capital gains tax relative to the amount reinvested will qualify for relief.

---

**Example 3.11**

James Moran disposed of a chargeable asset in 2012 for €300,000, on which he paid €25,000 capital gains tax. On 1 July 2015 he acquired a new business at a cost of €275,000 using the net proceeds of €275,000 from the 2012 disposal. That new business proved to be successful and on 1 October 2018 he disposed of it for €400,000. Assuming the capital gains tax rate remains at 33%, the CGT calculation is (ignoring annual exemption):

€400,000 – €275,000 × 33% = €41,250

Entrepreneur relief provides for the lower of:

- CGT of €25,000 paid in 2012; or
- 50% of €41,250 (€20,625).

---

If the individual further reinvests the proceeds of the disposal of the chargeable business assets in further new chargeable business assets, the relief can also be claimed on any capital gains tax payable on a subsequent disposal of those chargeable business assets.

**Revised Entrepreneur Relief – Section 597AA**

Section 597AA TCA 1997 outlines the revised entrepreneur relief and provides that a lower rate of CGT, i.e. 20%, applies to an individual who disposes of "**chargeable business assets**" and that individual is a "**relevant individual**" or "**qualifying person**". The relief applies to disposals on or after 1 January 2016.

Chargeable business assets include:

- assets including goodwill used for the purposes of a **qualifying business** carried on by the individual; or
- ordinary shares in a qualifying company carrying on a qualifying business (or ordinary shares in a holding company of a qualifying group), provided that the individual selling the shares owned 5% or more of the ordinary share capital in the company being sold.

A **relevant individual** is a person who has beneficially owned the chargeable business assets for a continuous period of not less than three years in the five years immediately before the disposal of the assets.

A **qualifying person** is an individual who:

- has been a director or employee of the company; and
- who was required to spend 50% or more of their working time in that company in a managerial or technical capacity and has done so for a continuous period of not less than three years in the five years immediately before the disposal of the assets.

A "**qualifying business**" is a business that does not include:

- the holding of shares/securities held as investments;
- the holding development land; or
- the development or letting of land.

The relief operates by applying the 20% CGT rate to disposals of chargeable business assets by a relevant individual or qualifying person on or after 1 January 2016. There is a lifetime limit of €1 million chargeable gains that qualify for the 20% rate. Chargeable gains that exceed €1 million will be taxable at the current rate of 33%.

## 3.12   The Knowledge Development Box

The Knowledge Development Box (KDB) was introduced by section 32 Finance Act 2015 and it amends Part 29 TCA 1997 by inserting a new Chapter 5 – sections 769G–769R. The existing R&D credit relief provides incentives for qualifying companies to carry out R&D activities in Ireland. The new KDB is a follow-on from that to provide a special tax rate on profits generated from related R&D or intellectual property activities. The KDB rate is effectively a tax rate of 6.25%, which takes effect from 1 January 2016 to include accounting periods up to and until 31 December 2020.

Ireland's KDB is seen as the first such scheme that complies with OECD (Organisation for Co-operation and Economic Development) guidelines in the world. The KDB's compliance is hoped to offer businesses, both foreign and indigenous, certainty and confidence in investing in Ireland.

The KDB applies the 'Modified Nexus Approach', which calculates the relief using the proportion of qualifying R&D expenditure expended by the Irish company, in comparison with the entity's overall R&D spend worldwide. Therefore the higher the proportion of R&D that takes place in the Irish entity, the greater the proportion of qualifying income/profits from a "qualifying asset" that may qualify for the 6.25% rate. The company must be carrying on a "specified trade".

"**Specified trade**" is one which satisfies one or more of the following criteria:

1. The managing, developing, maintaining, protecting, enhancing or exploiting of intellectual property.
2. The researching, planning, processing, experimenting, testing, devising, developing or other similar activity leading to an invention or creation of intellectual property.
3. The sale of goods or the supply of services that derive part of their value from activities described in 1 and 2 above, where those activities were carried on by the relevant company.

Where the above activities form part of the trade of a company, the specified trade will be deemed to be a separate trade and the results for this specified trade must be separated from the overall activities of the company.

"**Qualifying assets**" are specific qualifying intellectual property:

- computer programs, within the meaning of the Copyright and Related Rights Act 2000 (this includes computer programs that represent a derivative work or an adaptation of an original work);
- inventions protected by a qualifying patent or certain supplementary protection certificates; and
- medical or plant breeders' rights within the meaning of section 4 of the Plant Varieties (Proprietary Rights) Act 1980.

"**Qualifying expenditure**", under the KDB, is expenditure that must be incurred "wholly and exclusively" in the carrying on of R&D activities in an EU Member State, the consequences of which lead to the development, improvement or creation of the qualifying asset. When R&D activities are outsourced to a third-party entity that is not a member of the corporate group, this also constitutes as qualifying expenditure. However, when R&D activities are outsourced to a member of the corporate group, this may qualify as 'uplift expenditure', provided it does not exceed 30% of qualifying expenditure, but it will not constitute qualifying expenditure itself. Costs of acquiring the qualifying asset also comprise qualifying expenditure.

"**Qualifying profit**" is the profit of the specified trade relevant to the qualifying asset. In the case of the KDB this includes royalties, licence fees, insurance, damages or compensation, and the portion of income from sale of a product or service that relates to the intellectual property (calculated on a "just and reasonable" basis). Companies must also deduct costs expended in earning the income; therefore, the amount that qualifies for the effective rate of 6.25% is the net profit attached to the qualifying asset and is achieved as follows:

$$\frac{(QE + UE) \times QA}{OE}$$

where:

QE is the qualifying expenditure on the qualifying asset;

UE is the uplift expenditure;

OE is the overall expenditure on the qualifying asset; and

QA is the profit of the specified trade relevant to the qualifying asset.

### 3.12.1  Operation of the Relief

The qualifying profits of the specified trade calculated using the above formula equal the profits qualifying for the KDB relief. The KDB relief is calculated in such a way that it gives the company an 'allowance' of 50% of qualifying profits (treated as a trading expense) in that period. This 50% allowance is how the effective corporation tax rate of 6.25% is achieved.

Where the specified trade results in a loss, the above formula is used to calculate the 'qualifying loss'. When these losses are utilised they are reduced by 50%.

A claim for KDB relief must be made within 24 months of the end of the accounting period to which the claim relates.

## 3.13  Other Means of Funding a New Business

Other means of funding or managing the cash flow of a new business could include the following:

- The shareholders could introduce interest-free loans to the company. The loans can be repaid tax free to the shareholders at a time when the business has sufficient funds.
- If tax refunds are due to the company, the relevant tax returns should be submitted to the Revenue Commissioners as soon as possible. This will ensure a speedy issue of the tax refund.

- The company should maximise any available loss relief. For example, if a current year trading loss is generated and there were taxable profits in the prior year, it may be wise to prepare the current year corporation tax return in a timely fashion and claim a carry back of loss relief. This could generate a corporation tax refund for the company.
- If the company exports more than 75% of its turnover, the company could make an application for "VAT 13B" authorisation, whereby all Irish suppliers would charge the company 0% Irish VAT (on receipt of a copy of the authorisation from the company). This authorisation could assist in the company's cash flow management.
- If the company is in a constant VAT refund position, it should apply to the Revenue Commissioners for authorisation to file monthly VAT returns (as opposed to bi-monthly filing). This could assist the company's cash flow planning. For example, a tax refund may constantly arise if a company's sales are liable at the 0% rate of VAT (e.g. sale of certain foods), while the company's operational costs are charged at the 13.5%/23% rates of VAT.
- The shareholders could consider the introduction of venture capital funding to the company. This could take the form of a share subscription (with a redemption clause after a fixed period of time) or interest-bearing loan capital.
- Government grant funding may be available to the company on application. Certain grants are tax exempt (e.g. certain employment grants).
- Accelerated capital allowances are available in respect of the acquisition of certain plant/equipment/vehicle types (e.g. energy-efficient plant). This may be a point for consideration if significant asset expenditure is required.

## Chapter 3 Summary

| **Rates of corporation tax** | • Most trades 12.5%<br>• Certain trades and passive income 25% |
| --- | --- |
| **Reliefs available for companies** | • Start-up exemption<br>• Relief for trading losses<br>• Other losses<br>• Entrepreneur relief |
| **Funding a new company** | • Seed capital and EIIS<br>• R&D tax credits<br>• Intangible assets scheme<br>• Government grants<br>• Accelerated capital allowances<br>• Use of "VAT 13B" |

# Questions

## Challenging Questions
(Suggested Solutions to Challenging Questions are available through your lecturer.)

### Question 3.1

Greg and Edel are clients of your firm and have operated a successful bakery and retail partnership for many years. They have an opportunity to buy a café business (Café Limited) cheaply, as the owner is fed up of the current market and wants to move to Spain as quickly as possible to open a bar there. The company, which has several key outlets in prime shopping malls, has been trading at a loss and has accumulated trading losses of €150,000.

Greg and Edel have visited the outlets and were shocked at the poor quality of the food on offer and feel that this is turning potential business away. Both feel that their bakery produce would make a significant difference to the trade and allow the cafés to capitalise on their key locations.

Greg's son is in the coffee and tea importing business and wants to theme the cafés into coffee or tea houses selling specialist coffees and teas. Edel is a bit unsure of this but is willing to try with one café and see how it goes.

Greg is keen to buy the company but Edel is thinking about buying the assets of the trade. Edel has heard about income tax relief for investment in a company and was wondering if this could apply to their situation.

**Requirement**
Advise Greg and Edel on the advantages and disadvantages of a purchase of shares or a trade sale taking all circumstances into account. In addition, briefly outline the possible ways of tax efficient investment in the company and whether this company could be a suitable vehicle for such relief.

# Cash Extraction from the Company

## Introduction

A company is a separate legal entity to its shareholders. Therefore, the money earned by the company does not constitute immediate earnings by the shareholders. The funds earned by a company must be extracted in an appropriate manner. There are strict tax law (in particular, close company legislation) and company law rules in respect of cash extraction from companies.

The extent to which cash will be extracted from a company will depend on a number of factors. One shareholder may be happy to leave the cash to accumulate in a company for many years, and another shareholder may want immediate access to the cash. If cash is extracted on a frequent basis, it is most likely paid out by way of salary or annual dividend. This income, in the hands of the shareholder, will be liable to income tax.

## 4.1 Dividend versus Salary

The company is obliged to operate PAYE/PRSI/USC on any salary paid to its shareholders. Note also that employer's PRSI will apply in respect of salary paid to a non-controlling shareholder. The rate of employer's PRSI is 10.75% on salary above €356 per week. Employer's PRSI will not be levied on a salary paid to a controlling shareholder. This could represent a significant saving to the company if large salaries are paid to controlling shareholders.

If a dividend is paid by a company to a shareholder, the company may be obliged to withhold 20% dividend withholding tax (DWT) on the dividend. The practical differences between salary and dividends are summarised as follows:

| Salary | Dividend |
|---|---|
| Salary is subject to PAYE/PRSI/USC at source and the shareholder receives a net income. Salary income is therefore not likely to be liable to any further taxes in the hands of the shareholder. | The shareholder receives 80% of the dividend after 20% DWT is applied. The dividend is liable to income tax plus USC and possibly PRSI in the hands of the shareholder, with a credit available for the 20% DWT. |
| The company must remit the PAYE/PRSI/USC in its P30 return. | The company must remit the DWT to the Revenue Commissioners in the month following the distribution. |
| The salary (and employer's PRSI where applicable) is deductible for tax purposes against the company's profit. This represents a 12.5% tax benefit to the company (i.e. an allowable deduction). | A dividend is not deductible for tax purposes against the company's profit. |
| Employer's PRSI is payable by the company if the salary is paid to a non-controlling shareholder. | Employer's PRSI will not arise on dividends paid to shareholders. |
| Ongoing/set salary payments represent a significant cash outflow for a company as cash may be required for working capital purposes. | A dividend may be declared at year end, when the company is in a position to establish the extent to which a dividend can be paid (by reference to the previous trading period and future trading projections). |
| Salary can increase the capacity to boost pension contributions and can also increase the SCSB figure if a termination payment is being made in the future. | The dividend will reduce the distributable after-tax investment income of the company and hence lower/eliminate the close company surcharge liability. |
| The shareholder's income tax burden in respect of this income will be accounted for through the company's payroll. The shareholder will, however, have to make a declaration of this salary in an annual tax return. | The shareholder will have to declare this dividend in their annual tax return and pay any additional tax/PRSI/USC where due. |

A computational example of salary versus dividend is as follows:

| Company Cash Position | Salary | Dividend |
|---|---|---|
| | € | € |
| Profit before corporation tax | 100,000 | 100,000 |
| Salary | (100,000) | 0 |
| Taxable profit | 0 | 100,000 |
| Corporation tax @ 12.5% | 0 | (12,500) |
| After-tax profits | 0 | 87,500 |
| Pay dividend (assume gross) | 0 | (87,500) |
| Cash left in company | 0 | 0 |

**Shareholder's Cash Position**

|  | € | € |
|---|---|---|
| Salary/dividend received | 100,000 | 87,500 |
| Income tax @ 40% * | (40,000) | (35,000) |
| Net income – shareholder | **60,000** | **52,500** |

\* USC and PRSI would also be deducted from the above income. These liabilities have not been considered for the purposes of the illustration.

If, however, the company qualified for the new start-up company exemption, the computation would be as follows:

| **Company Cash Position** | **Salary** | **Dividend** |
|---|---|---|
|  | € | € |
| Profit before corporation tax | 100,000 | 100,000 |
| Salary | (100,000) | 0 |
| Taxable profit | 0 | 100,000 |
| Corporation tax @ 0% | 0 | (0) |
| After-tax profits | 0 | 100,000 |
| Pay dividend (assume gross) | 0 | (100,000) |
| Cash left in company | 0 | 0 |

| **Shareholder's Cash Position** | | |
|---|---|---|
| Salary/dividend received | 100,000 | 100,000 |
| Income tax @ 40% | (40,000) | (40,000) |
| Net income – shareholder | 60,000 | 60,000 |

In other words, there is no real difference in tax terms between dividend and salary. In fact, if this were a close company with a surcharge issue where, due to the level of profits, it did not make sense to extract profits in full, a dividend might be a better option than a salary as it would reduce, or perhaps eliminate, the surcharge.

## 4.2 Loans to Directors/Shareholders

A shareholder may decide to take a loan from his company. Obviously, repayment terms will be at the shareholder's discretion in most cases. There is, however, significant legislation in respect of loans to shareholders. Company law prohibits loans in excess of 10% of the company's net assets. If loans exceed this level, the shareholder's loan will be illegal and the company's auditors will have to report that shareholder to the Director of Corporate Enforcement. This is therefore a very serious offence.

From a tax perspective, close company tax legislation also contains restrictions in respect of a company's ability to make loans to directors/participators (and their associates). A close company is a company controlled by five or fewer participators.

**(Note: students should be familiar with all key aspects of close company legislation.)**

Where a company makes a loan to a shareholder/participator (or an associate of the participator), it must also make a withholding tax payment to the Revenue Commissioners. The loan will be treated as being a net annual payment, and subject to a re-grossing adjustment. The payment due to the Revenue

Commissioners is 20/80ths of the loan. Revenue will refund this withholding tax when the loan is repaid by the shareholder.

The above withholding tax treatment will not apply where:

- the amount of the loan (taking into account any other loans to that person and their associates) does not exceed €19,050; and
- the borrower works full time for the company; and
- the borrower does not have a material interest in the company (a material interest being defined as more than 5% of the ordinary share capital of the company).

---

**Example 4.1: Shareholder Loan**

Joe Malone took an interest-free loan of €12,000 from his company in December 2016.

When preparing Form CT1 of his company, the tax treatment will be as follows:

|  | € |
|---|---|
| Deemed net loan | 12,000 |
| Re-grossing adjustment | 15,000 |
| Income tax to be withheld | 3,000 |

This withholding tax of €3,000 must be paid to the Revenue Commissioners unless the loan is repaid to the company by Joe Malone within six months of the accounting year end. When the loan is repaid in full, or in part, the appropriate portion of the withholding tax will be repaid to the company.

Benefit in kind (BIK) rates apply to benefits given by a company to its employees. An interest-free loan would constitute a BIK. Tax/PRSI/USC on BIKs are collected through company payroll.

As Joe Malone's loan is interest-free, the BIK rules will also apply and the company must account for BIK on the loan. The deemed interest rates are 4% for a loan related to a principal private residence and 13.5% in all other cases.

---

If, at a later date, the company writes off the loan advanced to the individual, then the individual is assessable to income tax under Case IV on the amount of the loan advanced and then written off. The amount assessable is the gross loan (i.e. the cash advanced plus the income tax withheld by the company). A credit is available for the income tax paid by the company in computing the individual's tax liability.

---

**Example 4.2**

M Ltd is a close company and made interest-free loans to the following shareholders during the accounting period ending 31 December 2016.

|  | € |
|---|---|
| Mr X, who owns 30% of the share capital | 50,000 |
| Mr Y, full-time director with 3% share capital | 10,000 |
| Mr Z, who owns 2% of the share capital and is not a director/employee | 15,000 |

*Mr Y*

The loan to Mr Y is not subject to the withholding tax provisions as he is a full-time working director of the company, his shareholding does not exceed 5% and the loan does not exceed €19,050.

Mr Y will be liable to BIK on the interest deemed to apply to the loan. If the loan is not a principal private residence-related loan, a BIK will arise at an interest rate of 13.5%. The BIK will be accounted for through the company's payroll operation. The BIK will be liable to income tax, PRSI and the USC.

*continued overleaf*

---

*Mr X and Mr Z*

Income tax is payable by the company in respect of loans to Mr X and Mr Z. The income tax due will be computed as follows:

|  | € |
|---|---|
| Mr X | 50,000 |
| Mr Z | 15,000 |
| Total | 65,000 |
| *Tax due (20/80)* | *16,250* |

We assume that all of this income tax will have been paid to the Revenue Commissioners by 23 September 2017 (the date by which all corporation tax must be paid). If, for example, Mr X repays €25,000 on 30 December 2017, the company would be entitled to the following refund of income tax paid (to be collected by way of inclusion in the company's next CT1 return and reduction of corporation tax payments):

|  | € |
|---|---|
| Loan repaid | 25,000 |
| Withholding tax repaid | 6,250 |

---

## 4.3    Dividends to Shareholders

A company may make a distribution to its shareholders by way of dividend. The key points to bear in mind in respect of dividends are as follows:

- The dividend **is not deductible for corporation tax purposes.**
- DWT must be withheld by the company, unless there is an exemption. The current rate of DWT is 20%.
- There is no employer's PRSI on a dividend. This represents a saving to the company.
- The company must remit this withholding tax along with the appropriate declaration in the month following the distribution.
- The company must take into account whether it has sufficient distributable reserves to make a distribution. This is a key requirement for company law purposes as distributable reserves must exist.
- The dividend may be required to avoid a close company surcharge in the company. A close company avoids a 20% surcharge on its after-tax investment/estate income where it distributes this income to its shareholders.
- A distribution could include the transfer of assets at less than market value from the company to the individual (i.e. does not just apply to cash dividends).
- The shareholder must remit any balance of income tax due to Revenue and declare the dividend income in their annual tax return. The dividend may also be liable to USC and PRSI. The liability where due is payable by 31 October in the year following the year of assessment in which the dividend is paid (assuming sufficient preliminary tax was paid for that prior year, otherwise the due date is 31 October in the year of payment of the dividend).

In relation to close companies, certain payments or deemed payments from the company could be classified as a distribution to its shareholders. It is therefore important that, when there is a value shift in the company, consideration is given as to whether a distribution is deemed to occur. For example, the transfer of an asset at less than market value to a shareholder would be considered a distribution to that shareholder. Another example would be consideration for a buy-back of shares (unless the share buy-back is treated as a CGT item – this treatment is covered at **Section 4.7**).

(Students should be familiar with the close company legislation and should be able to recognise where such companies are deemed to have made distributions in respect of certain expenses of participators and their associates, or interest paid to directors or their associates above a certain level.)

## 4.4 Patent Income

Royalty income paid to a resident of Ireland from a "qualifying patent" was exempt from income tax and corporation tax under section 234 TCA 1997, subject to certain conditions. Effective from 24 November 2010, income from patents paid after that date is no longer exempt.

### 4.4.1 CGT, VAT and DWT Obligations

The following CGT and other tax problems arise if a company that is owned by the inventor incurs the costs of developing, testing, etc. a patent and then the company transfers the rights to the individual at nil cost or at undervalue:

- CGT arises on the disposal by a company of its capital asset at market value, i.e. rights under the patent;
- any undervalue element is treated as a distribution for a shareholder; and
- a benefit in kind (BIK) arises if a director or employee is deemed to receive a benefit.

VAT at 23% is chargeable on:

- patent royalty income;
- capital sum received on the licensing of patent rights; and
- outright sale of patent rights.

The amount of royalties and/or capital sum for granting licence is subject to 20% withholding tax at source, unless the payment is made within a 51% group.

## 4.5 Termination Payments

The payment of a tax-free termination payment could offer a tax-efficient method of extracting funds from a company. Termination payments apply where the working shareholder is ceasing active involvement in the company either by way of resignation or retirement. The tax-exempt portion of a termination payment is computed using the **highest** of the following options:

1. the "basic exemption" of €10,160 plus €765 for each complete year of service; or
2. the "increased exemption" being the basic exemption (1. above) plus €10,000, less any tax-free payment received or receivable from a pension scheme (assuming the individual has not previously claimed either the increased exemption or 3. below); or
3. the standard capital superannuation benefit (SCSB).

Any employee who is entitled to a tax-free pension lump sum (either now or in the future) will not benefit from the full increased exemption as the additional €10,000 will be reduced by this tax-free pension sum. These three exemptions determine the highest amounts the employer (i.e. the company) may pay **tax-free** to the individual who is leaving.

Where the amount of the termination payment exceeds the limits as calculated above, the excess is treated as salary subject to PAYE and USC. Employee and employer PRSI are not due on this excess.

The exemption under the SCSB is based on the length of service and level of remuneration of the employee. Therefore, individuals who have both a significant number of years of service with a company and a high salary would typically benefit from the SCSB. However, the value of a tax-free lump sum from a pension scheme is deducted in arriving at the SCSB amount. The SCSB is computed by reference to the formula:

$$\frac{E \times Y}{15} - L$$

where, E = Average remuneration* for the three years prior to termination of employment;

Y = Number of complete years of service of the person with the company; and

L = Tax-free lump sum** which the person is entitled to receive from the company pension scheme on retirement (or the actuarial value of any future right to receive a tax-free lump sum).

\* Remuneration means pay, before pension deductions, plus any BIK.

\*\* An individual may make an irrevocable claim to waive entitlement to the tax-free lump sum that would increase the value of the SCSB.

When used as a planning tool, if the SCSB is being considered, the level of Schedule E salary being received in the employee's final years may be adjusted to maximise the level of the SCSB relief.

---

**Example 4.3: Termination payment**

John Swan is a director and non-controlling shareholder of Swanlake Ltd. He is due to retire on 30 November 2016 and will immediately begin to draw down his pension. He commenced employment with the company on 1 January 1996. His average salary for the last three years has been €90,000. He is due to receive a tax-free lump sum from the company pension scheme of €100,000, which you can assume is the present value of this sum. On retirement, he is to receive a lump sum payment of €200,000 from Swanlake Ltd. You can assume the €200,000 settlement does not include taxable remuneration, such as holiday pay, bonus, etc. to which he may also be entitled.

Compute the net amount of his termination package (ignoring USC).

John has 20 complete years' service. It does not seem to make sense to waive the right to receive a tax-free lump sum from his pension scheme. If he does, then the lump sum remains in the fund and will be taxable as "normal" pension.

*Basic Exemption*

10,160 + (765 × 20) = 25,460

*Increased Exemption*

This is a negative figure, i.e. (25,460 + 10,000) − 100,000

*SCSB*

$$\left(\frac{90,000 \times 20}{15}\right) - 100,000 = 20,000$$

| | € |
|---|---|
| Gross termination package | 200,000 |
| Tax-free portion | (25,460) |
| Taxable termination payment | 174,540 |
| Income tax @ 40% | 69,816 |
| **Net termination package** | **130,184** |

---

The taxable portion of the termination payment is taxable in the year in which the employment ceases. In this regard, the date on which the payment is made to the employee will establish the period in which the tax is due. The company will not receive a tax deduction in respect of termination payments where:

- the termination payment relates to the proceeds from the sale of shares in the company; and
- the termination payment is made after the company ceases to trade.

Finance Act 2011 introduced a lifetime cap of €200,000 regardless of whether the tax-free amount is calculated using the basic exemption, increased exemption or SCSB (options 1–3 above).

## 4.6 Corporate Pension Schemes for Directors/Employees

There are significant benefits in setting up a Revenue-approved corporate pension scheme. The main tax advantages are as follows:

1. The contributions paid by the company (as employer) to the pension scheme are fully tax deductible (subject to a restriction where the contributions are excessive).
2. The company receives a tax deduction by reference to the pension payments made.
3. The contributions paid by the company are not subject to the same restrictions as those for personal contributions by the employee/director.

**Note**: if amounts are accrued in the accounts for pension contributions at year end, the accrual movement will have to be added back in the tax computation, as relief is only available on a paid basis.

---

*Example 4.4: Pension accruals*

|  | € |
| --- | --- |
| Opening pension accrual at 1 January 2015 | 50,000 |
| Closing pension accrual at 31 December 2015 | 200,000 |

The increase in the accrual of €150,000 must be added back in the tax computation to arrive at the tax-adjusted profit/loss. The accrual movement would be reflected in the profit and loss account as an expense.

---

### 4.6.1 Restrictions for Personal Pension Contributions

The tax relief for personal pension contributions is subject to certain restrictions, which take the form of an age limit and an earnings limit. These two limits apply for both sole traders paying into a PRSA/personal pension plan and for personal contributions paid by an employee/director to a corporate pension scheme. As stated at **Section 4.6** above, corporate contributions are not subject to the same restrictions where paid to a Revenue-approved corporate pension scheme. Therefore, the use of a corporate pension scheme can facilitate much higher contributions to a pension scheme for the company's director/employee. This has a big advantage over the sole trader contributor.

The personal tax relief limits are based on the taxpayer's age, and are as follows:

| | |
| --- | --- |
| Under 30 | 15% of net relevant earnings |
| 30 to 40 | 20% of net relevant earnings |
| 40 to 50 | 25% of net relevant earnings |
| 50 to 55 | 30% of net relevant earnings |
| 55 to 60 | 35% of net relevant earnings |
| 60 or older | 40% of net relevant earnings |

The director's/employee's personal pension contributions are also subject to an earnings cap of €115,000.

---

*Example 4.5*

John Sheridan is a 32-year-old with net relevant earnings of €200,000. He is a member of his employer's Revenue-approved corporate pension scheme. The maximum personal pension contribution John can make and qualify for tax relief is €23,000 (€115,000 × 20%). If John makes a contribution of €40,000 in a tax year, he can only get tax relief in that year of €23,000. The excess €17,000 contribution can be carried forward for tax relief to the following tax year.

---

The key issues in relation to company pension schemes are as follows:

▦ A corporate pension scheme provides a means of extracting cash in a tax-efficient manner in the future. The amounts invested in the pension scheme can be invested solely for the benefit of the relevant director/employee.

▦ A commercial advantage is that the company pension scheme is protected from the creditors of the company should the company experience trading difficulties or even go into liquidation.

▦ All contributions made by the company to a Revenue-approved pension scheme do not give rise to a BIK for the employee/director.

▦ Revenue-approved pension schemes are permitted to not only fund pensions but also life cover, disability cover and permanent health insurance. Therefore, such benefits can be provided to the employee/director on a tax-efficient basis.

▦ Contributions by the director/employee benefit from "net pay arrangement", i.e. tax is only payable on the net of pension pay.

---

**Key Issue**

Pension contributions to a Revenue-approved corporate pension scheme are not subject to the same level of tax restrictions as those of individual contributions by its directors/employees. This is a significant issue for the sole trader who cannot avail of such a scheme unless he incorporates.

---

### 4.6.2 Top-up Pension Fund ("Lump Sum Pension Payments")

In a corporate occupational pension scheme, it is possible to make special lump sum payments to top-up a pension fund (in order to meet the future pension requirements of the employee/director).

Revenue limits on company contributions make it possible to provide for a maximum fund of two-thirds of the employee/director's final pensionable salary. The pension fund may not be sufficiently funded to provide for such a pension (i.e. two-thirds of the individual's final salary), and the company may make lump sum top-up payments on a periodic basis to meet the fund's future requirements/obligations.

These top-up pension payments may not be fully tax deductible in the accounting period in which they are paid, and may be subject to a spreading adjustment for corporation tax purposes. If the spreading adjustment is to apply, the tax deduction for the lump sum pension payment will be spread over a period of up to five years. The actual period of the spread is determined by taking the lesser of five years or a sum under the following formula:

Once-off lump sum payment/annual recurring pension contributions = years of spread

---

**Example 4.6**

PC Futures Ltd pays a pension contribution of €200,000 per annum on behalf of its three key directors and equal shareholders. The pension fund will be required to pay two-thirds of the directors' final pensionable salary on their retirement. In 2016, in order to meet future pension requirements, the company pays a lump sum of €1 million to the pension fund. This lump sum is inclusive of the annual ordinary pension contribution of €200,000. The 2016 tax deduction for total pension contributions will be as follows:

|                                       | €                          |
|---------------------------------------|----------------------------|
|                                       |                            |
| Ordinary pension contribution         | 200,000                    |
| Special lump sum contribution         | 200,000*                   |
| Total tax deductible payment in 2016  | 400,000 (50% = €200,000)   |

*The lump sum contribution of €800,000 is to be spread as follows for corporation tax deductibility purposes:

800,000 / 200,000 = four years spread (i.e. €200,000 per annum × 50%)

*Note:* if the above computation produced a result above five years, the lump sum would be spread over five years for tax deductibility purposes.

---

### 4.6.3   On Retirement – Pension Issues and Planning

On retirement of the employee/director, a portion of the pension fund may be paid as a tax-free lump sum. Broadly, there are two options:

1.   If a director/employee has 20 years of pensionable service with the company, this entitles the director/employee to a maximum tax-free lump sum payment from their pension fund of 1.5 times their "final pensionable remuneration". In some cases this can be the entire accumulated fund. Where there is a fund remaining, this is used to purchase an annuity (which will effectively be the investment that will fund the pension).

2.   The alternative is to take up to 25% of the accumulated fund as a cash lump sum and with the balance, either:
     (a)   invest in an approved retirement fund (ARF);
     (b)   purchase an annuity;
     (c)   take as taxable cash; or
     (d)   a combination of (a), (b) and (c).
     Again, the ARF or the annuity will effectively be the investment that will fund the pension.

The tax-free lump sum amount is, however, subject to a lifetime limit of €200,000 and the excess up to €500,000 is taxed at 20%. Where the individual's 'lump sum' exceeds €500,000, the excess is taxed at the individual's marginal rate of income tax. Effectively, the pension provider operates 'PAYE' for the year of assessment in which the lump sum is paid.

**Final Pensionable Remuneration**

For an employee or director who does not hold more than 20% of the ordinary share capital, there are three different methods of determining final pensionable remuneration. It can be based on:

(a)   basic remuneration of any 12-month period of the five years preceding the retirement date, to include the average of any fluctuating emoluments of three or more consecutive years ending on the retirement date; or

(b)   the average of the total emoluments for any three or more consecutive years ending not earlier than 10 years before the retirement date; or

(c)   the rate of basic pay at the retirement date or at any date within the year ending on that date plus the average of any fluctuating emoluments calculated as in (a) above.

However, for a director who holds more than 20% of the ordinary share capital, final pensionable remuneration must be the average of the total emoluments for any three or more consecutive years ending not earlier than 10 years before the retirement date.

The above computed final pensionable remuneration forms the basis of computing the relevant tax-free lump sum.

Note that, if steps are put in place in respect of the directors'/employees' final levels of remuneration (either in the final year or in the final 10-year period), the tax-free lump sum can be maximised. This should be a key planning step put in place for executives within the corporate scheme who are due for retirement; however care must be exercised to ensure that the pension scheme rules are not contravened.

### 4.6.4   Pension Planning and Sale of a Business

If a sale of a business is planned, pension planning can be used in conjunction with any other tax relief associated with the future sale of a business (e.g. retirement relief). If, for example, a sale of an existing business is planned in the foreseeable future, the current shareholders/directors may take proactive steps to maximise cash extraction from the business prior to its sale. In addition to retirement relief, pension planning could (indirectly) achieve significant tax-efficient cash extraction from the business.

---

**Example 4.7**

Tim Mullane is 57 years of age with no children. He runs a transport and haulage business, Trans-Speed Ltd, which he has operated for 25 years. Tim is a 100% shareholder in the company.

Tim has never invested in a pension scheme. Instead, he retained all surplus funds in the company to build it up. The company is now valued at approximately €1 million. Tim has taken an annual salary from the company of €50,000 for the last 10 years. The company currently has €400,000 in cash.

Tim plans to sell the company by his 60th birthday. He is confident that a buyer can be easily found as he has received many offers from local investors over the years to purchase the business from him. Tim will sell the company by way of 100% share sale.

Tim is conscious that the company has significant cash holdings and would like to utilise this cash in a tax-efficient manner prior to the sale of the company. He does not want to draw all the cash down as a salary immediately, as he knows that this will lead to a large income tax liability etc.

Taking into account Tim's lack of pension provision and his intention to sell the business within the next three years, the following steps could be put in place to maximise the tax-efficient extraction of the €400,000 cash holding from the business:

- The company sets up a Revenue-approved pension scheme.
- By increasing Tim's salary to €120,000 per annum for the next three years, the company could invest €180,000 in a corporate pension scheme, i.e. the amount that he could receive tax-free (average annual remuneration of €120,000 × 1.5).

On Tim's retirement, assume he could take a tax-free pension lump sum of €180,000 (being 1.5 times final salary). Assuming a corporation tax rate of 12.5%, the net cost (after tax) to the company over the three years would be:

|                              | €        |
| ---------------------------- | -------- |
| Additional salary            | 210,000  |
| Allowable pension lump sum   | 180,000  |
|                              | 390,000  |
| Less: corporation tax relief | (48,750) |
| Company's after-tax cost     | 341,250  |

Tim would personally receive the following cash from the company over the three-year period:

|                          | €        |
| ------------------------ | -------- |
| Additional salary        | 210,000  |
| Less: PAYE* on salary    | (84,000) |
| Net income               | 126,000  |
| Tax-free lump sum**      | 180,000  |
| Tim's total after-tax funds | 306,000 |

\*   Assuming marginal tax rate at 40% and ignoring PRSI/USC.

\*\* Ignoring costs and income/gains/losses earned.

*continued overleaf*

If Tim had withdrawn the company's significant cash holding by way of salary or dividend, the tax rate alone applicable to that income would be 40%. Following the above pension/tax planning steps, the effective tax rate applying to the funds paid to Tim would be as follows:

€84,000/€390,000 = 21.5% effective tax rate

Tim may, on his 60th birthday, dispose of his shares in his trading company. Tim should qualify for retirement relief for CGT purposes. This will provide an additional tax saving for Tim.

Let us further consider what would happen if the company wishes to pay him a termination payment and he is to receive a tax-free lump sum of €180,000 and his pay has been increased to €120,000 for three years. Tim has 25 complete years' service.

*Basic Exemption*

10,160 + (765 × 25) = 29,285

*Increased Exemption*

This is a negative figure, i.e. 29,235 + 10,000 − 180,000

*SCSB*

$$\left(\frac{120,000 \times 25}{15}\right) - 180,000 = 20,000$$

As can be seen, the amount of termination payment is significantly reduced due to the tax-free sum from the pension. Therefore, while the pension tax-free lump sum is attractive, it does significantly reduce the tax-free sum under a termination payment.

(Students should be able to identify opportunities for an individual or a company to utilise the available tax relief in respect of pension planning opportunities.) **Key issues that might identify an opportunity for pension planning** are as follows:

- Director/shareholder has sufficient funds for his personal lifestyle and the company has excess cash holdings. There may be scope to implement a corporate pension scheme and invest the excess cash.
- Director/shareholder has been building up his business for a number of years and has neglected his pension planning. A corporate pension scheme could be put in place to fund his retirement.
- Consider the level of remuneration being paid to key directors/employees in the final years of employment. This is relevant to the level of tax-free lump sum payments that can be made to them on their retirement. This is particularly relevant if the individual has more than 20 years of service with the company.
- A sole trader is operating a profitable business and is making the maximum allowable pension contributions but is still subject to significant income tax on the remaining taxable profits. There may be benefit in transferring that trade to a company and setting up a corporate pension scheme to maximise tax relief.

## 4.7    Buying and Selling a Business: Cash/Proceeds Issues

A business may be sold by means of the following:

- a trade/asset sale by the company; or
- a share sale by the company's shareholders.

In the above transactions, the proceeds received in either scenario will be subject to 33% tax (either as CGT or as corporation tax on a chargeable gain). While this area is considered in detail in **Chapter 7,** a summary of the main points is set out below.

### 4.7.1  Asset Sale by a Company

If an asset/trade sale occurs, the company will receive the consideration. The company will be liable to corporation tax at a rate of 33% on the chargeable gain arising. The company may also be liable to a balancing charge on the sale of assets if capital allowances have been claimed (e.g. industrial building, plant, etc.). The issue at hand will then be how the shareholders can extract the cash from the company in a tax-efficient manner. If the funds are extracted by way of dividend or salary, the funds will be subject to an additional 40% income tax and PRSI/USC. If the company is liquidated, a 33% CGT charge will arise for the shareholders on the disposal of their shares. There is therefore a double tax charge if the funds are extracted in this manner.

### 4.7.2  Share Sale by a Shareholder

If a share sale occurs, the shareholder will be subject to 33% CGT on the chargeable gain arising. The benefit to the shareholder in this case is that funds are received directly by the shareholder following the sale. The exposure to a double tax charge (in the case of a company trade/asset sale as demonstrated above at **Section 4.7.1**) is avoided.

The benefits/disadvantages of a **share sale** can be summarised as follows:

| Advantages to the Seller – Share Sale | Disadvantages to the Seller – Share Sale |
|---|---|
| No balancing charge liability in respect of assets on which capital allowances have been claimed. | Requirement to provide warranties/indemnities in respect of potential future liabilities of the company. |
| No double charge to tax on disposal (compared to an asset/trade sale by a company). | May need to discount selling price to take account of latent tax liability associated with assets held by the company (i.e. the purchaser is buying shares and the base cost of underlying company assets remain at their original cost). |
| No need to liquidate the company to extract cash funds post-sale. Cash is received directly by the shareholder. | A due diligence will be undertaken by the purchaser and this may take time to complete or indeed factors identified could discourage the purchaser from buying the company. |
| If the seller is a company, the sale of a trading subsidiary may be exempt (i.e. section 626B TCA 1997 Participation Exemption). | |
| Avoids delay and cost of liquidation. | |
| 1% stamp duty on the acquisition of shares, as opposed to a rate of 2% applying to an acquisition of assets/trade. | The need for adequate warranties. |
| Possible benefit arising from the purchase of tax losses. | Requirement to do a comprehensive due diligence, which can be a costly exercise. |
| VAT will not arise on the acquisition of shares. | Possibility of clawback of group relief previously claimed (in the event of the company leaving a group, that company is liable for the clawback of group relief). |

---

**Example 4.8**

The concept of a latent gain can be best illustrated by way of example:

- Assume Mr A holds 100% of X Ltd.
- X Ltd owns a property now worth €10 million which was acquired for €1 million.
- In theory, the value of shares of X Ltd are €10 million (being the value of its property asset).
- If Mr A sells the shares for €10 million, the purchaser will then own shares which have a future base cost of €10 million. If X Ltd (under new ownership) sells that property in the near future, its base cost will be €1 million (and not the €10 million paid for the shares). Ignoring indexation, the "latent gain" is €9 million which, at the 33% rate, gives rise to a CGT liability of €2.97 million.

---

The benefits/disadvantages of an **asset sale** can be summarised as follows:

| Advantages to the Seller – Asset Sale | Disadvantages to the Seller – Asset Sale |
|---|---|
| As company assets are being sold, there should be no need to provide significant tax warranties/indemnities to the purchaser. | Exposure to corporation tax on balancing charges arising on the sale of assets on which capital allowances were claimed. |
| Sale price may be higher as the purchaser is taking on no latent/historical risk when compared to share purchase. This must be compared to the purchaser seeking to reduce the purchase price due to higher stamp duty. | Exposure to corporation tax on chargeable gains arising on the disposal of chargeable assets. |
| An asset sale may be a quicker process, compared to a share sale. | Higher stamp duty for purchaser may lead to a lower sale price being negotiated. |
| An asset sale should not require a restructuring or reorganisation of the company's group structure. | VAT will arise, which may be unattractive to a potential purchaser if they do not have full VAT recovery. |
| | Shareholders will still have the problem of getting the cash proceeds out of the company in a timely and tax-efficient manner. Liquidation can be a long and expensive process. |
| The purchaser's base cost for future disposal of the assets will be the current price paid. | A higher rate of stamp duty will apply to purchase of assets. |
| Less concern on warranties/indemnities and the risk of acquiring a future commercial/tax liability is minimal. | Tax losses, if any, cannot be acquired by way of asset purchase. |
| Due diligence may not be required and thus professional fees should be lower. | |
| Capital allowances can be claimed on relevant assets by reference to the price paid on purchase. | |

The acquisition or disposal of a business can often mean a reorganisation or restructuring of the company's affairs. There is provision for tax relief where a company reorganises its corporate structure for bona fide purposes. There are other tax reliefs such as retirement relief (i.e. a CGT relief) on the disposal of a trade/shares in a trading company. All of these reliefs are considered in later chapters.

## 4.8 Liquidations

### 4.8.1 Tax Implications of a Liquidation

Salary, dividends and corporate pension contributions are the methods of cash extraction while the business is in the continuing ownership of the shareholders. If the business or assets are sold by the company or the company ceases to trade, liquidation will typically follow as a means of extracting the assets/cash left in the company, if any. A liquidation can arise in the following circumstances:

- a compulsory winding up by a court; or
- a voluntary winding up either by the company's creditors or the company's members.

For the purposes of this text, we will assume that liquidation will occur by reference to a member's voluntary winding up. Typically, this will be done to terminate the company and distribute any remaining assets to the shareholders/members.

On the date of going into liquidation, the accounting period of the company will end, and a new period will commence (being the period while the company is in liquidation). Liquidation is deemed to be a disposal of the shares in the company. The proceeds of the disposal is the amount realised by the shareholder/ shareholders on liquidation (being the net funds received by the shareholder).

A double tax exposure can exist where a company makes a disposal of its trade/assets, and the post-tax funds left in the company are extracted by way of liquidation. This charge to double tax occurs because:

1. A tax charge will arise first in the company's hands on disposal of assets/business, etc. The company is left with net after-tax funds available for distribution to its shareholders.

    Other tax issues to consider on a sale of a business by a company:

    (a) Balancing charges on the sale of assets qualifying for capital allowances.
    (b) Cessation to trade and tax adjustments thereon (e.g. terminal loss relief).

2. A liquidation is treated as being a disposal of shares by the shareholders. Therefore, a second CGT charge will arise on the uplift in the value of those shares (i.e. being the net funds which the company holds for distribution on the liquidation).

### 4.8.2 Cash Extraction by Way of Liquidation

The effective tax rate that will apply to the distributed funds from the liquidation will depend on the value of the base cost of the shares held by the individual shareholders. If the base cost is very high, the tax charge (if any) will be much lower than where the base cost is low.

To the extent that the proceeds received exceed the base cost, CGT at the 33% rate will arise.

---

**Example 4.9: Cash Distribution on Liquidation**

A Ltd and B Ltd both sold a property asset. After discharging the tax liability on the sale of the property, both companies had €1 million available for distribution to their shareholders.

Assume:

|  | A Ltd | B Ltd |
|---|---|---|
| Issued share capital | €1 | €100,000 |
| Index factor | 5.0 | 5.0 |
| Cash in company for distribution | €1,000,000 | €1,000,000 |

*continued overleaf*

---

| On liquidation, the company will make a capital distribution to its shareholders: | | |
|---|---|---|
| | € | € |
| Capital distribution | 1,000,000 | 1,000,000 |
| Base cost (indexed) | (nominal) | (500,000) |
| Taxable gain | 1 million | 500,000 |
| CGT @ 33% | (330,000) | (165,000) |
| After-tax cash received | 670,000 | 835,000 |

You will observe from the above that the higher the base cost, the higher the post-tax funds are on the liquidation of a company.

### 4.8.3 Liquidation and Interactions with other Tax Reliefs

**Double Charge to Tax – Exceptions to General Example**
Note that we have identified an issue whereby a double charge to tax can arise. There may be instances where the first charge to tax (on a disposal of a business prior to liquidation) can be avoided.

---

*Example 4.10*
Take the following corporate structure:

Holding Company "Hold Co. Ltd"

Trading Company "Trade Co. Ltd"

Hold Co. Ltd decides to sell its 100% holding in Trade Co. Ltd for, say, €1 million. This disposal can be made tax free if the conditions of section 626B TCA 1997 (Participation Exemption) are met. Broadly speaking, this section provides that the disposal of a trading subsidiary is a tax-exempt sale for CGT purposes.

A summary of the main conditions to be met are:

▪ A parent/subsidiary relationship exists by virtue of a minimum 5% shareholding.
▪ The subsidiary is a wholly or mainly trading company.
▪ The parent company has held the shares for a minimum of 12 months.
▪ The greater part of the value of the "subsidiary" does not derive from Irish land, mineral or exploration rights.

In this example, Hold Co. will receive €1 million tax free, which is available for distribution by way of liquidation. Only one charge to tax will arise and funds can be extracted by the shareholders at the CGT rate of tax (as opposed to income tax rates). This creates a favourable tax result.

---

**Example 4.10** is also indicative of why many businesses put a holding company structure in place. An anticipated future sale of a business is generally a sufficient reason for putting such a structure in place at an early stage.

You should bear in mind that retirement relief can apply to liquidations, thus providing the potential to reduce/exempt the shareholder from additional CGT on the deemed disposal of shares on liquidation. However, retirement relief will not apply where assets are transferred *in specie* to the shareholders.

### 4.8.4 *Distribution of Assets* In Specie

Stamp duty will not arise in respect of transfers of assets *in specie* to the shareholders of a company in the course of a winding up. This can often be a substantial saving, especially where valuable land or property is being transferred out of a company. Ordinarily, stamp duty of 2% could arise on the transfer of ownership of commercial property.

It is important to note, however, that the transfer of assets *in specie,* in a situation where there is not a winding up of the company, will give rise to stamp duty as a conveyance on sale. The same treatment will apply where, for example, there is a transfer of assets out of a company in satisfaction of a cash dividend due for payment.

When a company goes into liquidation, the assets of the company are held for the benefit of discharging all of the company's liabilities. When all liabilities have already been discharged (i.e. all creditors have been paid, etc.), the remaining assets will be available for distribution to the company's shareholders. A distribution of a company's assets *in specie* in the course of a winding up will not be chargeable to stamp duty.

---

**Example 4.11**
Referring back to Example 4.10, assume, instead of selling the property, a distribution *in specie* of the property was made to the shareholders on a liquidation. The value of the property is €1 million and there is sufficient cash to discharge all liabilities:

|  | A Ltd | B Ltd |
|---|---|---|
| Issued share capital | €1 | €100,000 |
| Index factor | 5.0 | 5.0 |
| Value of property for distribution | €1,000,000 | €1,000,000 |
| Distribution *in specie* | €1,000,000 | €1,000,000 |
| Base cost (indexed) | (nominal) | (€500,000) |
| Taxable gain | €1 million | €500,000 |
| CGT @ 33% | (€330,000) | (€165,000) |
| Stamp duty if a distribution *in specie* on a winding up: exempt | Nil | Nil |
| Stamp duty if it were purchased from the company @ 2% | €20,000 | €20,000 |

---

## 4.9 Share Buy-back

Prior to 1991, the two constraints for a company buying back its own shares were company law and tax law. The Companies Act 1990 substantially liberalised company law to facilitate a company buying back its own shares. Finance Act 1991 made the necessary tax amendments to complement the company law changes.

Prior to 1991, any consideration passing to a shareholder of an unquoted company in respect of their shares was a deemed distribution and taxed as income under Schedule F. Post-Finance Act 1991, where the necessary conditions are satisfied, such consideration is now taxed as a chargeable gain and liable to CGT treatment. Currently the CGT tax rate is 33% versus a potential 55% rate (income tax, PRSI and USC) if liable under Schedule F.

While this publication refers to "share buy-back", which is the commonly used expression, students should note that the same tax provisions apply to a company on a "redemption, repayment or purchase of its own shares".

The relevant tax legislation is:

- section 175 TCA 1997, which deals with quoted companies (and their subsidiaries); and
- section 176 TCA 1997, which deals with unquoted companies (and their subsidiaries).

Section 176 TCA 1997 (which deals with unquoted companies) contains detailed preconditions and requirements in order to qualify for the CGT treatment. However, section 175 TCA 1997 does not have the same level of preconditions and requirements. Therefore, what follows will only concentrate on section 176 TCA 1997 (unquoted companies).

### 4.9.1 Conditions

To qualify for CGT treatment in the hands of the shareholder (i.e. the vendor), broadly speaking, the share buy-back must be for:

- the benefit of the company's trade or the trade of its 51% subsidiaries (therefore the company must be a trading company or an unquoted holding company of a trading group); or
- the discharge of inheritance tax where the inheritance tax is due following an inheritance of the shares.

Examples of "for the benefit of the company's trade" (also known as the "trade benefit test") are:

- where there is a disagreement between shareholders over the management of the company which could adversely impact on the business and it is necessary to remove the dissenting shareholder; or
- to ensure that the shares are not sold to a third party who might not be acceptable to the other shareholders.

To satisfy the trade benefit test, the following conditions must be adhered to:

1. the vendor must be resident **and** ordinarily resident in Ireland in the year of the share disposal;
2. the vendor must have owned the shares for a period of five years up to the date of disposal (where the shares were previously transferred from a spouse, that spouse's period of ownership is counted. If acquired on a death, the deceased's period of ownership is also counted but, in this case, the holding period is three and not five years. The holding period is also three years if the shares were appropriated under an approved profit-sharing scheme.);
3. following the share buy-back, the vendor's shareholding in the company must have been reduced by at least 25% (see **Example 4.12** below);
4. following the share buy-back, the vendor must not be connected with the company, i.e. not own more than 30% of issued share capital or voting power or assets available on a winding up of the company; and
5. the share buy-back must not be part of any scheme whose purpose is to enable the owner of the shares to participate in the profits of the company without receiving a dividend.

---

**Example 4.12**

Mr X owns 2,000 shares in Xtra Ltd out of a total issued share capital of 10,000 shares. He has agreed with his fellow shareholders that Xtra Ltd will buy back 500 of his shares. On the face of it, 500 shares represents a disposal of 25% of his overall holding. However, the following is the position:

|  | Total Issued Share Capital | Held by Mr X | Cannot exceed % | % held by Mr X |
|---|---|---|---|---|
| Before | 10,000 | 2,000 |  | 20.00% |
| After | 9,500 | 1,500 | 15.00% | 15.79% |

*continued overleaf*

Therefore, Mr X has not sufficiently reduced his holding. After the share buy-back, the revised holding does not represent a 25% reduction in his original holding. He will not qualify for CGT treatment on the disposal. If he sells 600 shares, however, he will have reduced his holding by a minimum of 25%:

| | Total Issued Share Capital | Held by Mr X | Cannot exceed % | % held by Mr X |
|---|---|---|---|---|
| Before | 10,000 | 2,000 | | 20.00% |
| After | 9,400 | 1,400 | 15.00% | 14.89% |

**Key Issue**

Note that, to qualify for CGT treatment, the shareholding after the share buy-back must represent a minimum 25% reduction in the original holding. When calculating the former as a percentage of the total issued share capital, remember that the issued share capital is reduced by the amount of shares bought back.

**Example 4.13**

Mark has been a director of ABC Ltd since the company was incorporated in June 1991. Mark is 50 and intends to retire. His original investment was €10,000 in €1 ordinary shares. His brothers Sam and Billy own 10,000 €1 shares between them and they will continue to run the business after Mark retires. Mark had his shares valued and they are worth €500,000. How can these shares be sold tax efficiently and control kept within the family? You can assume that Sam and Billy cannot raise the funds to buy the shares from Mark.

If the conditions are met for share buyback, Mark is liable to CGT:

| Mark | € |
|---|---|
| Proceeds | 500,000 |
| Cost €10,000 × 1.442 | (14,420) |
| Gain | 485,580 |
| Less: annual exemption | (1,270) |
| Taxable | 484,310 |
| CGT @ 33% | €159,822 |

If conditions are not met for share buy-back, Mark is liable to income tax, USC and possibly PRSI as follows:

| | € | |
|---|---|---|
| Schedule F | 490,000 | (€500,000 − €10,000 cost) |
| @55% | 269,500 | |
| Tax saving when liable to CGT | €109,678 | |

The company will also be obliged to deduct DWT.

**Example 4.14**

The facts are the same as in Example 4.13, except Mark is 60 years old and intends to retire. Would your answer be any different?

As we have already seen, if the conditions are met for share buy-back, Mark is liable to CGT. If, however, in addition to that relief he also meets the conditions for retirement relief, since the proceeds are less than €750,000 they are exempt from CGT. In that case, the CGT calculation would be as follows:

*continued overleaf*

| Mark | € |
|---|---|
| Proceeds | 500,000 |
| Retirement relief exemption | (500,000) |
| Gain | NIL |
| CGT @ 33% | NIL |
| CGT saving | 159,822 |

## Chapter 4 Summary

| | |
|---|---|
| **Cash extraction from company** | • There are many ways to extract cash from a business, each with its own tax implications<br>• Consider need and tax position of shareholders and company combined<br>• Salary versus dividend decision – the advantages and disadvantages of both<br>• Pension contributions are a good, tax-efficient way of extracting cash<br>• Termination payments have advantages in limited circumstances |
| **Selling the company** | • Consider share sale versus asset sale from vendor and purchaser point of view<br>• Advantages and disadvantages to both methods<br>• Retirement relief<br>• Share buy-back |
| **Liquidation of company** | • Tax implications of a liquidation<br>• Cash extraction by way of liquidation<br>• Distribution of assets *in specie* |

# Questions

## Challenging Questions
(Suggested Solutions to Challenging Questions are available through your lecturer.)

### Question 4.1

Mr and Mrs Jones are equal shareholders in their trading company, Jones Limited. The company was set up over 10 years ago when Mr Jones incorporated his shoe shop trade. Mr Jones takes a salary of €80,000 and Mrs Jones does not take anything. The dividend policy of the company has been to pay an annual dividend of €5,000 per shareholder.

Mr Jones is the major influence on the business, but Mrs Jones helps out with the company's administrative duties, such as taking phone calls, following up orders and sorting payments as required. She has no other income. The company currently employs 20 staff and Mr Jones is keen to incentivise his key members of staff in a tax-efficient manner, but is unsure if this is possible.

Mr Jones advises you that he has not started to plan for the future yet, but anticipates that he will require an annual income of €30,000 on retirement to maintain his current lifestyle.

The couple has been made an offer of €1 million for the business.

**Requirement**
Prepare a report for Mr and Mrs Jones addressing the following issues:

(a) The tax efficiency of the present remuneration arrangements from the company.
(b) Other forms of cash extraction from the company.
(c) The tax consequences of selling the business for €1 million.

# Investment Companies – Special Tax Treatment

## 5.1 Investment Companies

Special tax rules exist for Irish investment companies. An investment company is one that, as the name suggests, makes investments.

An investment company is defined in section 83 Taxes Consolidation Act 1997 (TCA 1997) as being:

"…any company whose business consists wholly or mainly of the making of investments, and the principal part of whose income is derived from the making of investments…"

Therefore, it is vital that:

1. the company's business "wholly or mainly" consists of making investments; and
2. the principal part of its income is from that investment business.

The concept of "wholly and mainly" has been comprehensively dealt with by the courts over the years. A degree of investment activity is required to have a business in the making of investments.

When considering the income of the company, it is reasonable to take a long-term view of income projections, rather than merely one accounting period.

The question can arise as to whether a company is an investment company, or merely a holding company (holding shares, etc.). A holding company will not qualify for the special tax rules pertaining to investment companies. The mere holding of investments by a company does not automatically qualify it for investment company status. A degree of investment activity is required.

An Irish resident investment company may, in computing its taxable profits, deduct **management expenses** incurred during a taxable period. The entitlement to this deduction is a key benefit attaching to investment company tax status. Without this specific tax treatment, an investment company could not obtain a tax deduction for its costs of operation.

### 5.1.1 Deduction for Management Expenses

"**Management expenses**" are not defined in TCA 1997. Once again, the concept of what a management expense is has been the source of extensive case law. The following expenditure has been determined as being deductible for tax purposes:

- Costs such as the keeping of the investment company share register, annual accounts and the holding of annual shareholder meetings.
- Costs incurred in respect of stock exchange quotations.
- Maintenance and repair costs in respect of premises used by the investment company.
- Director's remuneration (**subject to not being in excess of 10% of the company's gross investment income**).
- Payments in respect of Revenue-approved retirement schemes.
- Redundancy costs.
- Charges on income (e.g. interest, etc.).

The following are specifically **not** considered an expense of management:

- Professional fees in respect of land held as investments.
- Cost of appraising investments.
- Brokerage, commissions and stamp duty in respect of investments.
- Costs of raising capital.

The **management expenses** of an investment company are deductible against investment income (e.g. dividends, bank interest, etc.) in the applicable taxable period. An excess of unused/unutilised **management expenses** may be carried forward to the next accounting period. It is also possible to surrender excess **management expenses** to a fellow group member and claim group relief.

---

**Example 5.1**
Quasi Investments Ltd reported the following results for the year ended 31 December 2016 in its management accounts.

| Investment Income – 2016 | € |
|---|---|
| Irish dividend income | 20,000 |
| Bank interest (received gross) | 2,000 |
| Chargeable gain on disposal of shares (adjusted for corporation tax purposes) | 50,000 |
| Foreign dividend income from non-Treaty country | <u>8,000</u> |
| Gross income | 80,000 |

| Management Expenses – 2016 | € |
|---|---|
| Director's remuneration | 10,000 |
| Appraisal costs | 2,000 |
| Shareholder meeting costs | 3,000 |
| Rent of office | 2,000 |

*continued overleaf*

---

| Repairs to office door | 1,000 | |
| Total expenses | (18,000) | |
| Net profit per management accounts | 62,000 | |

The **tax computation** of Quasi Investments for the year ended will be as follows:

| | € | € |
| --- | --- | --- |
| Irish dividend income | Exempt | |
| Bank interest | 2,000 | |
| Foreign dividend income | 8,000 | |
| Total taxable gross income | 10,000 | |
| Chargeable gain | 50,000 | |
| Total profit | 60,000 | 60,000 |
| | | |
| Less: management expenses: | | |
| Shareholder meeting costs | 3,000 | |
| Director's remuneration (limit of 10%) | 3,000 | |
| Office rent | 2,000 | |
| Repairs | 1,000 | |
| Total management expenses | (9,000) | (9,000) |
| | | |
| Taxable profit | | 51,000 |
| Corporation tax @ 25% | | 12,750 |

An investment company, like any other company, returns details of its income in an annual corporation tax return (Form CT1). This return must be submitted approximately nine months after the company's year end.

## 5.2 Property Rental Companies

The Revenue Commissioners accept that a property rental company can come within the definition of an investment company for corporation tax purposes. However, it has also been indicated by the Revenue Commissioners that a property rental company should contain some of the following characteristics in order to obtain the same tax treatment as an investment company:

- The company must hold more than one property.
- A company which holds one property must also hold other classes of investment assets.
- The company must derive its income from the property (i.e. there must be an active rental operation carried on by the company).

The expenses deductible by a property rental company are:

- Those normally deductible for Case V purposes (i.e. bank interest, repairs, property management fees, insurance, letting fees, etc.).
- Management costs deductible under the investment company rules (as detailed above in **Section 5.1**)

A tax deduction for a director's remuneration is limited to 10% of the company's gross income. There is, however, an increased deduction of 15% for a director's remuneration where the director devotes a substantial part of their time to the management of the company's investment properties.

---

**Example 5.2**

Quasi Property Ltd, whose director devotes a substantial part of her time to the management of the company's investment properties, reported the following results for the year ended 31 December 2016 in its management accounts.

| Investment Income – 2016 | € | € |
|---|---|---|
| Irish dividend income | 20,000 | |
| Bank interest (received gross) | 2,000 | |
| Rental income | 50,000 | |
| Foreign dividend income from non-Treaty country | 8,000 | |
| Gross income | 80,000 | 80,000 |

| Management Expenses – 2016 | € | € |
|---|---|---|
| Director's remuneration | (12,000) | |
| Appraisal costs | (500) | |
| Shareholder meeting costs | (2,500) | |
| Property management fees | (2,000) | |
| Repairs to premises | (1,000) | |
| Total expenses | (18,000) | (18,000) |
| Net profit per management accounts | | 62,000 |

The **tax computation** of Quasi Property Ltd is as follows:

| | € | € |
|---|---|---|
| Irish dividend income | Exempt | |
| Bank interest | 2,000 | |
| Rental income | 50,000 | |
| Foreign dividend income | 8,000 | |
| Total taxable gross income | 60,000 | 60,000 |

| Less: management expenses: | € | € |
|---|---|---|
| Shareholder meeting costs | (2,500) | |
| Director's remuneration (limits of 10% and 15%) | (10,500) | |
| Property management fees | (2,000) | |
| Repairs | (1,000) | |
| Total management expenses | (16,000) | (16,000) |
| Taxable income | | 44,000 |
| Corporation tax @ 25% | | 11,000 |

---

## 5.3 Close Company Surcharge Issues

The close company surcharge is a mechanism to discourage the rolling up of investment and estate income in a close company. A close company is a company that is controlled by five or fewer individuals and their associates.

An investment company, or indeed a property rental company, comes within the scope of a close company surcharge. Therefore, an additional 20% tax may also arise on a company's undistributed investment and estate income net of tax. This close company surcharge issue should be borne in mind when reviewing the tax liability of an investment company.

---

**Example 5.3: Quasi Property Ltd with close company surcharge**

The close company surcharge position is as follows:

- the company's rental and investment income is calculated;
- the company's FII is then added to this figure and a deduction taken for non-trade charges and expenses of management; and
- the tax payable is deducted from this result to arrive at the distributable rental and investment income.

The relevant figures for Quasi Property Ltd for year ended 31 December 2016 are:

|  | € |
|---|---|
| Rental and investment income | 60,000 |
| Allowable expenses of management | (16,000) |
|  | 44,000 |
| Less: Corporation tax | (11,000) |
| Net after-tax income | 33,000 |
| Add FII | 20,000 |
| Distributable total | 53,000 |
| Surcharge @ 20% | 10,600 |

The surcharge of €10,600 is payable UNLESS distributions are made in respect of this accounting period. Distributions made up to 30 June 2018 will reduce or eliminate the surcharge.

---

## Chapter 5 Summary

| | |
|---|---|
| **What is an investment company?** | •Defined in statute as "any company whose business consists wholly or mainly in the making of investments"<br>•The concept of "wholly and mainly" has been comprehensively dealt with by the courts |
| **Relief for management expenses** | •Management expenses can be deducted to the extent that they relate to the management of the company's investment business<br>•Limit on the amount of directors' remuneration allowable |
| **Rate of corporation tax** | •Investment companies do not pay tax at the same rate as trading companies<br>•Rate is 25% versus 12.5% for trading companies<br>•Close company surcharge issues |

# Overview of Corporate Groups

**Learning Objectives**

By the end of this chapter you will be able to:

- Analyse and evaluate all the taxation implications at all stages of a company's business life cycle, including:
  - use of trading losses and excess charges in a group scenario;
  - CGT provisions relating to group transfers;
  - stamp duty relief on transfers between associated companies;
  - exemption from tax in case of gains on certain disposals of shares.
- Consider the implications of business taxation decisions at the individual entity level.

**Note:** group relief is covered extensively in prior studies, and students should review this material before reading this chapter. However, the key points relevant to group relief claims are also discussed below.

## 6.1    Reasons for Groups

**Why would one not just carry on a trade in a single company?** A business could form a group structure to coordinate/operate its business for both commercial, practical and tax reasons. For example, if a company has a number of trading interests, or indeed very distinct activities, it may wish to separate those trading interests into separate companies to:

- Operate separate trades capable of individual measurement.
- Separate strong and weak trades.
- Manage the performance of each entity.
- Isolate certain activities from other group activities.
- Manage any exposure to bad debts/trade failure, creditor pressures, etc.
- Separate companies/trades/assets for sale to third parties.
- Separate poorly performing trades for liquidation/cessation.
- Form one company to hold all employees.
- Form a company to hold all assets/shares in other subsidiaries.
- Form a company to facilitate once-off commercial transactions (often known in practice as "special purpose companies").
- Create a holding company structure to avail of reliefs such as the "Participation Exemption" (section 626B TCA 1997 – CGT exemption in respect of a disposal of shares in a trading subsidiary; **Section 6.14** below).
- Claim interest as a charge for investment in subsidiaries by a holding company.

While the above list is not exhaustive, nevertheless it demonstrates the numerous reasons why a corporate group may exist. In practice, as a business expands, additional companies are often created to facilitate growth/expansion or new business ventures.

## 6.2 Corporation Tax Group: Key Tax Issues

A company is a distinct legal entity. There are tax reliefs available where a qualifying group exists. An example of a corporation tax group can be illustrated as follows:

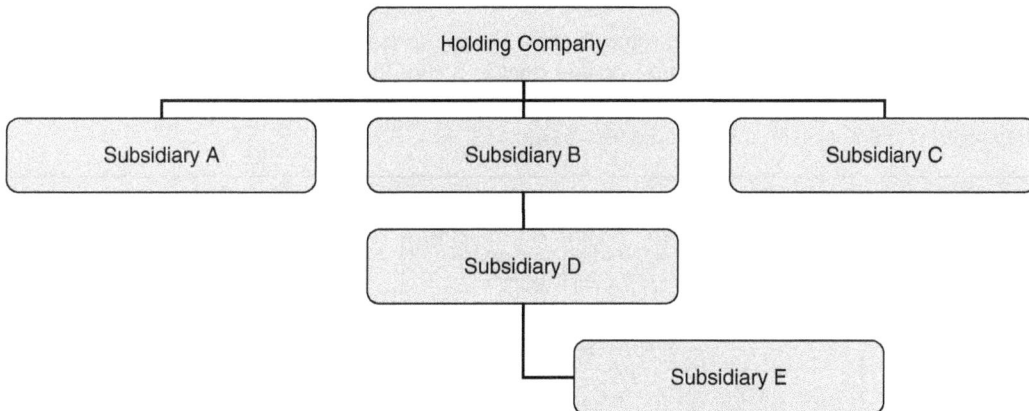

```
                    ┌──────────────────────┐
                    │   Holding Company    │
                    └──────────────────────┘
         ┌───────────────────┼───────────────────┐
┌─────────────────┐ ┌─────────────────┐ ┌─────────────────┐
│   Subsidiary A  │ │   Subsidiary B  │ │   Subsidiary C  │
└─────────────────┘ └─────────────────┘ └─────────────────┘
                    ┌─────────────────┐
                    │   Subsidiary D  │
                    └─────────────────┘
                         ┌─────────────────┐
                         │   Subsidiary E  │
                         └─────────────────┘
```

In general, the specific tax reliefs available in qualifying group situations can be summarised as follows:

- Relief from withholding tax obligations on annual payments between group members.
- Group loss relief for tax losses.
- Relief from tax on the transfer of capital assets between group companies.

For corporation tax loss relief and CGT group relief purposes, a minimum 75% relationship must exist between group members. This requirement is discussed in further detail below (**Section 6.4**).

## 6.3 Group Payment Relief: Obligation to Withhold Income Tax

Certain payments made by one company to another company may create a withholding tax obligation on the paying company. The withholding tax rate is the standard income tax rate (currently 20%). The payments on which there is a requirement to withhold income tax include:

- yearly interest;
- annuities;
- patents; and
- other annual payments.

The withholding tax liability is returned and paid by the payer company as part of its annual Form CT filing.

A company is not required to withhold the 20% tax when there is a 51% shareholding relationship between the paying company and the recipient company. Up to 2013, non-Irish companies had to be resident in the EU or an EEA country with which Ireland has a double taxation treaty (DTT). Finance

(No. 2) Act 2013 provides that a non-Irish company can be resident in any country with which Ireland has a DTT, or that the non-Irish parents' shares are traded on a recognised stock exchange. The payment must also be taxable in the recipient's country (if not resident in Ireland).

> **Key Issue**
> Students should pay particular attention to situations where annual payments are being made by a company. There may be a requirement to withhold 20% tax by the payer company, if it is not a 51% group member.

## 6.4 Corporation Tax Group: Loss Relief

When a corporate group exists, a key tax objective for the group is to efficiently manage its overall tax liability. If one company in the group makes a loss, that loss should, if possible, be available for use in another group entity that has profits to shelter. The group would seek to ensure that tax is payable only on net group profits (and not on an individual entity basis).

---

**Example 6.1**

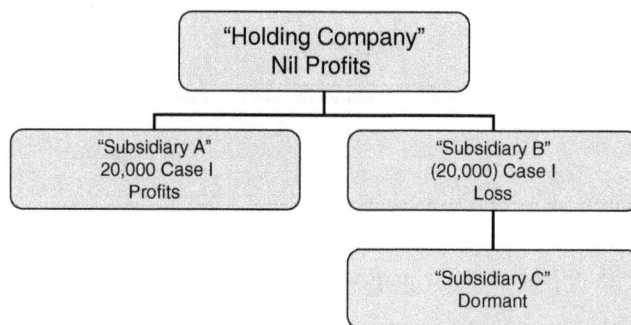

**Tax Position**

| | |
|---|---|
| Holding Company | Nil Profits |
| Subsidiary C | Dormant |
| Trading Subsidiary A | €20,000 Case I Profits |
| Trading Subsidiary B | (€20,000) Case I Loss |

In the absence of group relief, Subsidiary A would be liable to corporation tax at 12.5% on its €20,000 profits. Subsidiary B would not have a corporation tax liability as it is in an overall loss position.

---

Group relief allows for an off-set of losses in one group company against the profits of another group company.

Section 420 TCA 1997, and the related sections 420A and 420B, legislate for the utilisation of group relief. The following are available for surrender to other group members:

- Trading losses.
- Certain excess capital allowances.
- Management expenses (i.e. of an investment management company).
- Charges on income (e.g. yearly interest, patents, etc.).

To claim group loss relief, a 75% relationship must exist between the relevant group members. This 75% relationship is satisfied if one company holds, directly or indirectly, at least 75% of the ordinary share capital of the other company. It will also apply where two or more companies are 75% subsidiaries of a company (usually known as a parent or holding company). The parent must be entitled to 75% of the profits on a winding up and 75% of the assets on distribution.

A qualifying group structure may include indirect shareholdings, provided they are owned by a company that is either:

- resident in Ireland;
- resident in an EU Member State;
- resident in an EEA state that has a DTT with Ireland; or
- resident in any country, provided the company's principal class of shares are substantially and regularly traded on a recognised stock exchange.

---

*Example 6.2: Group relief*

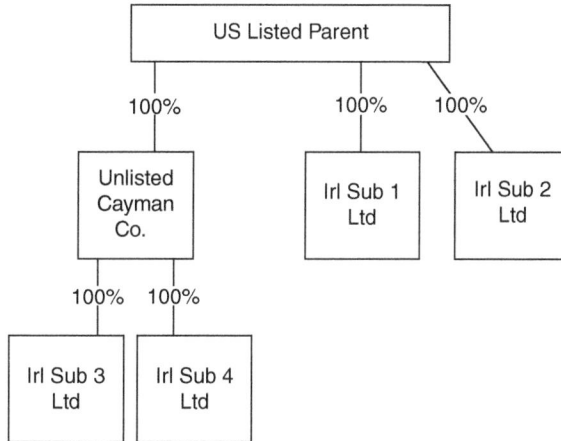

Only two of the Irish subsidiaries (Sub 1 and Sub 2) form part of a group since their immediate parent is listed on a recognised stock exchange. Sub 3 and Sub 4 do not form part of a group since their immediate parent is not resident in a country with which Ireland has a DTT.

---

In addition to the 75% shareholding test, for group relief to apply, the company must also:

- be entitled to not less than 75% of the profits of another company; and
- be entitled to not less than 75% of the assets of another company if that company were wound up.

Losses can be surrendered up through the group, down through the group or sideways through a group. The key requirement at all times is the 75% tests must be met.

---

*Example 6.3*

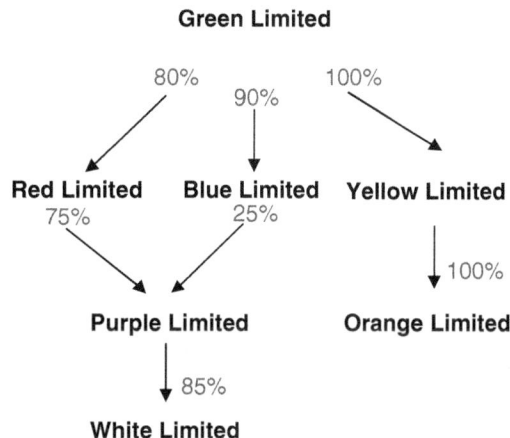

*continued overleaf*

> The Green Group consists of the following members:
>
> Green Ltd, Red Ltd, Blue Ltd, Yellow Ltd, Purple Ltd and Orange Ltd.
>
> Purple Ltd is a member of the group as Green Ltd owns more than 75% of the shares once the combined shareholding is taken into consideration.
>
> **White Ltd does not satisfy the 75% overall shareholding condition. However, as there is a group relationship between Purple Ltd and White Ltd, group relief applies between those two companies.**
>
> **Residency Issues**
> When dealing with tax issues, the question of residency will always arise. The companies seeking group relief must be either resident in Ireland or be an Irish branch of a DTT company. The claimant company must be liable to Irish corporation tax to avail of the relief.
>
> **Foreign Subsidiary Losses**
> Group relief in respect of Case I losses incurred outside of Ireland is only available for relief *upwards*, i.e. from the foreign subsidiary to its Irish parent. This, in effect, means that the surrendering company is either DTT resident and is 75% related to the Irish claimant company. This form of relief is only available where relief in the surrendering foreign country has been exhausted in that foreign country. This form of loss relief was introduced following the outcome of the *Marks & Spencer v. Inspector of Taxes* (2006) (Case C–446/03).

### 6.4.1 Key Questions to Ask when Considering Group Relief

- Does the company have current year trade losses? If yes,
- is the company a member of a tax group, i.e. is there the required 75% common relationship? If yes,
- is there another group member with taxable profits? If yes,
- does the company meet the required residency rules? If yes,
- are there any issues which might impact on the use of group relief (e.g. late filing of returns, failing to meet time limits, etc.). If no,
- group relief applies and the trading losses may be offset against trading profits or used on a value basis against corporation tax of the group.

**(As noted above, FAE students will have studied group loss relief in detail in earlier studies and a review of past material is recommended.)**

## 6.5 Group Loss Relief

As with all loss relief, there is an order by which losses must be utilised. A company with a Case I trading loss must first set that loss against its own income. The balance may then be considered for group relief purposes. Both the surrendering and claimant company must agree to the utilisation of group relief. A claim for group relief can be made on the company's CT1 Form (for both the surrendering company and the claimant company).

> **Key Issue – Time Limits**
> The relief must be claimed within two years of the end of the relevant accounting period (a claim for group relief is not available beyond that period). This includes amendments of previous claims for group relief.

Losses brought forward from a prior period must also be utilised by a claimant company before it can avail of group relief.

Group relief in respect of Case I trading losses is claimed in the following order:

1. Relevant trading losses against other group trading income (section 420A TCA 1997).
2. Group relief as a credit against corporation tax on a "**value basis**" (section 420B TCA 1997).

---

**Example 6.4**

|  | € |
|---|---|
| Subsidiary A Case I loss | (€80,000) |
| Subsidiary B Case I profit | €100,000 |
| Subsidiary B Case I loss b/f | (€50,000) |

Subsidiary B must first utilise the Case I loss brought forward, and then use the available loss relief, best illustrated as follows:

| Subsidiary B | € |
|---|---|
| Case I profit | 100,000 |
| Less: loss b/f | (50,000) |
|  | 50,000 |
| Less: loss relief surrender from A | (50,000) |
| Taxable profits | Nil |

Subsidiary A has a Case I loss for carry forward of €30,000.

---

### 6.5.1 Value Basis Relief

Students will recall from prior studies that the "value basis" for loss relief involves an offset of a 12.5% trading loss against other income and gains liable to 25% tax. Due to the different corporate tax rates, it is not possible to allow each euro of loss against the equivalent euro of 25% income. Therefore a tax credit for the trading losses is calculated to offset the tax payable on the other income.

---

**Example 6.5**

|  | € |
|---|---|
| Subsidiary A Case I loss | (100,000) |
| Subsidiary B Case III profit | 40,000 |

Subsidiary A must surrender:

- €80,000 of its trading loss (i.e. €80,000 × 12.5% = €10,000) to shelter.
- Subsidiary B's Case III income (i.e. €40,000 × 25% = €10,000).

Subsidiary A now has a trading loss balance for carry forward of €20,000.

---

## 6.6 Payments for Group Relief

One might encounter in practice a situation whereby a claimant company will pay for group loss relief. There is no requirement or obligation to do so, but it can be encountered from time to time. For example, where a third party owns a 10% minority interest in a company that is a group member, they may wish to see some benefit accruing to the surrendering company if it is surrendering tax losses to that company.

The amount paid is typically the same value as the tax benefit received by the claimant company. If the payment for the group relief does not exceed the amount of loss relief actually claimed, then:

- the payment is not considered to be taxable income or a deductible expense in the hands of either company; and
- the payment is not considered a dividend to the recipient of the payment.

## 6.7 Impact of Accounting Periods

Group relief can only be availed of where the accounting period of the surrendering company (i.e. the loss-maker) and the claimant company (i.e. the profit-maker) correspond wholly or partly. If both companies have, for example, a year end of 31 December, no further consideration is required as the accounting periods correspond equally. If, however, the accounting periods correspond partially, group loss relief is computed on a time-apportionment basis.

The steps required are:

- the corresponding accounting period for both companies is identified;
- the losses and profits for those corresponding periods are computed; and
- group relief is surrendered to the extent that profits are exhausted, or the full amount of available loss relief is claimed.

Note that, although the claimant and surrendering companies must be in a group throughout any overlapping accounting period, they need not be in a group relationship at the time the relief is claimed.

---

**Example 6.6**

Take Example 6.4 above, but assume that A's accounting period is the 12 months to 30 September 2016 and B's is the 12 months to 31 December 2016.

|  |  | € |
|---|---|---|
| Subsidiary A | Case I loss | (80,000) |
| Subsidiary B | Case I profit | 100,000 |
| Subsidiary B | Case I loss b/f | (50,000) |

Subsidiary B must first utilise the Case I loss brought forward, and then use the available loss relief, best illustrated as follows:

| Subsidiary B | € |
|---|---|
| Case I profit | 100,000 |
| Less: loss b/f | (50,000) |
|  | 50,000 |
| Less: loss relief surrender from A (note) | (37,500) |
| Taxable profits | 12,500 |

Subsidiary A has a trading loss carryforward of 42,500.

**Note:** establish the profit and loss of the corresponding accounting period and take the lower figure:

$9/12 \times 80,000 = €60,000$

$9/12 \times 50,000 = €37,500$

---

However, in the above example, you would also need to consider the extent to which the accounting periods immediately before and after these periods correspond. For example, A's loss for the three months to 31 December 2015 might be available for offset against any profits of B for the corresponding accounting period. Similarly, if A has losses for the year ended 30 September 2017, the portion that corresponds with B's period to 31 December 2016 could be used.

## 6.8 Restriction of Group Loss Relief

Group relief may not always be available to companies. There is a restriction on group relief where a company files a late corporation tax return (section 1085 TCA 1997). This applies where either the surrendering company or the claimant company files a late return. It is very important, therefore, that all companies within a group that wish to claim group relief file their tax returns on time. The restriction is as follows:

- Where the return is less than two months late, the group relief claim is restricted to 75% of the relief, subject to a maximum restriction of €31,740.
- Where the return is more than two months late, a 50% restriction applies, subject to a maximum restriction of €158,715.

## 6.9 Computational Example: Group Loss Relief

*Example 6.7*
Take the corporation tax group below, where X Ltd is the parent company and the year end for all group members is 31 December 2016. All profits/losses shown are Case I trade related.

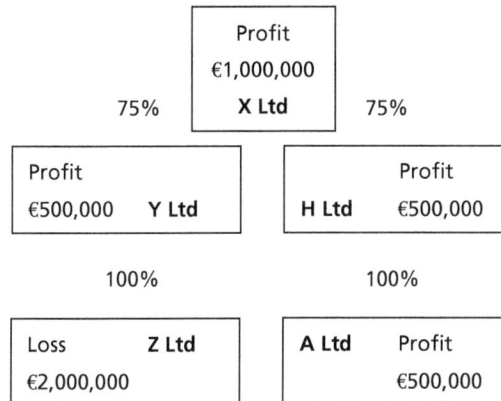

Loss relief can be surrendered as follows:

| X Ltd | € |
|---|---|
| Case I profits | 1,000,000 |
| Less: surrender of loss – Z Ltd | (1,000,000) |
| Profits liable to CT | 0 |

| Y Ltd | € |
|---|---|
| Case I profits | 500,000 |
| Less: surrender of loss – Z Ltd | (500,000) |
| Profits liable to CT | 0 |

| H Ltd | € |
|---|---|
| Case I profits | 500,000 |
| Less: surrender of loss – Z Ltd | (500,000) |
| Profits liable to CT | 0 |

| *Z Ltd* | |
|---|---|
| **Tax Loss Memo** | € |
| Current year loss | (2,000,000) |
| Surrender to X Ltd | 1,000,000 |
| Surrender to Y Ltd | 500,000 |
| Surrender to H Ltd | 500,000 |
| Balance c/f at 31/12/2016 | 0 |

The key points to note in the above example are:

1. Z Ltd did not have profits in the prior year that could have benefited from a carry back of the loss.
2. Z Ltd did not have other income that would have been reduced by loss relief before group relief.
3. There is no particular order to claim the group relief; the above example could have started with A Ltd benefiting from the group relief.

4.  If Z Ltd was paid by the group members for the relief, a charge to tax would not arise for Z Ltd on the payment (subject to the required conditions discussed previously).
5.  If any of the corporation tax returns of the relevant companies were late, group relief would be restricted. This is a key point to be aware of when claiming relief.

## 6.10 Consortium Relief

A consortium exists where at least 75% of the share capital of a company is owned by:

- five or fewer companies;
- all of which are EU resident or resident in a country within the EEA and with which Ireland has a double taxation treaty; and
- no single investor company on its own owns 75% or more of the company.

The company owned by a consortium must be:

- a trading company; or
- a holding company that owns a minimum 90% holding in trading entities.

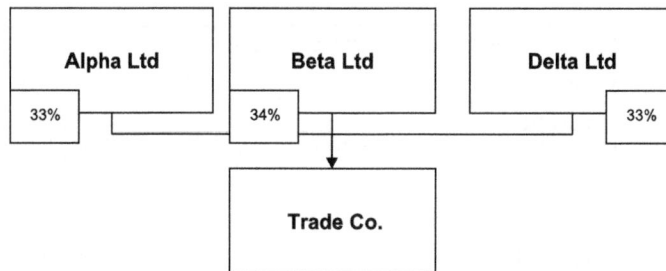

Another possible consortium structure could be as follows:

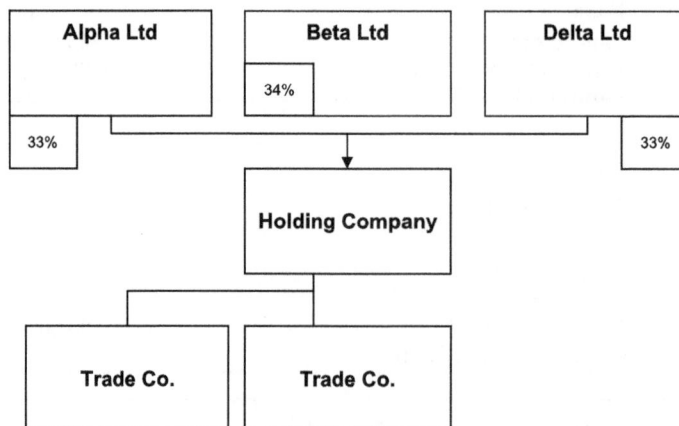

Consortium loss relief is a type of group relief. The first thing that is apparent is that the 75% group relationship between one parent and the trading company does not exist. In fact, for consortium relief to apply, one company alone must not own 75% or more of the trading subsidiary. The consortium members (of which there will be five or less in number) must hold at least 75% of the trading company. A member's share in a consortium is the lower of:

- its % holding in the trading company/holding company of a trading group;
- its % entitlement to profits available to equity holders; or
- its % entitlement to assets on a winding-up.

The second issue to note is that losses may only be surrendered upwards (which is different to normal loss relief). In effect, this means that Trade Co. will surrender losses to its consortium owners in proportion to their % holdings. Take a simple example:

---

**Example 6.8**
Trade Co., which incurred a trading loss of €2 million, is owned as follows:

| | |
|---|---|
| A Ltd | 20% |
| B Ltd | 40% |
| D Ltd | 30% |
| G Ltd | 10% |

The €2 million loss generated by Trade Co. can be surrendered upwards as follows:

| | |
|---|---|
| A Ltd | €400,000 Loss relief |
| B Ltd | €800,000 Loss relief |
| D Ltd | €600,000 Loss relief |
| G Ltd | €200,000 Loss relief |

---

## 6.11 Capital Gains Tax Group

Group relief also exists in respect of the transfer of chargeable assets between group members. Remember, where ownership of a chargeable asset changes, there will be a disposal of that asset for tax purposes. Also, where that disposal occurs between connected parties, the transaction will be deemed to happen at the market value of the asset passing. As a reminder, examples of chargeable assets can include property, goodwill, shares and other such capital assets.

The transfer of revenue items (e.g. stock or debtors) does not give rise to CGT issues. The group relieving provisions provide that the transfer of the chargeable asset is to occur as if a no gain/no loss situation were to arise. The purchaser or recipient of a property will take on the original base cost and date of acquisition. If an asset is transferred intragroup numerous times, the base cost and date of acquisition attaching to that property will not change until the company leaves the group or the property is sold to a third party.

### 6.11.1 Intragroup Sales/Transfers of Capital Assets

A principal company and its effective 75% subsidiaries form a CGT group. Where a principal company itself is a member of a group (as being itself an effective 75% subsidiary), that group comprises all of its effective 75% subsidiaries.

A "principal company" is a company of which another company is an effective 75% subsidiary (directly or indirectly). A company is an effective 75% subsidiary of another company, the parent, if the parent:

1. owns, directly or indirectly, not less than 75% of its ordinary share capital;
2. is beneficially entitled to not less than 75% of any profits available for distribution; and
3. would be beneficially entitled to not less than 75% of the assets of the company available for distribution on a winding up.

The distinction between a group for loss relief purposes and for CGT purposes is that, where a principal company is itself an effective 75% subsidiary, it and all its effective 75% subsidiaries will be part of the same CGT group as its parent, even though a sub-subsidiary of the ultimate parent may be less than 75% owned by that parent. For example: P Ltd owns 75% of S Ltd. A Ltd acquires 75% of P Ltd. Even though A Ltd does not control 75% of S Ltd, it is in the A Ltd CGT group.

The member companies must be resident in Ireland or in a DTT country, or be a company quoted on a recognised stock exchange. The thrust of CGT group relief is that, where an asset is transferred between members, the transfer is deemed to occur at a price that would give rise to a no gain/no loss position. It is compulsory. Therefore, there cannot be a capital loss on intragroup transfers of capital assets.

For accounting purposes, the transfer may occur at the book value of those assets. For tax purposes, the consideration (if any) that actually passes is ignored. The tax relief is structured in such a manner that it is deemed to be a no loss/no gain scenario.

Subsequently, if there is a disposal of an asset by a member of a group to a person outside the group and that asset had been acquired by the company making the disposal from another group member, the acquisition cost for the disposal is the original base cost and date of acquisition of the first member to acquire the asset.

### 6.11.2 Clawback of Relief

As with most tax reliefs, there is a provision for clawback of that relief, which is in section 623 TCA 1997. In general, the clawback will occur where there is a break in a group relationship between the company holding the asset and the transferor company. The clawback period exists for 10 years following the transfer of that asset.

---

**Example 6.9**
Company A transfers a building to Company B on 1 July 2009. If the 75% relationship between Company A and Company B is broken before 1 July 2019, there will be a clawback of group relief in Company B.

---

Where a company ceases to be a member of a CGT group, the assets it has acquired on which group relief was claimed will be deemed to be sold and immediately reacquired by the company holding the asset. Note therefore that CGT group relief is effectively, for that 10-year period, a deferral of the CGT that should have arisen on that intragroup transfer. It is not a full exemption without further implication to the CGT group.

If the 10-year period expires, there will not be a clawback of group relief if the 75% relationship is broken. Group relief clawback should be considered if any of the following occurs:

- New investors into a group (i.e. the 75% relationship is broken).
- Disposal of a subsidiary to a third party.
- Liquidation of a subsidiary and the passing of assets to members (see **Section 6.11.3** for exception).

The above scenarios could give rise to clawbacks of group relief.

### 6.11.3 Occasions where a Group Relief Clawback Does Not Occur

A clawback of group relief will not typically occur where:

- the asset has been held by the company leaving the group for more than 10 years; or
- a company leaves the group by virtue of being wound up or dissolved. This dissolution of the company must occur for bona fide commercial reasons and not for the purposes of tax avoidance.

**Example 6.10**
Take the following group structure:

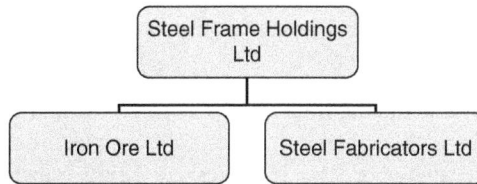

```
        ┌──────────────────────┐
        │  Steel Frame Holdings │
        │          Ltd          │
        └──────────┬───────────┘
          ┌────────┴────────┐
 ┌─────────────────┐  ┌─────────────────────┐
 │   Iron Ore Ltd  │  │ Steel Fabricators Ltd│
 └─────────────────┘  └─────────────────────┘
```

The two subsidiaries are owned by Steel Frame Holdings Ltd. It purchased a property in 2008 for €20 million which is now (2016) valued at €30 million and is the factory where the group's steel products are manufactured. In recent years, Iron Ore Ltd has reduced its activity, as Steel Fabricators Ltd now directly sources all materials used for the business. Steel Fabricators is the main trading entity with turnover of €200 million per annum, and it is profitable.

To streamline the business, Steel Frame Holdings Ltd is going to transfer the property to Steel Fabricators Ltd. Without group relief, the following would occur:

▨ Steel Frame Holdings would be deemed to dispose of the property at market value. A chargeable gain of €10 million would arise, taxable at an effective rate of 33%.

▨ Steel Fabricators Ltd would acquire the asset and its base cost would be €30 million.

Group relief provides that the following applies:

▨ Steel Frame Holdings Ltd will dispose of the property for a deemed consideration that will give rise to a no gain/no loss situation. This company will not have a tax liability on the transfer.

▨ Steel Fabricators Ltd will acquire the asset and will take on the base cost and date of acquisition of Steel Frame Holdings Ltd (i.e. €20 million and acquired in 2008).

If Steel Fabricators Ltd leaves the group within 10 years, the following will occur:

▨ Steel Fabricators Ltd will be deemed to dispose of and immediately reacquire the property (by reference to the date it took ownership – 2016). A chargeable gain of €10 million will arise and, as such, Steel Fabricators Ltd will trigger a €3.3 million tax liability for itself in the absence of loss relief.

If Steel Fabricators Ltd does not leave the group, but sells the property to a third party in the future, the following will apply:

▨ Steel Fabricators Ltd will be liable to CGT on the disposal of the property. For computational purposes, it will have a base cost of €20 million and an original date of acquisition of 2008.

## 6.12 Stamp Duty: Associated Companies Relief

Stamp duty relief is also available for the transfer of assets between group members. If two companies involved in a property/asset transfer are **90%** related by virtue of:

▨ direct or indirect ownership of 90% of ordinary share capital,
▨ entitlement to not less than 90% of any profits available for distribution, and
▨ entitlement to not less than 90% of assets available on a winding up,

then an exemption from stamp duty can be claimed.

Section 79 of the Stamp Duty Consolidation Act 1999 (SDCA 1999) legislates for this exemption. The exemption will apply to an instrument that executes for the transfer of any of the following:

- Conveyance or transfer on the sale of any stocks or marketable securities.
- Conveyance or transfer on sale of a policy of insurance or a policy of life insurance where the risk to which the policy relates is located in the State.
- Conveyance or transfer on the sale of any property other than stocks or marketable securities, a policy of insurance or a policy of life insurance

In practice, one is most likely to encounter a transfer of shares, stocks and property.

This stamp duty exemption is a valuable relief, and if, for example, property is the asset that is passing, the exemption can mean a tax saving of 2%. If shares are being transferred, the stamp duty saving would be 1%.

---

**Key Issue**
Where there is a transfer of assets intragroup, there may be an entitlement to an exemption from stamp duty if the provisions of section 79 SDCA 1999 are met. This is a valuable relief.

---

This stamp duty relief is subject to clawback if the two companies cease to be associated within two years of the transfer.

---

**Key Issue**
A stamp duty clawback will not arise if the property is sold within two years, and the clawback will arise if the group relationship is broken within two years.

---

An application to the Revenue Commissioners is required to claim this stamp duty exemption.

---

**Example 6.11**
Take the A Ltd Group. All entities within the group are 100% subsidiaries of A Ltd.

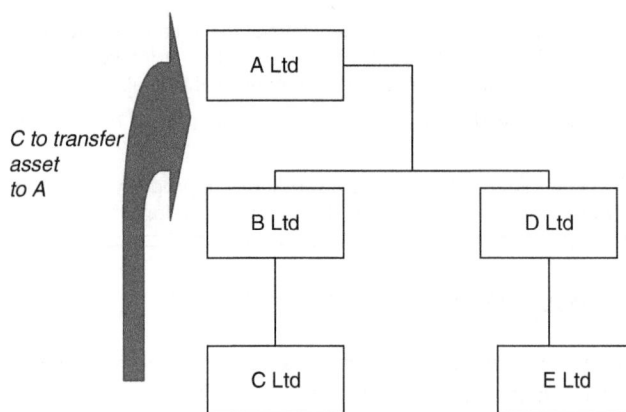

*C to transfer asset to A*

If C Ltd is to transfer a property asset to A Ltd, a claim for stamp duty associated companies relief is available.

Note that CGT group relief can be claimed and the transfer can effectively take place tax free.

If the 90% association between C Ltd and A Ltd is broken within two years of the transfer, there will be a clawback of the stamp duty associated companies relief.

---

**Note:** CGT group relief can also be claimed, so the transfer can effectively take place tax free.

## 6.13 Benefits of Holding Company Structure: Commercial/Practical and Tax Benefits

There may be limited benefits in holding various business interests in separately owned companies (i.e. not within a group structure). However, problems can arise using this type of structure, for example in respect of the financing of each individual entity. Therefore, a holding company structure is often put in place to maximise commercial and tax efficiencies.

The benefits of a holding company can be summarised as follows:

- Interest as a charge may be claimable by the holding company.
- Section 626B TCA 1997 (participation exemption) may apply on a future disposal of shares by the holding company.
- Facilitates group loss relief in respect of tax losses between subsidiaries.
- Facilitates CGT group relief in respect of the transfer of assets between members.
- Creates a vehicle to allow third-party investors entry at the top company level.

## 6.14 Participation Exemption

Section 626B TCA 1997, "participation exemption", is an important tax relief. This relief involves complete exemption from CGT on the disposal of shares in a subsidiary.

For the purposes of this relief, a subsidiary can consist of a company in which the "parent" has a minimum 5% holding. Note therefore that this exemption can be claimed where the parent has only a minority holding. The exemption will apply where:

- A parent company makes a disposal of shares in a subsidiary.
- The investee company (i.e. subsidiary) must be tax resident in Ireland (or the EU or in a country with which Ireland has a DTT).
- The subsidiary must be a wholly or mainly trading subsidiary, or a holding company owning shares in wholly or mainly trading subsidiaries.
- The investor company must, throughout an uninterrupted period of 12 months, have held at least a 5% shareholding in the subsidiary.

For example, if Parent Co. owns a 55% shareholding in Subsidiary Co. and it wishes to make a disposal of 20% of that shareholding, the disposal should (subject to the above conditions being met) qualify for the section 626B exemption.

This exemption does not apply where the shares in the subsidiary derive the greater part of their value from land, minerals or exploration rights in Ireland (i.e. Irish "specified assets").

---

**Key Issue**

If there is a disposal of shares in a subsidiary, students should always consider if that disposal is exempt from CGT by virtue of the section 626B TCA 1997 participation exemption. Students should also consider this exemption if setting up or restructuring a business. It may be beneficial to isolate trading entities intended for sale at some point in the future. This is a key aspect of long-term tax planning. In fact, this exemption could be an incentive to incorporate and set up a holding company structure if a future trade sale is anticipated as part of a long-term business plan.

---

## Chapter 6 Summary

| | |
|---|---|
| **Corporation tax losses for groups** | • Reasons for groups<br>• Need a 75% relationship overall<br>• Losses available include trading losses, excess management expenses and excess capital allowances and charges on income<br>• Impact on loss relief where tax returns are filed late |
| **Consortium relief** | • Surrender/claim losses in proportion to ownership<br>• Needs consent of all members<br>• Group relief takes priority over consortium relief |
| **Capital gains groups** | • Need 75% ownership, with overall control of the group<br>• Assets are transferred at no gain/no loss<br>• Clawback may apply on member leaving the group |
| **Other group issues** | • Stamp duty – relief where 90% relationship exists<br>• Clawback of relief if member leaves group<br>• Participation exemption – relief from CGT on sale of subsidiary |

# Questions

## Review Questions
(See Suggested Solutions to Review Questions at the end of this textbook.)

### Question 6.1

In the year ended 31 March 2016, GAS Limited is a 75% subsidiary of OIL Limited. The accounts and computations of the companies for the 12-month accounting period to 31 March 2016 show the following:

| OIL Limited | € |
|---|---|
| Current year management expenses | 15,000 |
| Management expenses brought forward | 2,500 |
| Case III income | 3,200 |

| GAS Limited | |
|---|---|
| Trading profits | 10,000 |
| Charges paid | 600 |

GAS Limited claims group relief from OIL Limited, with the consent of OIL Limited.

**Requirement**
(a)  Calculate the amount of group relief available to GAS Limited.
(b)  Calculate the revised profits chargeable to corporation tax for the group for the year ended 31 March 2016.

### Question 6.2

Company A is a 75% subsidiary of Company B. Both companies make up their accounts to 31 December. The accounts and computations of the companies for the 12-month accounting period to 31 December 2016 show the following:

| Company B | € | € |
|---|---|---|
| Management expenses | | 2,000 |
| Capital gain | 3,200 | |
| Less: capital losses brought forward | (1,800) | |
| | | 1,400 |
| Case III income | | 1,000 |
| Non-trade charges paid | | 5,500 |

| Company A | | |
|---|---|---|
| Case I profit | | 1,000 |
| Case III income | | 500 |
| Non-trade charges paid | | 200 |

**Requirement**
Calculate the maximum amount of a group relief claim between Company A and Company B.

## Question 6.3

Tree Limited is owned as follows:

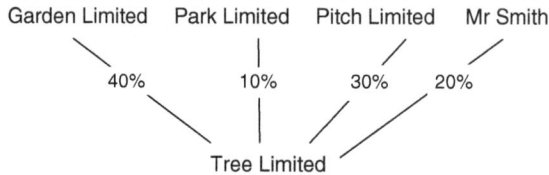

The following information in respect of the members of the consortium is available:

▨ Garden Limited had trading profits of €290,000 in respect of the year ended 31 December 2016.
▨ Park Limited had trading profits of €200,000 in respect of the year ended 31 March 2016. In addition, Park Limited had a non-trade charge of €75,000.
▨ Pitch Limited had trading profits of €160,000 and Case III income of €40,000 for the year ended 31 March 2016.

Tree Limited has trading losses of €400,000 and Case III income of €45,000 in respect of the year ended 31 March 2017.

### Requirement

1. Calculate the maximum amount of losses available for consortium relief.
2. Calculate the corporation tax liabilities for the above companies, assuming all relevant claims and elections are made.

# Challenging Questions
(Suggested Solutions to Challenging Questions are available through your lecturer.)

## Question 6.1

QuikPhones Group

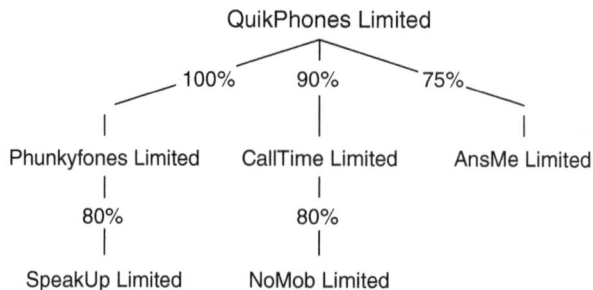

During the year ended 31 December 2016, the group had the following trading results:

▓ QuikPhones Limited is a trading company, involved in the manufacture of mobile phones.During the year ended 31 December 2016, it had trading profits of €256,065 with capital losses brought forward of €60,000.

▓ Phunkyfones Limited has Schedule D Case I profits of €67,994 before deducting capital allowances of €34,000. The company also has trading losses of €446,086 brought forward, together with capital losses of €44,000.

▓ CallTime Limited incurred trading losses of €369,402 during the year.

▓ SpeakUp Limited had trading profits of €72,100 and a capital gain of €135,000.

▓ The shareholding in AnsMe Limited was acquired by QuikPhones Limited on 1 August 2016. Its results for the year ended 31 December 2016 showed a Schedule D, Case I profit of €155,866.

The financial controller advises you of the transactions that are due to take place during the following months:

▓ An offer of €1,750,000 for a property owned by SpeakUp has been received by an unconnected third party. The property was originally transferred from NoMob Limited in January 2010 when an offer of €1.25 million was turned down, as it was needed in the trade of SpeakUp. Due to recent changes in the company, it is no longer required and the offer is too good to refuse. QuikPhones is to transfer a smaller property that is not currently being used to SpeakUp. The property was acquired in February 1983 and indexation from then to 2002 is 2.253.

▓ NoMob Limited is to be sold to an unconnected third party. The purchaser is interested in a property that is held by the company and which was originally bought by QuikPhones in January 1986 for €45,000. The property was transferred to NoMob in November 2005, when it was worth €178,000. Indexation from January 1986 to 2002 is 1.713.

**Requirement**
(a) State the members of the group relief CGT for corporation tax purposes.
(b) State the members of the CGT group.
(c) Calculate the corporation tax liability of the group, on the basis that all claims and elections are made to minimise the tax position.
(d) Advise on the actual and proposed capital transfers during the year.

# Acquisition and Disposal of a Business

**Learning Objectives**

By the end of this chapter you will be able to:

- Analyse and evaluate the taxation implications of an acquisition or disposal of a business, including:
  - share sales and asset/trade sales;
  - trading losses and loss-buying provisions;
  - tax relief on interest paid by companies and individuals;
  - need for taxation warranties and indemnities;
  - exemption from tax in the case of gains on certain disposal of shares; and
  - retirement relief.

## 7.1 Types of Acquisition and Disposal

The sale of a business can take various forms. Each method gives rise to different commercial, tax and legal consequences that influence the way in which the transaction is structured. In summary, the different forms of a business sale can include:

- Share sale/purchase.
- Sale/purchase of a trade as a going concern.
- Sale/purchase of assets.

The purchaser and vendor will have different requirements and may want to buy/sell different things to achieve a more favourable tax treatment for themselves. This chapter looks at several ways of acquiring/disposing of a business, both from the vendor's and the purchaser's point of view, having regard to the tax, legal and commercial consequences of the transactions.

How a business is eventually sold will be a matter for negotiation between the two parties. A restructuring or reorganisation of a business prior to a sale may be required to enable a particular type of sale (suitable from both a purchaser's and a vendor's perspective).

---

*Example 7.1*

A purchaser may only want to buy the share capital of a company and not specific business assets/trade from the company which were put up for sale. If so, steps will be required to enable the share sale. For example, assets not intended for sale will need to be moved out of the company and therefore a restructuring of the company will be required prior to the share sale.

---

*Example 7.2*

A purchaser may not wish to purchase the shares of a company to avoid acquiring any historical tax issues associated with the company. The seller must therefore take appropriate steps to ensure that an asset sale can be facilitated. The vendor must take into account how to extract the cash proceeds from the company following the sale. The issue of cash extraction is often a key issue associated with an asset sale for the vendor.

---

*Example 7.3*

A vendor is due to sell a 100% shareholding in a subsidiary. An issue could be that CGT and stamp duty group relief were claimed in recent months/years, and the sale of the subsidiary will trigger a clawback of tax relief claimed. Tax clawback matters will have to be considered.

---

*Key Issue*

Prior to the sale of a business, **the vendor** must consider the tax implications associated with the various sale options. If an asset/trade sale, the vendor should carefully evaluate how cash can be extracted from that entity. It may be the case that the vendor wishes to retain cash in the company for further investment. Issues such as the base cost of assets will be relevant as the vendor is likely to have to consider a CGT liability. Always remember retirement relief when considering a business sale. This is a key planning relief and if available can prove very beneficial to the vendor.

**The purchaser** should consider how to purchase a business at a minimum acquisition cost from a tax perspective. Consideration should also be given as to the purchaser's future or intended exit from the business. Stamp duty will be a key consideration for the purchaser, and very often a share purchase offers the most favourable stamp duty result. There are other considerations, such as latent tax liabilities, to consider when purchasing shares or capital allowances if purchasing assets.

---

## 7.2   Share Sale Analysis

### 7.2.1   Share Sale

A share sale is a disposal, for CGT purposes, by the individual shareholders and taxed accordingly. If the share sale is made by a company, the selling company may also be liable to tax on any chargeable gain arising. Always identify if:

▪ the vendor is an individual; or
▪ the vendor is a company.

The type of tax advice will vary according to the circumstances of the vendor. A vendor may prefer to sell the shares in their business for a number of reasons:

▓ They may be able to avail of retirement relief on the disposal of a shareholding in a trading company if the relevant conditions are met, thus reducing/eliminating the CGT liability on disposal.

▓ If the vendor is an individual, they will receive the cash personally from the share sale. CGT, at a current rate of 33%, will apply to the chargeable gain arising.

▓ It avoids a double tax charge (a) on the tax due on the disposal of assets by the company; and (b) CGT due by the shareholders on the subsequent cash distribution to them following the liquidation or winding up of the company. **This is a key tax planning issue to remember, as the asset sale by a company does not give the individual the direct benefit of the sale proceeds. Further steps are required to extract cash from the company.**

▓ If a holding company is disposing of one of its trading subsidiaries, the section 626B TCA 1997 participation exemption may be available, thus exempting the share disposal from tax.

A purchaser may wish to acquire shares for a number of reasons, for example because:

▓ The business can continue uninterrupted.

▓ The rate of stamp duty on the purchase of shares is lower at 1%, rather than at 2% on transactions in land and buildings.

▓ Unused tax reliefs, such as losses available for carry forward, continue to be available, subject to anti-avoidance provisions on the change of ownership.

▓ If the purchaser is a company, then the corporation tax reliefs for groups may be available (e.g. group loss relief on future tax losses); but note, it is not possible to use pre-entry losses for CGT group relief purposes.

▓ The vendor may not be willing to sell anything other than the shares.

### 7.2.2 Tax Consequences of a Share Sale

A sale of shares is a disposal for CGT purposes. If the entire sale consideration is in cash (as opposed to a swap for shares in another company – discussed in **Chapter 8**), the vendor is taxed on the full amount received after deducting the base cost, etc.

There is a continuation of the company's trade and therefore no balancing charges/allowances arise in respect of items eligible for capital allowances.

Existing tax losses may be carried forward within the company, subject to the anti-avoidance provisions i.e. if there is a change in the nature or conduct of a trade following the change in ownership. These provisions are discussed in more detail in **Section 7.4**.

There are no VAT consequences for a share sale because a sale of shares is not a VATable supply.

Note that a share purchase may not be the best choice for the purchaser, since a share purchase carries with it a number of risks for the purchaser, i.e. taking on the "history" of the company, including any bad debts and outstanding liabilities.

A restructuring of the business may be required to separate items held by the company that are not intended to form part of the sale. Corporate restructuring is considered in detail in **Chapter 8**.

### 7.2.3 Stamp Duty Considerations: Share Purchase

Stamp duty issues are likely to influence how the purchaser will want to structure the acquisition of a business. The main stamp duty considerations are:

▓ The rate of stamp duty on the purchase of shares is 1%.

▓ The rate of stamp duty on the purchase of assets is higher at 2%.

As stamp duty is a cost for the purchaser, they may seek to structure the transaction in a way to minimise stamp duty, most likely being a share purchase. The question of stamp duty will not arise in isolation, however, as other commercial and tax issues will impact on the transaction structure.

### 7.2.4 Commercial Consideration: Latent Gains Attaching to Property

A frequent tax consideration when dealing with a share sale/purchase, is the question of "latent gains" attaching to a company's assets. Remember that, on a share purchase, all assets remain in the ownership of the company and their base cost is unaffected. A latent gain can arise where the company (now under the ownership of the purchaser) incurs a capital gain on the disposal of an asset (e.g. property). This arises where the property has a low base cost but has appreciated in value while in the ownership of the company. Where such latent gains are identified before the share sale/purchase, the purchaser will no doubt want to be compensated for this potential liability by negotiating a lower price for the shares.

---

**Key Issue**

In valuing the shares for the share sale, the value comes from the market value of the underlying assets of the company at the date of sale. On a purchase of shares in a company, the base cost for a future disposal will be the price paid for the shares. However, if the company is disposing of its assets (e.g. property) subsequent to the share sale, the assets retain their original base cost.

---

**Example 7.4**

Steven Ryan purchased the shares of a trading company Blue Ink Ltd. He paid €15 million for the shares in the company. The assets of the company comprised a trade worth €5 million and a property worth €10 million. The property was purchased by the company many years ago for €100,000. Steven has now received an offer to acquire the trade and assets of the business for €16 million. The purchaser doesn't want to acquire the shares in the company. Steven thinks he is only liable to CGT on the gain of €1 million. Is that correct?

It is not. One of the key issues driving the high value of the company is that the property is worth at least €10 million. If that property is sold at its current market value, the company will be liable to corporation tax on a significant chargeable gain of at least €10 million. Why? The base cost is very low compared with the open-market value.

In other words, the €15 million paid by Steven is not considered when the company is making the asset sale. The €15 million paid by Steven is therefore the base cost of the shares, and the key asset, i.e. the property, within the company will still have a very low base cost.

Steven should try to negotiate a share sale rather than an asset sale. If properly advised, the purchaser may be reluctant to accept this without being adequately compensated as, at a future date, he is likely to face the same "latent gain" issue.

---

Where a latent gain is identified in advance of a share acquisition, a purchaser may decide instead to only buy the trade/assets of the company. There would, however, be the higher rate of stamp duty payable on the purchase of assets.

---

**Example 7.5: Latent gain**

Philip Loughran is considering the purchase of Travel Limited from an unconnected third party. Within the accounts of Travel Limited are premises that have an original base cost of €200,000. The current market value of the premises is €1 million.

*continued overleaf*

---

Philip knows that the premises will be surplus to requirements once the company is bought, as he has his own premises from which the new business will trade.

The latent gain in the company is as follows (ignoring any indexation):

|  | € |
|---|---|
| Current market value | 1,000,000 |
| Base cost | (200,000) |
| Potential gain | 800,000 |
| Corporation tax liability @ 33% | 264,000 |

Philip will want to ensure that this latent liability is reflected in the purchase price negotiations for Travel Limited, as ultimately it will be "his" liability.

### 7.2.5  Summary: Share Sale

Some of the key advantages/disadvantages associated with a **share** sale are:

| Vendor's Perspective | Purchaser's Perspective |
|---|---|
| Reduced consideration receivable due to company's latent gains (i.e. cost paid for shares is not the base cost of underlying assets). | Due diligence process is likely to be costly, but a key requirement in advance of completing the sale. |
| Shareholders benefit by receiving cash directly from the sale. | Sufficient warranties will be required. |
| Liable to once-off CGT rate of 33%. | Provision for latent gains should be reflected in the purchase price. |
| No balancing charges in respect of assets held by the company. | Lower stamp duty benefit (1% on shares). |
| No liquidation costs (when compared to a sale of trade/assets by a company and subsequent liquidation to distribute the net proceeds to the shareholders). | If purchasing a company from a group, is there potential for clawback of CGT/stamp duty reliefs previously claimed on intragroup transfers? |
| No VAT considerations as a share sale is not a VATable supply. | VAT will not arise on share purchase. |
| If the vendor is a company, section 626B TCA 1997 relief may be available. | May purchase tax losses within a company – **but bear in mind the anti-avoidance loss-buying provisions and restrictions applying.** |

## 7.3  Tax Implications of the Sale/Purchase of a Trade/Assets

### 7.3.1  Trade Sale/Purchase

A disposal of a trade and/or assets by a company may trigger a chargeable gain on the disposal. The chargeable assets for tax purposes are likely to be land and buildings and the goodwill of the business.

**The purchaser** may wish to only acquire the trade and/or assets of a company. It is often easier and more straightforward to acquire assets rather than shares and it may be less costly. For example, a due diligence is not likely to be required if an asset purchase is planned. The main reasons for the purchaser to acquire the trade/assets are as follows:

- A purchaser can choose which assets to acquire.
- The assets are acquired at their market value, rather than at their base cost as with a share purchase, therefore the issue of latent gains is not relevant.
- Capital allowances may be claimed on the purchase of plant/machinery/equipment, etc. on their purchase price
- The requirement for tax warranties and indemnities may not arise.
- Issues such as a clawback of CGT group relief or associated company stamp duty relief are not relevant.

### Purchaser's Disadvantage

The major disadvantage to the purchaser of acquiring assets is the increased stamp duty charge over the cost of acquiring shares (1% on share purchase versus 2% on trade/asset purchase).

### Vendor's Disadvantage

The proceeds on the sale of the trade and/or assets may be subject to corporation tax if a chargeable gain arises. If the shareholders wish to extract any of the proceeds, they must consider the tax implications. A second charge to CGT is likely to arise if the company is subsequently liquidated and the net proceeds distributed to the shareholders. If the company is not liquidated but cash is paid to the shareholders, this cash, whether a dividend or additional salary, is subject to income tax/PRSI/USC in the hands of the shareholders who are individuals. Tax planning is likely to be needed to achieve the CGT rate on cash extraction from the company.

---

**Example 7.6: Trade/asset sale**

Jones Limited is disposing of its trade and assets for €500,000 and John Jones will extract the remaining cash from the company post-sale by way of dividend.

|  | € |
|---|---|
| Proceeds of sale of assets | 500,000 |
| Cost of assets per balance sheet | (225,000) |
| Gain arising in company | 275,000 |
| Less: corporation tax on gain @ 33% | (90,750) |
| Proceeds available for distribution | 409,250 |
| Less: DWT @ 20% | (81,850) |
| Additional income tax due on distribution* | 81,850 (@ 40% − 20%) |
| Net proceeds received by shareholder | 245,550 (taking account of taxes due) |

* Assume John Jones is a 40% rate taxpayer and ignore PRSI/USC for illustrative purposes.

---

**Note:** in the above example, the sale of assets and subsequent cash extraction by way of dividend has been very tax inefficient for the vendor. A tax charge has arisen twice on the proceeds received from the sale. If it is the intention of the shareholders to keep the cash in the company for further investment, then an asset sale may well give the best tax result. If immediate cash extraction from the company to individual shareholders is planned, then a share sale has obvious advantages over a trade/asset sale.

---

**Key Issue**
Always establish the intention of the vendor if an asset sale is planned. Students may be in a position to highlight the benefits of a share sale and change the intended structure of a transaction.

---

### 7.3.2 Tax Consequences of Sale of Trade and/or Assets

The sale of a trade and assets by a company will result in a cessation of the trade for corporation tax purposes and will be the end of an accounting period. Any unused tax reliefs brought forward may be lost and any trading losses cannot be carried forward. Terminal loss relief may be available on cessation of the trade. The sale of a trade and assets by an individual will result in a cessation of the trade for income tax purposes. The tax implications of a cessation to trade have been considered in **Sections 1.11** and **1.12**.

Capital gains may arise on the disposal of chargeable assets, such as property or goodwill. If there are current year trading losses available in the company, these may be used to reduce the corporation tax on the gains arising.

There may be balancing charges on the sale of plant and machinery. This should be considered if the business has a significant holding of plant and equipment. The sale of stock may give rise to a profit, which will be taxed as a trading receipt.

VAT is chargeable on the sale of assets, unless the transfer of a business as a going concern exemption applies. For this relief to apply, the purchaser must also be a VAT-registered entity.

As stated above, there are a number of reasons why a purchaser may wish to only acquire the trade and/or assets of a company. The tax implications for such a purchase are as follows:

- Capital allowances will be based on the acquisition price paid for plant/machinery, etc.
- Base cost for CGT purposes will be the acquisition price paid for assets.
- VAT is not an issue if the purchaser is also a VAT-registered entity and the transfer of a business exemption applies. Otherwise VAT is chargeable by the vendor.
- Stamp duty may be payable on the acquisition of the assets (e.g. property, goodwill, etc.) at a rate of 2%.

### 7.3.3 Commercial Considerations

It is important to identify precisely the assets/liabilities being taken over from a legal point of view. Leases may need to be reviewed. The assignment of a lease may require a VAT review. Employee legislative and pension rights must be considered so as to avoid any potential liabilities arising after the sale if a business is being purchased as a going concern.

### 7.3.4 Stamp Duty Considerations: Asset/Trade Purchase

Stamp duty issues are likely to influence how the purchaser will want to structure the acquisition of a business. As previously identified, stamp duty considerations for the purchaser are as follows:

- The rate of stamp duty on the purchase of shares is 1%.
- The rate of stamp duty on the purchase of assets is higher at 2%.

Stamp duty is a cost for the purchaser. If an asset purchase is planned, the stamp duty arising could be significant if the value of assets being acquired is high. Note that items such as plant and stock can pass by delivery and where they do should be excluded when computing the stamp duty due to arise. Typical examples of assets liable at 2% stamp duty are property and goodwill. The issue of stamp duty will not arise in isolation, as other commercial and tax issues will be considered by reference to the particular structure of the sale/purchase.

### 7.3.5  Summary: Trade/Asset Sale

In summary, some of the key advantages/disadvantages associated with a trade/asset sale are:

| Vendor's Perspective | Purchaser's Perspective |
|---|---|
| Vendor likely to benefit from higher price as the question of latent gains and significant warranties may not arise if the assets are sold directly to purchaser. | Due diligence process is not likely to be required and this may represent a cost saving to the purchaser. |
| Further tax planning may be required to extract cash proceeds from the company – this may be a key disadvantage. | Warranties may not be critical. |
| The company making the sale will be liable to an effective corporation tax rate of 33% on any chargeable gain arising. | The question of latent gains will not arise, as the purchase price will be the base cost of the assets on a future disposal. |
| Possible balancing allowances/charges in respect of assets being disposed of. | Higher stamp duty charge is likely to be an issue. |
| Liquidation of the company may be required post-sale, which could be a lengthy and costly process. | Capital allowances will be based on the acquisition price paid for assets. |
| VAT will need to be considered as part of the sale of the trade/assets. | VAT recovery should be considered if it is going to arise on the purchase of assets/trade. |
|  | Tax losses will not be purchased if assets are purchased. |

## 7.4  Loss-buying Provisions

An investor buying shares in a company may invest in a company that has existing tax losses. If the investor is confident that they can make the company profitable, then the existing tax losses constitute a future benefit or asset to the company (i.e. the tax losses can be used to shelter future profits). Case I trading losses can be carried forward and set against future profits from the same trade. However, where there is a change in ownership of a company, existing trading losses can sometimes be disallowed. This is commonly known as the loss buying anti-avoidance rules. The losses will be disallowed where, within a three-year period:

▪ there is a change in the ownership of the company; **and**
▪ there is also a major change in the activities carried on by that company; **or**
▪ where, at the time of the change in ownership, the company was almost dormant in terms of activity.

A major change in the nature of the trade of the company can include a change in the stock/property/services sold by the company or a major change in the company's customer/market base.

---

**Key Issue**
The purchaser of shares may be confident that they can turn a loss-making business into a profitable one. If the company has significant tax losses accumulated (which could be common in companies that require significant growth/development investment), these tax losses represent an asset to the purchaser of shares. The key issue is to ensure that losses carried forward by the company are not jeopardised by any change in the nature of the trade or level of activity in the three years following the change of ownership.

---

## 7.5 Due Diligence Process

If a share purchase is to take place, the purchaser will carry out a due diligence review of the company to ascertain the level of any hidden/potential liabilities within the company.

The due diligence review of a company will normally involve a detailed review of the accounts of the target company for at least the previous three years. It plays a vital part of a share sale. As well as discovering any potential liabilities, it is also an important tool for assessing whether or not to proceed with the deal. The intention is to see what potentially hidden liabilities exist in the company. The purchaser will typically use this information to arrive at a more realistic sale price.

If the investor's confidence in the company is reduced following the findings of a due diligence review, the investment may not take place.

Due diligence tax checks can:

- Elicit the history of outstanding tax returns across all tax heads.
- Establish if tax returns have historically been submitted on time (to establish exposure in respect of potential interest and penalties).
- Conduct a review of the company's VAT history from records available.
- Ensure that the company has applied the correct VAT rate to its supplies.
- Establish the extent to which the company is entitled to VAT recovery (and compare that to what has actually been recovered).
- Establish the key VAT history of property within a company/group.
- Establish if the PAYE/PRSI affairs are in order, including the extent to which payments have been made to individuals without operation of PAYE.
- Obtain confirmation of the last period in which there was a Revenue audit and the outcome.
- Cross-check VAT and PAYE records to key financial data (e.g. the financial statements).
- Establish indicators of any aggressive tax planning in the company.
- Analyse intragroup/inter-company transactions to establish if the share sale will trigger a clawback of reliefs such as group relief and stamp duty relief.

The due diligence process is similar to an audit of the company's affairs.

## 7.6 Tax Warranties and Indemnities

Tax warranties are an important part of a share purchase agreement. The rationale of the tax warranties is to impose legal liability on the vendor if there are any discrepancies between the tax position as reported and the actual tax position.

If, as part of the due diligence process, any outstanding or potential future liabilities are discovered, the purchaser will want a commitment from the vendor that the vendor will be responsible (indemnify) for these should any such liability arise. These are known as the tax warranties and indemnities that can be included as part of the share purchase agreement or covered in a separate legal document.

---

**Key Issue**

If shares in a company are being purchased, it is very important that the history of the company is checked. For example, if you purchase a company on 1 July 2016, and one week later that company receives notification of a PAYE and VAT audit for the 2013 year, any tax liabilities that arise from that audit may be your problem. Suitable warranties for such a situation should be documented in the share purchase agreement or a similar legal document.

---

Examples of tax warranties are:

◾ VAT compliance is up-to-date and no historical filing penalties will accrue in the hands of the new investors.

◾ PAYE obligations have been met and no historical filing penalties will accrue in the hands of the new investors.

◾ Historical corporation tax affairs are in order and no historical filing penalties will accrue in the hands of the new investors.

◾ Computation of tax losses forward is accurate and correct.

◾ Warranties in respect of prior year CGT/stamp duty group relief claims.

◾ Who will benefit from tax refunds by reference to the periods prior to the share purchase (e.g. a back-dated claim for tax relief, etc.)?

## 7.7 Group Relief Clawback Provisions: Consideration Required if Shares are Purchased

As outlined in **Section 6.11**, transfers of chargeable assets (e.g. property, goodwill, shares, etc.) between group companies related by virtue of 75% common ownership can happen without triggering a charge to tax on any gain. This is commonly known as "CGT group relief". The assets are deemed to transfer between the group members in such a way that would give rise to a "no gain/no loss position".

There is a clawback of CGT group relief if the 75% group relationship is broken prior to the expiry of a 10-year period following the asset transfer. If the group relationship is broken, the company holding the asset is deemed to sell and immediately reacquire the asset at the market value on the date it took ownership. The company leaving the group will be liable to tax on the chargeable gain arising, and this tax must be remitted to the Revenue Commissioners.

This is an issue therefore for an investor purchasing a company which holds an asset on which group relief was previously claimed (e.g. where group relief was claimed on an asset transfer within the previous 10 years).

It might not be obvious to the investor that group relief had been claimed previously. Sufficient investigation, as a part of the due diligence process, should be undertaken and, in addition, warranties should be put in place in the share purchase agreement.

A similar issue might arise for stamp duty associated companies relief – see **Section 6.12**. In this situation, if the 90% relationship is broken between the transferor and the transferee of property within two years, a clawback of stamp duty relief will arise.

## 7.8 Participation Exemption

As previously noted (**Section 6.14**), the participation exemption is a valuable tax relief. The exemption applies where a company makes a disposal of shares in a trading subsidiary. In view of its significance for a disposal of a business, the main points are repeated below:

◾ The investor company (i.e. the company making the disposal) must be a parent of the subsidiary at the time of the disposal. Note that the parent/subsidiary relationship is defined as being a 5% holding (in terms of share capital and in respect of entitlement to profits/assets).

◾ The parent company is required to have held the minimum holding for a continuous period of at least 12 months.

▨ The investee company (i.e. the subsidiary) must be wholly or mainly carrying on a trade, or if a group is being purchased that group must be wholly or mainly a trading group.

▨ At the time of the disposal, the subsidiary must be resident either in Ireland or in another EU Member State or in a country with which Ireland has a tax treaty.

If all of the relevant conditions are met, a parent company can sell all or part of its shareholding in a subsidiary tax free. This is a significant relief, and students should be in a position to apply the relief where appropriate.

---

**Key Issue**
If a company is selling all or part of its interest in a subsidiary, the CGT participation exemption relief may be available. If so, the transaction will be exempt from CGT.

---

## 7.9 Retirement Relief on Disposal of a Business

Retirement relief can provide a full or partial exemption from CGT on the disposal of an interest in a trading company/business. The relief will apply to:

▨ disposal of business assets by an individual; or

▨ disposal of shares in a wholly or mainly trading company by an individual.

Students should ensure they are in a position to compute the retirement relief computation.

---

**Key Issue**
Retirement relief is available in respect of the disposal of either trading assets by a sole trader or shares in a family trading company. Restructuring or reorganising a company in advance of a future sale (or if gifting the assets/shares) may in certain circumstances be required to maximise the relief available.

---

A detailed analysis of the relief follows.

### 7.9.1 Capital Gains Tax Retirement Relief

Retirement relief under sections 598 and 599 TCA 1997 is a CGT relief on certain disposals of business assets by an individual aged 55 years or over. Companies and trusts do not qualify for the relief. If the conditions are satisfied, gains realised on the disposal of relevant business assets are exempt from CGT. Where the disposal is to a child of the person disposing of the assets, there is no upper limit on the consideration for the relief under section 599 TCA 1997. However, transfers by a parent who is aged 66 years or older carry a cap on the value of the assets being transferred at €3 million, where the transfer occurs after 1 January 2014. If the disposal is to any other person/entity, the relief only applies to disposals generating proceeds totalling €750,000 under section 598 TCA 1997. The €750,000 threshold is a lifetime limit for disposals an individual makes after reaching age 55. This limit of €750,000 is reduced to €500,000 for persons aged 66 years or older, where the transfer occurs after 1 January 2014. Note that the value of any disposals to children under section 599 TCA 1997 is disregarded for the purpose of calculating the total consideration received for section 598 TCA 1997.

Typically, the relief is claimed where an entire business is being sold. However, the relief also applies to disposals of individual assets, even when the person making the disposal continues to trade. For example, a farmer aged over 55 years could sell sites while continuing to carry on his farming business and retirement relief may apply to any gains on the disposals of the sites. While the relief is referred to as retirement relief, there is no requirement that the person actually retires.

There are, however, wide-ranging anti-avoidance provisions associated with this relief to protect against abuse.

### 7.9.2  Conditions for Relief

The relief applies where the disposal is made:

- by an individual,
- aged 55 years or more at the time of the disposal.

And the disposal is:

- of a qualifying asset as outlined in **Section 7.9.3**, and
- owned by that individual for the qualifying period as outlined in **Section 7.9.4**.

### 7.9.3  Qualifying Assets for Retirement Relief

The relief applies to the disposal of qualifying assets. Qualifying assets may comprise actual assets used in a trade or profession or shares in trading companies. Investment assets such as quoted shares and rental properties do not qualify for the relief. If these assets are held within a trading company, an apportionment would be required to see what amount of the consideration would qualify for the relief.

Qualifying assets comprise:

1. **Land, buildings and goodwill** owned for at least 10 years and used for the purposes of the trade or profession continuously throughout the 10-year period.
2. **Plant, machinery or motor vehicles** used for the purposes of the trade or profession. Plant, machinery and motor vehicles do not have to be owned for a 10-year period prior to disposal. This is in recognition of the fact that such assets rarely have a useful life of up to 10 years. In practice, it would be very rare for a capital gain to arise on a disposal of plant, machinery or motor vehicles as they are wasting assets. However, it is very important to bear in mind that they are qualifying assets and the value of such assets must be included in the calculation of the €750,000/€500,000 threshold.
3. Farmers who transfer land for the purpose of complying with the terms of Revenue's **Scheme of Early Retirement from Farming**, provided the farmer used the land for the purpose of farming for a continuous period of 10 years ending on the date of the transfer. EU single-farm payment entitlements are also qualifying assets.
4. **Farmland that has been let** by the individual at any time in the 25-year period ending with the date of disposal, provided:
   (a) that immediately before the time the land was first let, the land was owned by the individual and used for the purpose of farming throughout the period of 10 years; and
   (b) the land was disposed of to a child of the person claiming retirement relief.
5. **Farmland that has been let** by the individual at any time in the five-year period ending with the date of disposal, provided:
   (a) that immediately before the time the land was first let, the land was owned by the individual and used for the purpose of farming throughout the period of 10 years; and
   (b) the land is disposed of under a compulsory purchase order to the local authorities for the purposes of road widening, etc.

Section 50 FA 2014 provides that where there is a disposal to a third party of land that has been let, each letting of the land must be for a period of not less than five consecutive years. Land let under a conacre arrangement may, in certain circumstances, also qualify for retirement relief. Land that is let under conacre prior to a disposal to:

▪ a child, at any time, or
▪ a third party where the disposal occurs on or before 31 December 2016

will qualify for retirement relief.

6. **Shares in a family trading company or farming company or holding company of a trading group** where the shares have been held by the individual making the disposal for a period of not less than 10 years ending on the disposal and the individual has been a working director of the company for 10 years, five years of which they have been a full-time working director of the company. A company is a family company in relation to an individual who is disposing of the shares, if:

   (a) he/she owns at least 25% of the shares; or
   (b) he/she owns at least 10% of the shares and his/her family, including the individual's own holding, owns at least 75% of the shares. Family means a spouse, a relative and relative of a spouse. A relative means a brother, sister, ancestor and lineal descendants.

   In order for the shares to be qualifying assets, tests (a) or (b) must be satisfied throughout the 10-year period immediately prior to the disposal of the shares.

7. **Assets owned by the individual but used by the family company**. Therefore, assets such as buildings, plant and equipment owned personally by a controlling shareholder for a period of 10 years ending on the disposal, but used by the company for the purposes of carrying on its trade or profession, qualify for relief if the assets are transferred at the same time as the shares in the company in which the assets are used. This provision mirrors a similar provision for the CAT relief, business property relief.

---

**Example 7.8**
Mark is aged 56. He sold his stationery business to Mary (an unrelated third party) for €770,000. The sales consideration comprised the following:

|  | € |
|---|---|
| Shop owned for 15 years | 440,000 |
| Delivery van owned for two years | 10,000 (cost €16,000) |
| Stock | 40,000 |
| Debtors | 20,000 |
| Shelving | 10,000 (cost €15,000) |
| Computer system | 20,000 (cost €30,000) |
| Goodwill | 230,000 |
| **Total** | **770,000** |

First, we must establish if the total proceeds in respect of qualifying assets (i.e. assets used for the purpose of the business and which could result in a capital gain on disposal) exceeds €750,000. If it does not, it is not even necessary to calculate any potential gains. The qualifying assets are the shop, goodwill, the van, the shelving and the computer system. The shelving, van and the computer system are chargeable assets for CGT purposes even though no chargeable gain arises on the disposal of these assets. Note that the stock and the debtors are not qualifying assets as these are not chargeable assets for CGT purposes.

*continued overleaf*

---

| Proceeds on qualifying assets | € |
|---|---|
| Shop | 440,000 |
| Goodwill | 230,000 |
| Van | 10,000 |
| Shelving | 10,000 |
| Computer system | 20,000 |
| **Total** | **710,000** |

As the proceeds in respect of qualifying assets are less than €750,000, retirement relief applies regardless of the level of any gains arising on the disposal of individual assets. A clawback of relief can arise for the seller of the business assets if the cumulative lifetime sale proceeds to third parties after the seller has reached 55 years of age exceeds €750,000.

### 7.9.4  Qualifying Periods of Ownership

The following points should be noted in relation to the 10-year period of ownership rule:

1. The asset must be owned and actually used in the trade for the 10-year period immediately before the disposal. For example, an individual may have owned a warehouse for the last 20 years. For the first 18 years, it was let but had been used for the purposes of the trade for the last two years. Such an asset would not be a qualifying asset as, while it was owned for more than 10 years, it was not used for the purposes of the trade throughout the 10-year period immediately before the disposal.
2. A period of ownership of a spouse or a deceased spouse is taken into account in assessing the 10-year period of ownership. For example, a woman may have owned a building for seven years for the purposes of carrying on her trade before gifting the building and the trade to her husband. If he then disposes of the building after a further three years, having used the building for the trade, the asset would be a qualifying asset.
3. Where the qualifying assets are shares in a family company, which was previously run as a sole trade or partnership, and section 600 TCA 1997 relief on the transfer of a business to a company in exchange for shares was claimed, then the period the business was run as a sole trade will also qualify for the purposes of the 10-year test. The period the individual ran the business as a sole trade will also count for the purposes of assessing if the working director test of 10 years ending on the date of disposal is satisfied.

### 7.9.5  Marginal Relief

If the sales proceeds on disposals to third parties under section 598 relating to qualifying trading assets exceeds €750,000/€500,000, retirement relief is not available. However, a measure of marginal relief under section 598(2) TCA 1997 may be available provided that the total CGT payable on the various assets disposed is not zero. If so, then the CGT may be calculated as 50% of the excess of the proceeds over €750,000 (or €500,000).

It is first necessary to compute the total CGT arising on the disposal. The maximum CGT payable will be the lower of:

- the actual CGT computed; or
- 50% of the excess of the sales proceeds relating to qualifying assets over €750,000 (or €500,000).

**Example 7.9**

Martin, aged 59, disposed of his business to a third party in December 2016. He had commenced to trade in 1977. The total sales proceeds were €840,000, allocated as follows:

|  | € |
|---|---|
| Goodwill | 280,000 |
| Premises | 395,000 |
| Plant | 110,000 |
| Stock | 25,000 |
| Debtors | 30,000 |
|  | 840,000 |

He purchased the premises in June 1980 for €40,000. No capital gain arises on plant.

The proceeds in respect of qualifying assets are as follows:

|  | € |
|---|---|
| Goodwill | 280,000 |
| Premises | 395,000 |
| Plant | 110,000 |
| Total | 785,000 |

As the proceeds in respect of qualifying assets exceed €750,000, full retirement relief is not available. However, marginal relief may be available.

First, calculate the CGT payable.

*Goodwill*

Martin has no base cost for goodwill as it was not purchased. The full €280,000 represents a capital gain.

| Premises | € |
|---|---|
| Proceeds | 395,000 |
| €40,000 @ 3.240 (80/81 − 2004) | (129,600) |
| Gain | 265,400 |

*Summary of gains*

|  | € |
|---|---|
| Goodwill (no base cost) | 280,000 |
| Premises | 265,400 |
| Total | 545,400 |
| Less: annual exemption | (1,270) |
|  | 544,130 |
| CGT @ 33% | 179,563 |

*continued overleaf*

Second, calculate the excess of the proceeds of qualifying assets over €750,000.
As the proceeds in respect of qualifying assets are €785,000, the excess is €35,000. 50% of the excess is €17,500. As 50% of the excess is less than the CGT on individual assets of €179,563, the final CGT payable is €17,500.

If the marginal relief in this example did not provide a saving, then CGT under normal rules would be payable.

### 7.9.6 Clawback of Section 598 Relief

Provisions are made for a clawback of relief where an individual who has claimed retirement relief on disposals to persons other than a child makes a further disposal of qualifying assets, which would qualify for retirement relief, and the aggregate proceeds exceed the threshold (currently set at €750,000, or €500,000 for those age 66 and over) within a 10-year period. Therefore, if an individual claims retirement relief under section 598 TCA 1997 and subsequently makes a further disposal of qualifying assets, then CGT relief on the original claim will be clawed back. The clawback calculation would be based on the lower of the actual CGT liability on the aggregate disposals or CGT based on marginal relief.

### 7.9.7 Disposals to a Child

As noted above, section 599 TCA 1997 provides that disposals to a child of an owner of qualifying business assets are not limited to the €750,000/€500,000 threshold. For the purposes of retirement relief, a child includes a niece or a nephew who has worked substantially on a full-time basis in the business for the five years ending with the date of disposal. The definition of a child includes a qualifying foster child and a child of a deceased child. A qualifying foster child is a child who was under the care of the individual making the disposal and was maintained at the expense of the individual throughout a period of five years prior to the child reaching 18 years of age.

**Clawback of Section 599 Relief**
In the absence of anti-avoidance provisions, it would be possible to effectively use the unlimited proceeds threshold relating to disposals to a child to avoid CGT completely by first transferring the assets or shares to a child and then have the child sell on the assets or shares to the ultimate purchaser. As the child would acquire the asset at market value, no CGT would arise on a subsequent immediate disposal by the child.

Under section 599(4)(a) TCA 1997, if a child receives assets under a disposal that attracts retirement relief, he must not dispose of those assets for at least six years after the date of disposal. If there is a disposal within the six-year period, the CGT avoided on the disposal by the parent becomes payable by the child. There is no requirement that the child should continue trading with the asset on which retirement relief was claimed by the parent. For example, a child could lease the assets of the trade without triggering a clawback of the relief. If the assets received by the child are shares in a family company, the six-year holding period applies to the shares. There is no restriction on the company disposing of some of its trading assets within the six-year period.

In calculating the amount of clawback, it is necessary to first ascertain if the parent would have qualified for retirement relief under the normal €750,000/€500,000 threshold on that disposal. In computing a clawback on a child, any relief that would have been available to the parent had the original disposal been to a third party must be allowed. Marginal relief is also available when computing the clawback.

---

**Example 7.10**

Robert, aged 57, transferred all his business assets to his daughter Eleanor. The market value of the qualifying assets at the date of the transfer was €1.5 million. CGT of €100,000 was avoided by availing of retirement relief. Eleanor carried on the business for three years but then disposed of it.

Because Eleanor did not retain ownership of the assets for six years, she must pay the €100,000 CGT avoided by her father on his transfer of the business to her. It is clear that no form of retirement relief would have been available to the father had the original disposal been to a third party as the €1,500,000 proceeds means that marginal relief could not be claimed, i.e. (€1.5 million − €750,000) @ 50% = €375,000 > €100,000 actual CGT. It should be noted that Eleanor may also have a CGT exposure in relation to her own period of ownership of the assets.

---

There is no clawback of the relief if the child dies within the clawback period, i.e. six years. As you will recall, death is not a CGT event.

### 7.9.8 Disposals to Spouses

Normally, disposals between spouses are treated as a no gain/no loss with the transferee spouse deemed to have acquired the asset at the same date and cost as the transferor spouse. Where the asset disposed of is a qualifying asset and the transferor spouse is aged 55 years or more, the asset is deemed to be transferred at market value for the purposes of the €750,000/€500,000 limit. This is an anti-avoidance provision and is designed to prevent asset transfers between spouses, after age 55, to effectively increase the €750,000/€500,000 threshold. All disposals between spouses before reaching 55 years of age continue to be treated as transferred at no gain/no loss and do not utilise any part of the transferor's €750,000/€500,000 limit.

One exception to the rule arises where all of the qualifying assets of one spouse are transferred to the other spouse; in this case the transfer is made at cost regardless of age. This is a logical exception as the transferor spouse cannot avail of retirement relief as they have now divested themselves of all their qualifying assets.

### 7.9.9 Liquidation and Retirement Relief

A capital distribution of cash and assets to a shareholder following the appointment of a liquidator is broadly a CGT disposal by the shareholder of his shares. Retirement relief may be available on capital distributions if the necessary conditions are satisfied.

Technically, retirement relief does not apply as, at the time of liquidation, the assets of the company consist of the proceeds of disposal of the business and not the business itself. Section 598(7) TCA 1997 allows the relief in the case of capital distributions received by an individual in the course of the dissolution or winding-up of a family company in the same manner as if the individual had disposed of the shares or securities in the company. By concession, the relief will apply if the company assets are sold not more than six months prior to liquidation and were sold with the intention of liquidating the family company.

Retirement relief is not available if a shareholder receives a capital distribution *in specie*, i.e. physical transfer of ownership of assets without a sale of company assets by the liquidator. A distribution *in specie* can be still be a tax-efficient option because, in general, nominal stamp duty is payable on the transfer of assets *in specie* by the liquidator rather then the normal *ad valorem* rates of stamp duty.

### 7.9.10 Interaction of Retirement Relief with Other Tax Reliefs

**Transfer of a Business to a Company Relief**

If a sole trade is transferred to a company under section 600 TCA 1997 relief, then the period of ownership of the sole trade is recognised for the purposes of the 10-year tests applicable to qualifying shares and qualifying periods of directorship of a family company.

The interaction of the two reliefs can also yield negative results. For example, if a child takes a transfer of qualifying trading assets under section 599 relief and incorporates the business within six years from the date of the retirement relief claim, then the transfer of the business to the company is a disposal for CGT purposes. This will trigger a clawback of retirement relief originally claimed by the parent, notwithstanding the fact that the actual CGT arising on the transfer of the business to the company qualifies for CGT relief under section 600.

**Unquoted Company Buy-back of Shares**
Section 176 TCA 1997 provides that a distribution received under a scheme of buyback will be subject to CGT at 33%, provided certain conditions are met. The key test of the relief is to show that the buy-back of shares was carried out for the benefit of the trade. This test may be satisfied when a controlling shareholder is retiring as a director and wishes to make way for new management. The distribution treated as a CGT event may then qualify for retirement relief under sections 598 and 599, provided all the other conditions for the relief are fulfilled. Any payments received that qualify for the CGT treatment on the buyback of company shares, must be taken into account for the €750,000/€500,000 lifetime thresholds under section 598.

**CAT Business Relief and Agricultural Relief**
Retirement relief provides relief for gifts of businesses and farms which might otherwise give rise to a CGT liability on the disponer. However, the business and farm may be a taxable gift in the hands of the recipient for CAT purposes. Therefore, the provision of advice to a client on retirement relief may also involve a review of the recipient's circumstances in order to ensure that business relief or agricultural relief for CAT purposes can also be claimed.

### 7.9.11 Retirement Relief Planning Points

There are many planning points associated with maximising the benefit of retirement relief. The relevant planning points will depend on the facts of the particular case but, in general, the following points should be noted for implementation **before the individual's 55th birthday** (these actions are designed to minimise the disposals of qualifying assets after the age of 55):

1.  Gift assets or shares to spouse. In some cases, this will mean that two €750,000/€500,000 bands become available. Where it is not possible to make such a gift, it may be possible to ensure that maximum benefit is derived from one €750,000/€500,000 threshold by ensuring that the transferor spouse has exactly €750,000/€500,000 worth of assets that qualify for relief. Ideally, the assets which count for the €750,000/€500,000 threshold should attract the largest gain and CGT liability and thereby yield the greatest saving.

2.  Sell qualifying trading assets that are surplus to requirements. It may be possible that certain assets are no longer vital to the running of the business. For example, certain items of plant and motor vehicles could be disposed of in preparation for a retirement relief claim before age 55. Assets such as plant and motor vehicles are unlikely to generate capital gains, but these assets could eat into the €750,000/€500,000 threshold.

3.  Sell and lease-back certain trading capital assets on which there are either no latent gains or relatively small latent gains. If possible, certain trading assets with minimal gains should be disposed of before the owner's 55th birthday. For example, a premises used in a business may be worth €400,000 but, due to indexation relief/substantial base cost, no capital gain would arise on disposal. The premises could be sold to an investor and leased back for continued use in the business. A future claim for business relief would not include the leased asset.

4.  Where a disposal of a business to a third party would be for an amount significantly in excess of €750,000/€500,000, it may be possible to sell or gift some assets to a child on the basis that the child

will not sell the assets until after the requisite six-year holding period. The proceeds of the asset taken by the child under a section 599 claim are disregarded for the purposes of the €750,000/€500,000 test under the section 598 claim and are not aggregated with the proceeds of sale to third parties.

5. In the case of a business carried on through a company, long-term planning could be implemented by appointing a spouse as a working director for a minimum of 10 years and ensuring that spouse is a full-time working director for at least five years. A surviving spouse may aggregate the period of the deceased spouse's directorship but no aggregation is allowed for the period of directorship of a living spouse.

6. Where the value of shares exceeds the €750,000/€500,000 threshold, reduce the value of the shares by extracting value from the company in a tax-efficient manner. Tax efficiency means reducing the overall tax burden. For example, it may be possible to use available cash to increase the company's contribution to the pension fund or it may be possible to pay a tax-free termination payment or in some cases it may be tax-efficient to pay additional salary or directors' fees, thereby extracting cash and reducing the value of the shares that qualify for retirement relief to below the €750,000/€500,000 threshold.

7. Where it is intended to transfer or sell a business to a niece or nephew, employ that person in the business with a view to transferring or selling the business to them after five years.

## Chapter 7 Summary

**Share sale/purchase**

- Depending on the circumstances this may be the vendor's preferred method of sale
- Disposal for CGT purposes
- Will require a due diligence/warranties/indemnities
- Purchaser takes on history of the company, indemnity e.g. latent gains
- Various reliefs available
- Lower rate of stamp duty

**Sale of trade and assets**

- Depending on the circumstances, this may be the purchaser's preferred method of sale
- Disposal by company
- Increased stamp duty costs
- Double tax charge on the vendor

**Other considerations**

- Interest relief available to purchaser in limited cirumstances
- Losses of target company might be unavailable (anti-avoidance)
- Group relief clawback
- Participation exemption
- Retirement relief

# Questions

## Review Questions
(See Suggested Solutions to Review Questions at the end of this textbook.)

### Question 7.1

Rose Limited produces golf balls. The company has divisions in Ireland, the UK, France and Spain. However, recent trading results have been poor and accumulated trading losses amount to €400,000. In particular, the Spanish division has had extremely poor results.

McIlroy Limited wishes to buy Rose Limited and make the following changes:

- Change the machinery being used, as McIlroy Limited feels it is out of date and needs modernising.
- Close the Spanish division.
- Include a teaching DVD with each set of golf balls, with lessons on how to get the best value from the golf balls.
- McIlroy Limited sees Germany as a new market that could benefit from the product and will open a division there in the near future to help regenerate sales.

**Requirement**
Advise McIlroy Limited on whether it can utilise the trading losses.

### Question 7.2

Rover Limited owns 8% of Ford Limited and 70% of Porsche Limited. Porsche Limited also owns 4% of Ford Limited.

**Requirement**
(a) Rover Limited sells its entire shareholding in Ford Limited on 1 July 2016. Can the participation exemption apply?
(b) The directors of Porsche Limited are considering selling its shareholding in Ford Limited. Advise on the latest date the transaction should take place.

## Challenging Questions
(Suggested Solutions to Challenging Questions are available through your lecturer.)

### Question 7.1

Rattles Limited is involved in the manufacture and distribution of baby rattles. It is wholly owned by Sharon Williamson, who started the business over 10 years ago. Following a period of poor sales and results, Sharon now wishes to retire and has been approached by another company, Shakes Limited, that wishes to make an offer for the trade and assets of Rattles Limited.

Sharon is reluctant to sell the trade and assets, and would prefer a share sale, as she will have only one tax charge on the sale of the shares. Shakes Limited have indicated that a share sale might be possible, but at a reduced sales price to take account of various issues that could arise from the tax due diligence review.

Shakes Limited is involved in the production of baby milkshakes, but wishes to expand its operations into the baby market further and is confident that it can turn the trade of Rattles Limited around and make it profitable once again.

The balance sheet of Rattles Limited for the year ended 31 December 2016 is as follows:

| | € | € | | € |
|---|---|---|---|---|
| Fixed assets (Note 1) | | 150,000 | Share capital | 1,000 |
| Cash at bank | | 30,000 | Accumulated profits | 80,300 |
| Debtors | | 3,500 | | |
| Creditors: | | | | |
| Trade creditors | 60,000 | | | |
| PAYE (Note 2) | 23,750 | | | |
| VAT | 4,450 | | | |
| Other (Note 3) | 14,000 | (102,200) | | |
| Net assets | | 81,300 | | 81,300 |

*Notes:*

1. The fixed assets of €150,000 include:
   - Plant and machinery with a net book value of €5,000 and a TWDV of €2,250.
   - Goodwill of €25,000 relating to the goodwill of Sharon's trade on incorporation of the business in 1999. It has a current market value of €45,000.
   - Business premises which are included at a cost of €120,000 and have a market value of €500,000.

2. The PAYE liability includes €2,000 in relation to an additional liability as the result of a recent PAYE inquiry.
3. Other creditors of €14,000 relate to a contingent liability for a trade dispute between Rattles Limited and various customers over a faulty batch of rattles. This is the best estimate of the amount to be paid out.

In addition, Rattles Limited has trading losses carried forward of €87,000 and current year losses of €18,000.

**Requirement**
(a) Calculate the minimum price that Sharon Williamson should accept, and calculate the maximum amount that Shakes Limited should be willing to pay for the business. You can assume that the sale takes place on 31 March 2017.
(b) Advise how the sale proceeds should be allocated, and indicate how this will affect Rattles Limited.
(c) What tax indemnities should Shakes Limited include within the share purchase agreement?
(d) Advise Shakes Limited on whether the accumulated trading losses of Rattles Limited can be used.
(e) Assuming the two parties meet in the middle in respect of the sale consideration, calculate the CGT liability of Sharon Williamson, indicating any reliefs that may be available to reduce her gain.

# Reorganisations of a Business

**Learning Objectives**

By the end of this chapter you will be able to:

- Analyse and evaluate the taxation implications of a reorganisation of a business, with or without a change of ownership, including:

  - company reorganisations without a change of ownership;
  - paper-for-paper transactions and CGT implications;
  - company amalgamations by exchange of shares;
  - stamp duty relief for amalgamations;
  - implementation of a holding company structure; and
  - reconstruction/amalgamation relief and interaction with group relief.

- Consider the implications of business taxation decisions for each entity involved.

## 8.1 Company Reorganisations/Amalgamations: Overview

A business evolves over time. As the business grows and expands, the corporate structure of the business, with its inherent complexity, can also expand and develop. This can involve activities such as setting up new companies, creating a holding company structure, issuing different classes of shareholdings, separating assets and trades from one company to another, and amalgamations of companies, to name but a few.

The main tax implications for the above are CGT and stamp duty. However, there are specific tax reliefs where there is a company reorganisation or amalgamation effected for bona fide commercial reasons. Sections 584–587 TCA 1997 deal with CGT relief and section 80 Stamp Duty Consolidation Act 1999 (SDCA 1999) with stamp duty relief. The conditions for the reliefs and examples of their applications are considered in this chapter.

### 8.1.1 Company Reorganisations/Amalgamations: Tax Reliefs

As stated above, the main tax implications for company reorganisations/amalgamations are CGT and stamp duty.

**CGT Relief**

Sections 584–587 TCA 1997 deal with share reorganisation or the amalgamation or reconstruction of companies by way of the exchange of shares. These sections provide that, subject to certain conditions being satisfied, no CGT will arise where a shareholder (either individual or company) receives, in exchange for the shares they hold, a new form of shares in the company being reorganised or in a new company where there is an amalgamation or reconstruction. This is commonly known as a "paper-for-paper" transaction. The new shares are treated as if they are being acquired at the same base cost and the same date of acquisition as the original shares. If the shareholder receives "consideration" (e.g. cash) in addition to the new shares, the consideration is deemed a part disposal of the original holding and the normal CGT rules apply (i.e. no specific relief for the part disposal).

*Conditions for Relief*

The relief will only apply where it is clear that the exchange was for bona fide commercial reasons and does not form part of an arrangement whose main purpose is the avoidance of tax.

**Stamp Duty Relief**

Section 80 SDCA 1999 provides for a zero rate of stamp duty where company reorganisations or reconstructions/amalgamations involve the transfer of shares in one company to another.

*Conditions for Relief*

As for the CGT relief this relief will only apply where it is clear that the exchange was for bona fide commercial reasons and does not form part of an arrangement whose main purpose is the avoidance of tax. In addition, the following must apply:

- the acquiring company must be a limited company;
- the acquiring company must issue new shares in exchange for 90% or more of the shares in the target company;
- the shares being issued in the acquiring company must represent at least 90% of the value of the target company;
- the acquiring company must retain beneficial ownership of the shares in the target company for at least two years (unless it loses this as a result of reconstruction/amalgamation or liquidation);
- the relief applies where the acquiring company is registered in Ireland or an EU Member State, however the target company may be registered anywhere in the world.

Students should not confuse section 80 SDCA relief ("reconstruction or amalgamation of companies") with section 79 SDCA relief ("conveyances and transfers of property between certain bodies"). They are two separate and distinct reliefs.

## 8.2    Company Reorganisations Without a Change in Ownership

To facilitate further expansion, a reorganisation of a company's existing structure or affairs can arise. Similarly, a reorganisation of a shareholder's shareholdings can also arise. Often a reorganisation will not require a change in ownership of a company/group, but certain steps need to be put in place to make the commercial and tax affairs of the company more efficient.

> **Key Issue**
> If a change in ownership of an asset or an exchange of an asset for a different asset occurs, students will most likely have to consider CGT. Remember, all transfers of assets between connected persons are at market value for CGT purposes. Remember, a **share** is a chargeable asset.

---

***Example 8.1***

Joe Brown owns 100 shares in his company, Brown Property Ltd. Brown Property Ltd is a successful land dealing business worth €200 million. Joe Brown subscribed for the shares at par value many years ago. Joe is getting old, and is taking stock of his affairs.

Joe wishes to plan a future gift of shares to his family, but also intends to gift certain shares to key employees of his business, many of whom have worked for him for over 20 years and whom he considers loyal friends and valuable people.

Joe's dilemma is, how does he split up 100 shares worth €2 million each? He does not want to grant his employees shares of such significant value. The solution could be to exchange his 100 ordinary shares in direct return for a new holding of 1,000 ordinary shares plus 1,000 Class A non-voting shares (which are not as valuable as the ordinary shares).

Joe could gift the ordinary shares to his family, and the Class A shares to his employees, thus keeping the main value with the Brown family.

*Tax Issue*

If Joe is to dispose of his 100 shares (by whatever means or for whatever reason), he is making a disposal for CGT purposes. Does Joe have a €60 million CGT problem?

*For the purpose of the above illustration, we have ignored any implications of passing value/shares to employees of the company and related Schedule E tax issues.*

---

Where a bona fide reorganisation take place, tax relief is available. The various legislative tax reliefs consider situations such as Joe Brown's, and are designed to ensure that tax does not arise on such a reorganisation.

The general overriding proviso is that reorganisation relief is only available for a bona fide restructuring project. If tax avoidance is the motivation, reorganisation relief will be denied.

There are various issues to consider when a company reorganisation takes place (with or without a change of ownership), and tax relief is generally available to allow such a reorganisation take place in a tax-efficient manner. These are summarised below:

| Area to be considered | Consequences |
|---|---|
| Corporation tax – transfer of chargeable assets | ▓ No gain/no loss transfer takes place if within a CGT group, otherwise market value for connected parties. |
| Capital allowances | ▓ Continuation of ownership means continuation of capital allowances – no balancing charge event under section 312 TCA 1997. Assets are transferred at tax written down value (TWDV). |
| Trading losses | ▓ Losses associated with the trade transferred to transferee unless disallowed under section 401 TCA 1997. |
| Stock | ▓ Normally transferred at market value. |
| VAT | ▓ If in the same VAT group, no VAT charge. <br> ▓ If qualifying as a "transfer of a business as a going concern", outside the scope of VAT. <br> ▓ Otherwise, VAT is charged by the transferor. |
| Stamp duty | ▓ 1% on transfer of shares and 2% on other chargeable assets. <br> ▓ Stamp duty relief may be available, subject to conditions. |

## 8.3 Reasons for a Corporate Reorganisation

There are many commercial, business, legal and tax reasons for a corporate reorganisation. A reorganisation can be driven by any one reason or motivation, or a combination.

Some reasons for corporate reorganisation are:

- Removal of unnecessary layers of companies to reduce complexity and compliance costs.
- A new business has been or will be acquired.
- A shareholder dispute – split of business or exit of a significant shareholder.
- Estate or retirement planning – separation of holdings.
- Separation of poorly performing divisions from strong divisions.
- Create a more tax-efficient structure.
- Set up a holding company structure to admit new investors.
- A business or portion of a business is being sold and must be separated from assets to be retained.
- Separation of old business from new or more risky ventures.
- Separation of trades for administrative efficiency.
- EIIS relief – suitable corporate structure.
- Separation of trading assets from investment assets to maximise tax reliefs such as retirement relief or business asset relief (for CAT purposes).
- Separation of property assets from trading assets.
- Make a company/group more suitable or attractive for outside investors.
- Banking purposes – high-value assets may need to be separated from other assets/activities if finance is being raised against those assets.
- Takeovers or mergers.

Examples of typical outcomes from reorganisations include:

- Exchange of old shares for new shares.
- Exchange of old shares for new shares plus other consideration.
- Exchange of old shares plus consideration for new shares.
- Transfer of a business to a new company.
- Company amalgamations.
- Reductions in share capital.

---

**Example 8.2**

Take a scenario where a company has two trades that are carried on in a single company. They are being considered for separation to take account of the potential to sell either one of those trades to a third party. As both trades are within the one entity, it may be beneficial to transfer one trade to another company.

**Corporate Structure Before Restructuring:**

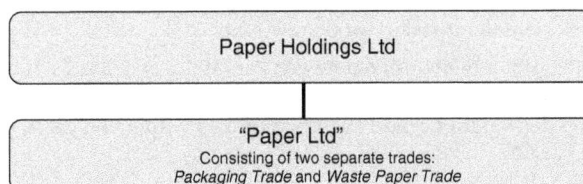

Paper Holdings Ltd

"Paper Ltd"
Consisting of two separate trades:
*Packaging Trade* and *Waste Paper Trade*

*continued overleaf*

---

***Restructuring Steps***

1. Incorporate New Co. as a 100% subsidiary of Paper Holdings Ltd.
2. Transfer the Packaging Trade to New Co.
3. New Co. will not give any consideration to Paper Ltd for this trade, other than taking over the liabilities of the business.
4. New Co. will issue shares to Paper Holdings Ltd in return for receiving the trade.

*Outcome:*

This series of steps will constitute a disposal of a business for CGT purposes, but restructuring relief can exempt the transfer.

Similarly, a stamp duty exemption can apply (saving 2% of the value of the assets, etc.).

Both exemptions require that the transfer be carried out for bona fide commercial reasons and the avoidance of tax must not be the main motive for the transfer.

Following the above, the trades have been split into two distinct entities.

***Corporate Structure after Restructuring:***

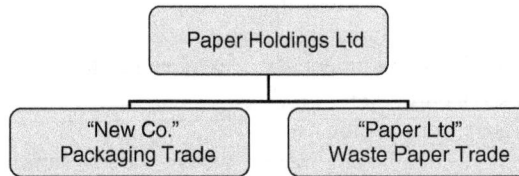

```
                    ┌─────────────────────┐
                    │  Paper Holdings Ltd │
                    └──────────┬──────────┘
              ┌────────────────┴────────────────┐
   ┌──────────────────────┐        ┌──────────────────────┐
   │      "New Co."        │        │     "Paper Ltd"      │
   │   Packaging Trade     │        │   Waste Paper Trade  │
   └──────────────────────┘        └──────────────────────┘
```

What has happened in the above example is that the packaging trade has been transferred to New Co. in exchange for New Co. issuing shares in itself to Paper Holdings Ltd, which now has two trading subsidiaries holding individual trades.

For tax purposes, a disposal of the trade by Paper Ltd has occurred and a CGT/stamp duty event arises. However, as restructuring relief is available, a tax charge is avoided where all the conditions are satisfied.

---

Reorganisations typically involve the transfer of either the shares or the trade/assets of the company and, on the face of it, bring the transaction within the charge to CGT and stamp duty.

In certain situations, group relief can be availed of for CGT and stamp duty purposes. While these reliefs are very advantageous and commonly used, there are circumstances where they are not entirely suitable. In the above example, while CGT group relief and stamp duty associated companies relief could have been claimed, the clawback period could be a disincentive.

---

***Example 8.3***

Parent Co. wants to transfer its property portfolio (being a number of properties held for rental purposes) to its subsidiary Sub Co. Assume there is a 100% relationship between both entities. That property portfolio can be transferred intragroup without attracting a CGT or stamp duty charge (assuming all the conditions for group relief and associated companies relief are met).

However, the clawback provisions in respect of group relief are:

▪ For CGT purposes, if the group relationship between Parent Co. and Sub Co. is broken within 10 years, there is a clawback of CGT relief. This will become due for payment by Sub Co.

▪ If the relationship between Parent Co. and Sub Co. is broken within two years, there is a clawback of stamp duty relief for Sub Co.

If, for example, the intention was to dispose of the shares in Sub Co. within 18 months of the property portfolio transfer, a clawback of CGT and stamp duty would arise, which could be a significant tax burden. This clawback could be a deterrent to a prospective buyer for the shares or could reduce the sales proceeds received.

> **Key Issue**
> A claim for group relief for tax purposes may not be suitable if a change in the 75% group relationship is expected in the near future.

## 8.4 Reorganisation of Share Capital in a Single Company

A reorganisation of share capital is not defined. Reorganisations typically involve an adjustment to existing shareholdings. However, following the process, the proportions of holdings among those shareholders will remain the same and the number of shareholders will remain the same. The shareholders may end up owning different shares, different classes of shares or indeed shares in a different company, but ultimately the ownership structure will have remained fundamentally the same.

For an exchange of shares, all that is happening is that one holding of shares is being exchanged for a different holding of shares. Tax reliefs are available in respect of a reorganisation or a reduction in share capital.

> **Key Issue**
> In any reorganisation, a transfer of shares is a disposal for CGT purposes. However, in the case of company reorganisations, there are specific reliefs for the shareholders, which will be addressed later in this chapter.

In simple terms, the CGT relief applies as follows:

- the old shares are not treated as being disposed of; and
- the new shares take on the same base cost and acquisition date as those of the old shares.

Typical share reorganisations, and the applicable tax treatment, can be summarised as:

1. Exchange of old shares for new shares.
2. Exchange of old shares for new shares plus other consideration.
3. Exchange of old shares plus consideration for new shares.

### 8.4.1. Exchange of Old Shares for New Shares

In an exchange of old shares for new shares, the unit quantity can be more or less, but the new shares will be of the same general proportion/value as those of the old shares.

**Tax Relief Available**
The original shares are being exchanged for new shares in the same company/another company. The tax relief provisions are such that there is no disposal of the old shares and the new shares are treated as if they are being acquired at the same base cost/date of acquisition as the original holding.

### 8.4.2. Exchange of Old Shares for New Shares Plus Other Considerations

In this type of reorganisation, the shareholder redeems his old shares for new shares but also receives other consideration (i.e. cash or other valuable assets).

**Tax Relief Available**
The original shares are being exchanged for new shares in the same company/another company and for some other consideration. The tax relief provisions are such that there is a deemed part disposal for the consideration equal to the cash/assets being received by the shareholder. The shareholder is not

liable to CGT on the full consideration, but on the part received in cash/assets. Using the part-disposal rules, part of the base cost of the original shares is deducted from the consideration. When the new shares are ultimately disposed of, the base cost of the new shareholding will be computed by reference to the base cost/date of acquisition of the old shares less the amount utilised in the part disposal.

---

**Example 8.4**

Patrick Ryan acquired 200 ordinary shares in Worldscape Software Ltd. These shares were acquired for €250,000 in June 2007. The share capital of Worldscape was reconstructed in June 2016. Patrick, in exchange for his 200 ordinary shares, received 20,000 non-voting preference shares, the market value of which was €12 each, plus €200,000 in cash. Patrick's CGT position for June 2016 is as follows:

| | € |
|---|---|
| Cash consideration received | 200,000 |
| Base cost apportioned | |
| $250,000 \times \dfrac{200,000}{200,000 + 240,000}$ | (113,636) |
| Chargeable gain | 86,364 |
| Less: annual exemption | (1,270) |
| Taxable gain | 85,094 |
| CGT @ 33% | 28,081 |

Patrick is liable to pay CGT of €28,081 by 15 December 2016 on the cash received on foot of the reorganisation of Worldscape.

He will also have a stamp duty liability – see **Example 8.5**.

---

**Example 8.5**

Joe Flynn owns 100 ordinary shares in Flynn Oil Ltd, acquired originally for €20,000. The market value of those shares was €250,000 in July 2014 when the company underwent a reorganisation. Joe was issued with 2,000 new "Class A ordinary shares" in exchange for his existing 100 ordinary shares. He was also paid €40,000 by the company on that date.

The value of the 2,000 new Class A ordinary shares immediately after the reorganisation was €210,000.

What is Joe's CGT and stamp duty position?

*CGT*

Assuming that the exchange was for bona fide commercial reasons and did not form part of an arrangement whose main purpose was the avoidance of tax, then the only implication is for the cash of €40,000, which is treated as a part disposal:

| | € |
|---|---|
| Consideration | 40,000 |
| Less: cost (ignoring indexation relief for illustration purposes) | |
| $€20,000 \times \dfrac{€40,000}{€40,000 + €210,000}$ | (3,200) |
| Chargeable gain | 36,800 |

*Stamp Duty*

One of the conditions of section 80 SDCA 1999 is that the consideration for the exchange is at least 90% in the form of shares. This means that any cash payment cannot exceed 10% of the value (at the time of the reconstruction) of the old shares. Since Joe received €40,000 in cash, this represents 16% of the share value and, therefore, he is liable to stamp duty of €2,100 (i.e. €210,000 × 1%).

### 8.4.3. *Exchange of Old Shares Plus Consideration for New Shares*

In this type of reorganisation, the shareholder redeems the old shares but must also pay consideration (i.e. cash or other valuable assets) in exchange for the new shares.

**Tax Relief Available**

Where the old shares and consideration are exchanged for new shares in the same company/another company, the new shares acquire the same base cost/date of acquisition as the original holding and the additional consideration is deemed to be enhancement expenditure at the date of the reorganisation.

---

**Example 8.6**

June Flaherty owns 100 ordinary shares in Flaherty Ltd, acquired originally for €20,000 in May 2005. The market value of those shares was €250,000 in July 2016 when the company underwent a reorganisation. June was issued with 2,000 new "Class A ordinary shares" in exchange for her existing 100 ordinary shares. As part of the reorganisation, she also paid €100,000 to the company on that date.

June sold her shares for €1 million on 3 December 2016. Her CGT is computed as follows:

Assuming that the exchange was for bona fide commercial reasons and did not form part of an arrangement whose main purpose was the avoidance of tax, then there was no disposal in July 2016 and the payment of €100,000 is treated as enhancement expenditure.

The disposal in December 2016 is taxable as follows:

|  | € |
|---|---|
| Proceeds | 1,000,000 |
| Less: cost | |
| Original shares | (20,000) |
| Enhancement expenditure | (100,000) |
| Gain | 880,000 |

---

## 8.5 Company Amalgamations by Exchange of Shares

The tax reliefs discussed above can also apply where the reorganisation involves more than one company. Company amalgamations involve an **acquiring company** and a **target company**. The amalgamation could be part of a planned exchange, or indeed part of a takeover attempt. Section 586 TCA 1997 states that:

> "Where a company issues shares or debentures to a person in exchange for shares in or debentures of another company, section 584 shall apply with any necessary modifications as if the two companies were the same company and the exchange were a reorganisation of its share capital."

Section 584 TCA 1997 also states that:

> "A reorganisation or reduction of a company's share capital shall not be treated as involving any disposal of the original shares or any acquisition of the new holding or any part of it; but the original shares (taken as a single asset) and the new holding (taken as a single asset) shall be treated as the same asset acquired as the original shares were acquired."

In the context of the above, a company amalgamation occurs where, for example, the acquiring company issues shares to another person by way of exchange for their shares in the target company.

---

**Example 8.7**

Zinc Mines Ltd has approached the shareholders of Kerry Mine Holdings Ltd. The shareholders of Kerry Mine Holdings Ltd have been offered four shares in Zinc Mines Ltd for each share held in Kerry Mine Holdings Ltd.

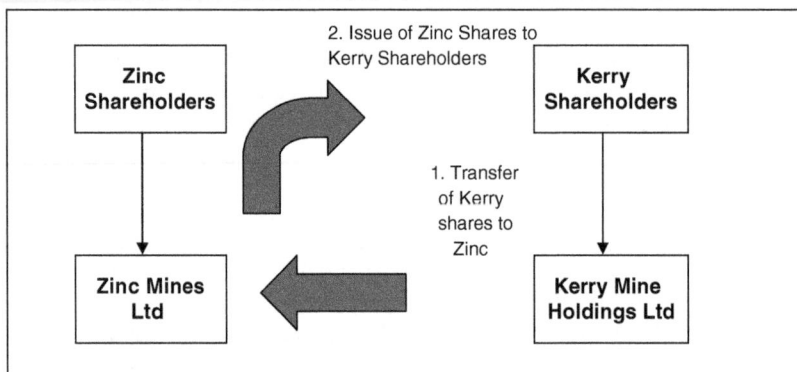

The share movements can be summarised as follows:

|   |   |
|---|---|
| 1. Transfer of shares by Kerry Shareholders in Kerry Mine Holdings Ltd to Zinc Mines Ltd | CGT/Stamp duty |
| 2. Issue of shares by Zinc Mines Ltd to Kerry Shareholders | No tax issues |

The revised corporate structure will be as follows:

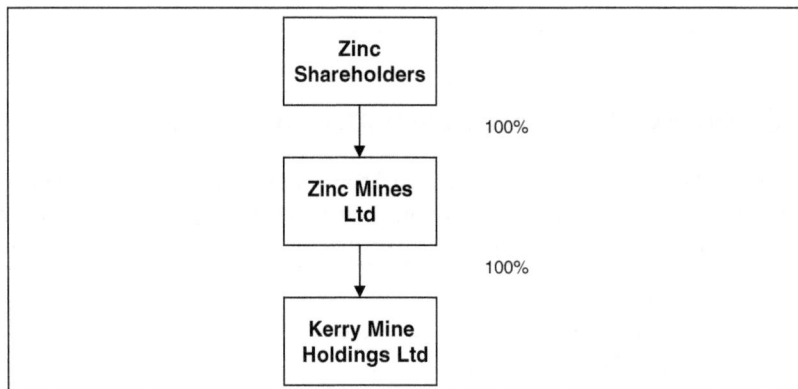

The disposal of shares by the shareholders of Kerry Mine Holdings Ltd will not be considered a disposal for CGT purposes if the transfer is part of a bona fide company amalgamation.

---

Relief from CGT, however, will **only** apply to the transferor of the shares if:

- the acquiring company, as a result of the exchange, has taken a controlling interest in the target company; **or**
- the exchange is part of a general offer made by the acquiring company to the shareholders of the target company. The offer must be designed to give the acquiring company the opportunity to take control of the target company.

The relief is available where the amalgamation is carried out for bona fide commercial reasons and does not form part of a scheme or arrangement the principal purpose of which is the avoidance of tax.

### 8.5.1 Stamp Duty Relief for Amalgamations

Stamp duty relief can also apply to amalgamations. Where conditions for the relief are not satisfied, a stamp duty charge of 1% arises on the transfer of shares. To revisit the example above:

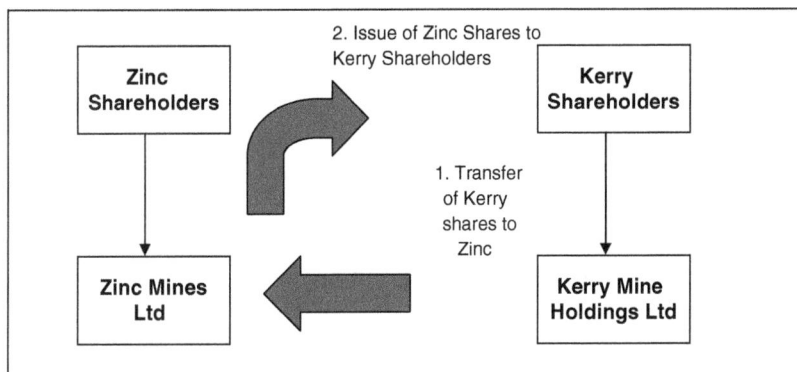

Stamp duty will not arise on the transfer of shares in Kerry to Zinc by virtue of section 80 SDCA 1999 – see **Section 8.1.1** for conditions.

**Note:** stamp duty relief will not be available unless the amalgamation is for bona fide commercial reasons and does not form part of a wider scheme whose main purpose is the avoidance of tax.

---

*Key Issue*
Where a business is being taken over, or a merger is being planned, subject to the necessary conditions being met, tax relief is available for each party transferring their shareholdings. Students should apply the available tax reliefs to the particular commercial scenario presented.

---

## 8.6 Implementation of a Holding Company Structure

The above restructuring relief can be used to implement a holding company structure. To implement a holding company structure, the shareholders would incorporate a new company with the intention that this company would become the new "group" holding company.

On the basis that New Co. has been incorporated, the following would exist:

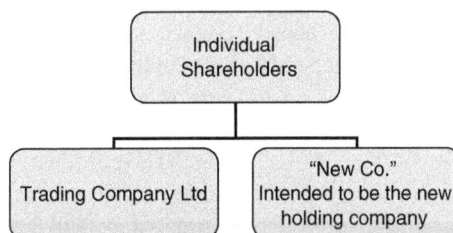

Assuming Trading Company Ltd is worth €1 million and the base cost of the shares is very small, there is a potential CGT liability of €330,000 if the shareholders transfer their shareholding to the new holding company. However "reorganisation relief" should permit the implementation of a holding company structure tax free as follows:

1. Each shareholder transfers their shareholding in Trading Company Ltd (the target company) to New Co. (the acquiring company), in exchange for New Co. issuing shares to them in New Co. in equal proportion to their original holdings.
2. New Co., as the acquiring company, will take a 100% holding of Trading Company Ltd (i.e. takes full control).
3. On the basis that this is a reorganisation for bona fide commercial purposes, the transfer of shares in Trading Company Ltd by the shareholders will not be considered a disposal for CGT purposes.
4. Stamp duty will not arise on the shares acquired by New Co. If the relationship between New Co. and Trading Company Ltd is broken within two years of the transfer, the stamp duty relief will be clawed back.

As a result of the above steps, the following structure will exist:

The benefits of the above holding company structure can be summarised as follows:

- New Co. allows for other investors to invest in the whole group. This would be more relevant, however, if there is more than one subsidiary within the group.
- Certain assets may be transferred between group members tax free (i.e. CGT and stamp duty group relief).
- Group loss relief can be claimed if applicable.
- If at some point in the future New Co. wishes to sell Trading Company Ltd, it should be able to sell the shares tax free under section 626B TCA 1997 (participation exemption).

Typical share reorganisations and the tax implications applying can be summarised as follows:

| Scenario | Tax relief available |
|---|---|
| Exchange of old shares for new shares, perhaps in more unit quantity but of the same general proportion/value. | The original shares are being exchanged for new shares in the same company. There is no disposal of the old shares and the new shares are treated as if they are being acquired at the same base cost/date of acquisition as the original holding. No stamp duty if all the conditions of section 80 SDCA 1999 are satisfied (see **Section 8.1.1**) |

| Scenario | Tax relief available |
|---|---|
| Exchange of old shares for new shares plus cash. | Deemed part disposal of the original holding. Base cost of the new shareholding will be computed by reference to the same base cost/date of acquisition of the old shares less the base cost used for the part disposal. CGT will be payable by reference to the consideration received (being a part disposal). No stamp duty if all the conditions of section 80 SDCA 1999 are satisfied. |
| Exchange of old shares plus cash for new shares. | The original shares are being exchanged for new shares in the same company. There is no disposal of the old shares and the new shares are treated as if they are being acquired at the same base cost/date of acquisition as the original holding. The cash paid as part of the exchange for the new shares is treated as enhancement expenditure. No stamp duty if all the conditions of section 80 SDCA 1999 are satisfied. |

## 8.7 Reconstructions: Transfer of a Business

A reconstruction will typically involve an exchange of shares for an "undertaking". An "undertaking" is not defined, but is usually described as a business or a trade. A transaction involving a disposal by a company of its business (or part of its business) to another company can be deemed a reconstruction. Share reorganisation relief (for CGT) and stamp duty relief will apply to the shares in the company acquiring the business issued to the individual shareholders of the target company (assuming all the conditions for the reliefs are met). These new shares will be issued in the same proportion to the shareholders' existing ownership in the target company.

Transfer of a business relief is commonly used to:

- Split up a trade or multiple trades within one company.
- Separate investment business or non-core business from trading operations.
- Separate property and non-property interests for tax-planning purposes.
- Effect a trade sale where it is anticipated that the purchaser will want to purchase the trade only (i.e. the purchaser will not wish to purchase the shares and therefore take on the historical issues associated with the company, e.g. past tax liabilities, legal claims, CGT clawback of prior group relief, etc.).

The typical reconstruction steps can be briefly summarised as follows:

1. Transfer of the business of a company ("Company A") to "New Co.".
2. Company A does not receive consideration for the transfer of the business.
3. Company A (or the shareholders in Company A) will instead receive shares in New Co. as consideration for the business transferred to New Co.

If the above steps are followed, and assuming all other conditions are satisfied, a charge to CGT and stamp duty can be avoided on the reconstruction.

The question of whether an undertaking exists will frequently arise. For example, an undertaking can be a trade, but it can also cover much more than a trade. An investment portfolio managed by a company will constitute an undertaking. A property portfolio, if shown to be a business in itself, can constitute an undertaking.

In principle, a business and its associated activity should exist. The lack of business activity may mean that the relief is not available.

To establish if an undertaking exists, you must ask the extent to which a business activity is actually taking place. An undertaking should consist of more than mere ownership of assets.

### 8.7.1   Legislative Analysis

Section 615 TCA 1997 provides that:

> "...where any scheme of reconstruction or amalgamation involves the transfer of the whole or part of a company's business (i.e. the undertaking) to another company, the company acquiring the assets is resident in the State at the time of acquisition, or the assets are chargeable assets in that company's hands immediately on receipt, the company transferring the assets is resident in Ireland, or the assets at that time were chargeable assets in its hands, and the transferor receives no consideration for the transfer other than the acquiring company taking over business liabilities..."

Then, for CGT/CT purposes only, both companies are treated as if the assets included in the transfer were acquired by one company from the other company for a consideration that would give rise to a no gain/no loss result on the disposal.

The transferor may not receive consideration other than the transferee taking over of the undertaking's liabilities.

## 8.8   Stamp Duty: Reconstruction/Amalgamation Relief

The document transferring a business to a new entity will have to be stamped. A potential charge to stamp duty will therefore arise. This could be a substantial charge if the undertaking has a significant value attaching to it. Take, for example, a trade with a valuable property worth €200 million. The stamp duty on a transfer would be significant enough to perhaps deter a reconstruction (given that there is ultimately no change in ownership and more a change in structure).

As advised previously, section 80 SDCA 1999 provides for reconstruction relief (for transfers between companies and not unincorporated entities/individuals) – see **Section 8.1.1** for conditions.

A conveyance or transfer of assets made in conjunction with a scheme of reconstruction of company/companies can avail of a full exemption from stamp duty. To qualify for the stamp duty exemption, there must be a:

1.   scheme of **reconstruction** or **amalgamation** carried out for bona fide reasons, and
2.   the purpose of the scheme must not be tax avoidance.

### 8.8.1   Relief for Reconstructions

Stamp duty reconstruction relief will involve:

- No substantial change in the makeup of shareholders before and after the reconstruction.
- The assets being transferred must constitute an "undertaking" or "part of an undertaking" (i.e. a business).

■ The undertaking (or part of it), being transferred must, following the transfer, be carried on by the acquiring company.

Two illustrative reconstructions are as follows:

1. Two-party share for undertaking swap – stamp duty
Shares are issued to the target company by the acquiring company in exchange for its business.

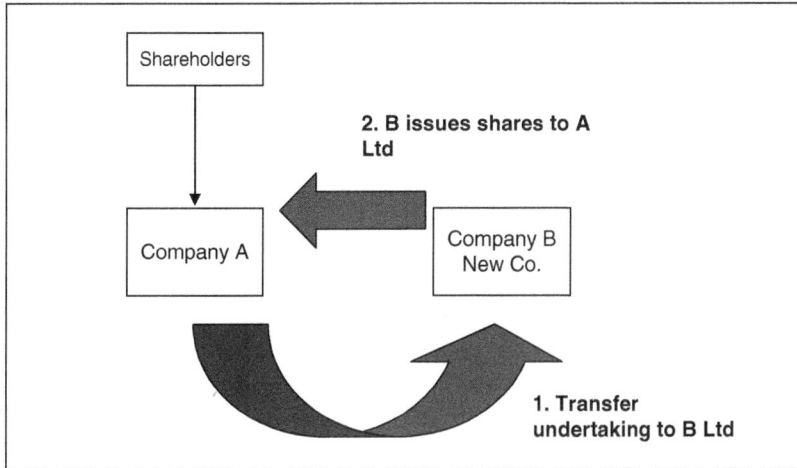

```
┌─────────────────────────────────────────────────────┐
│   ┌──────────────┐                                    │
│   │ Shareholders │        2. B issues shares to A     │
│   └──────┬───────┘        Ltd                          │
│          │                                             │
│          ▼            ◄═══════════                     │
│   ┌──────────────┐        ┌──────────────┐            │
│   │  Company A   │        │  Company B   │            │
│   └──────────────┘        │   New Co.    │            │
│          ╲_____╱└──────────────┘            │
│                  ═══════►                              │
│                           1. Transfer                  │
│                           undertaking to B Ltd         │
└─────────────────────────────────────────────────────┘
```

For stamp duty purposes, the stamp duty charge would not arise at Stage 1, being the transfer of an undertaking to B Ltd.

**Note:** the interaction with CGT reconstruction relief avoids a charge to CGT for Company A on the disposal of the undertaking to Company B.

2. Three-party share for undertaking swap
Shares are issued to the shareholders of the target company by the acquiring company in return for the business.

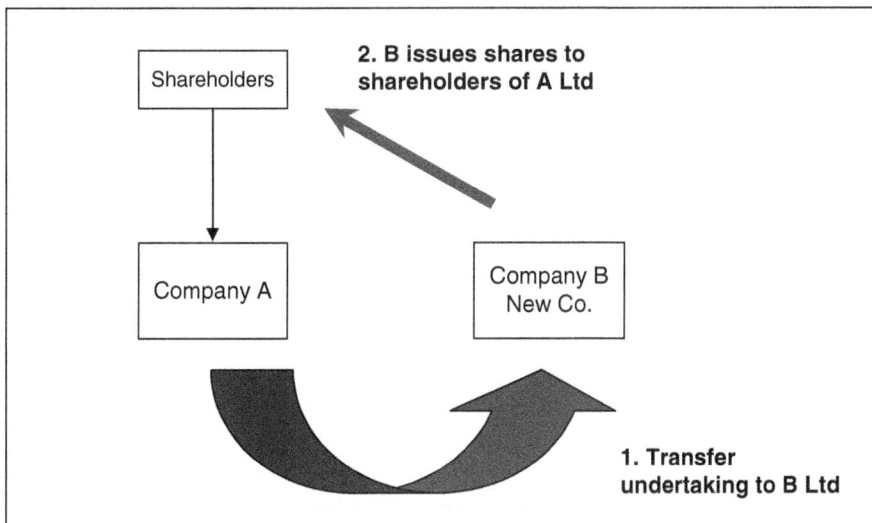

```
┌─────────────────────────────────────────────────────┐
│   ┌──────────────┐    2. B issues shares to           │
│   │ Shareholders │    shareholders of A Ltd           │
│   └──────┬───────┘                                     │
│          │          ◄════════                          │
│          ▼                    ═══                      │
│   ┌──────────────┐        ┌──────────────┐            │
│   │  Company A   │        │  Company B   │            │
│   └──────────────┘        │   New Co.    │            │
│          ╲_____╱└──────────────┘            │
│                  ═══════►                              │
│                           1. Transfer                  │
│                           undertaking to B Ltd         │
└─────────────────────────────────────────────────────┘
```

For stamp duty purposes, the stamp duty charge would not arise at Stage 1, being the transfer of an undertaking to B Ltd.

**Note:** the interaction with CGT reconstruction relief avoids a charge to CGT for Company A on the disposal of the undertaking to Company B.

---

**Example 8.8**

The transfer of a business can best be illustrated by way of example:

**Stage 1**

Blue Glass Ltd is a trading company that carries on two trades: a recycling trade and a glass manufacturing trade. Robert Robinson is the 100% shareholder and would like to separate the recycling trade from the manufacturing trade for commercial reasons. He would like to take a direct ownership in the recycling business if possible.

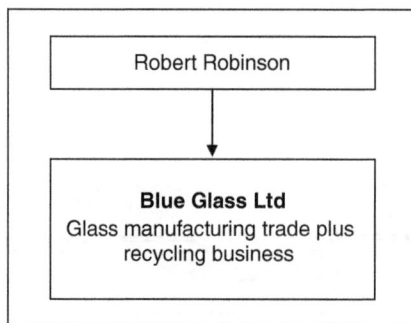

**Stage 2 – New Co. is incorporated**

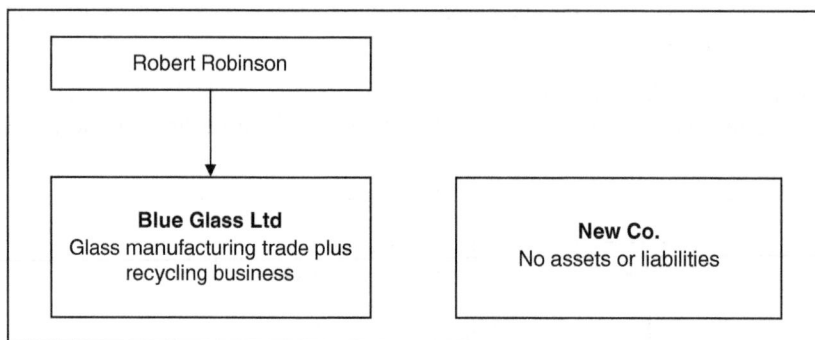

**Stage 3: Transfer of an undertaking to New Co. in exchange for the issue of shares to Robert**

Blue Glass Ltd will transfer its recycling trade (the "undertaking") to New Co. The disposal of the recycling trade would normally give rise to CGT for Blue Glass Ltd, being a disposal of chargeable assets. However, as this is a bona fide reconstruction of the business, the transfer is deemed to occur on a no gain/no loss basis.

Stamp duty in the hands of New Co. will also not arise for the same reason.

Blue Glass Ltd will not receive any consideration for the transfer, other than New Co. taking over the liabilities of the recycling business.

New Co. can either issue its shares to Blue Glass Ltd or to Robert Robinson in exchange for the business.

*continued overleaf*

As Robert would like to take a direct holding, the shares will be issued to him. The base cost of these shares will be computed by reference to Robert's original holding in Blue Glass Ltd. If Robert disposes of these new shares within two years, there is no clawback of the CGT relief (as it is reconstruction relief) or of stamp duty relief (as it is a three-party swap).

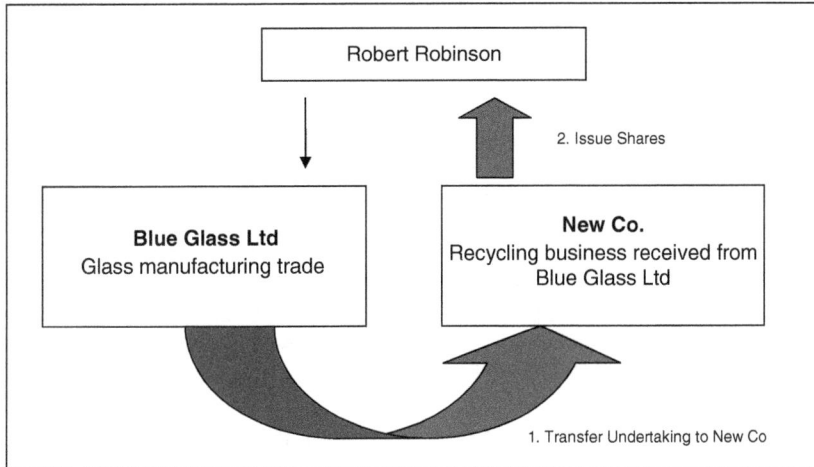

### 8.8.2 Reconstruction Relief versus Group Relief

You may ask why it is necessary to claim reconstruction relief when you could just transfer a business or undertaking to New Co. (being a new 100% subsidiary of the transferor) and claim CGT group relief. The key considerations are:

- There is a clawback of CGT group relief if the group relationship is broken within 10 years of the transfer.
- There is a clawback of stamp duty relief if the group relationship is broken within two years of the transfer.

Group relief, while being a valuable relief, is not always the most appropriate relief given the 10-year time constraint. Therefore, provided there is a reorganisation that satisfies the conditions in section 615 TCA 1997, the undertaking can be transferred to New Co. (at which time it is not in the group) in return for shares in New Co. and no CGT will arise as the assets transfer at no gain/no loss. When New Co. is sold, there is no clawback as there was no claim under CGT group relief. The claim was under section 615 TCA 1997 and there is no clawback of that relief.

> **Key Issue**
> Always take into account the subsequent clawback period when using group relief. If a break in the group relationship or a disposal of assets out of the group is anticipated, there may be little merit in relying on group relieving provisions. Reconstruction relief may be more suitable.

---

*Example 8.9: Group relief vs reconstruction relief*

Mullins Ltd operates a fruit distribution trade, but also has a number of property interests in Meath. A property business, consisting of 10 completed commercial retail units in Meath that are rented to well-known retailers, is held in Mullins Ltd, which actively manages the units, seeking suitable tenants and evaluates further property investment opportunities. It also employs four staff to manage the facility. Mullins Ltd is 100% owned by Francis Mullins, who does not want to complicate his corporate structure. He would like to separate his property business from his distribution business, as he feels that, if property values fall, this could impact on the results of his distribution business. Francis would like to set up a new subsidiary of Mullins Ltd and transfer the property business to a new company.

*Group Relief Option*

Take the scenario whereby Mullins Ltd transfers the property undertaking to New Co. (being a 100% subsidiary of Mullins Ltd). If a transfer to New Co. takes place and CGT group relief is claimed, a charge to tax will not arise (by virtue of that CGT group relief). However, if the group relationship is broken within 10 years of the transfer, a CGT charge will arise in the hands of New Co. A further stamp duty charge will become due in the hands of New Co. if the group is broken (i.e. associated companies stamp duty relief clawback) within two years.

*Transfer of an Undertaking – Reconstruction Option*

Take, however, the scenario whereby the property undertaking is to be transferred to a new company to separate it from the distribution trade (i.e. a scheme of reconstruction). In such a commercial scenario, Mullins Ltd would undertake to do the following:

- Mullins Ltd would transfer the undertaking to New Co. for zero consideration.
- New Co. could, in return, issue shares to Mullins Ltd as part of the reconstruction.

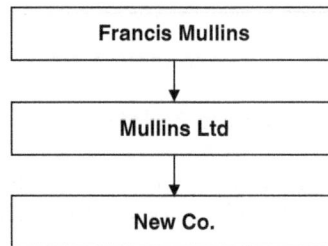

```
┌──────────────────────┐
│   Francis Mullins    │
└──────────┬───────────┘
           │
           ▼
┌──────────────────────┐
│     Mullins Ltd      │
└──────────┬───────────┘
           │
           ▼
┌──────────────────────┐
│      New Co.         │
└──────────────────────┘
```

*Outcome*

For stamp duty relief purposes, the "holding" period is two years, which is not necessarily prohibitive. However, for CGT group relief purposes, the holding period is 10 years if a clawback is to be avoided. Therefore it would make more sense for Francis Mullins/Mullins Ltd to avail of the CGT relief for "company reorganisation or amalgamation" as it does not have the 10-year time constraint.

---

*Key Issue*

Students should be aware that in any of the situations referred to in this chapter, where the setting up of a new company is required, notwithstanding the reliefs for CGT and stamp duty, the new company will be required to register for and operate such taxes as PAYE/PRSI, VAT, corporation tax, etc. where appropriate.

---

## 8.9    Bonus Issue

A bonus issue of shares occurs where existing shareholders are issued with new shares without an obligation to provide any consideration for the new holding. The bonus issue involves the capitalisation of part of the company's retained reserves. The impact of this is that reserves are reduced as the issued share capital of the company is increased.

A bonus issue may be implemented in order to limit the amount of the company's distributable reserves and therefore prevent the company from making large dividends to its shareholders. This situation could arise where restrictions are required on the level of distributions a company is capable of making. The value of the company effectively does not change (in terms of balance sheet value), but the amount of distributable reserves is reduced.

For CGT purposes, the bonus issue shares are considered to be a reorganisation of share capital with no CGT implications.

---

**Example 8.10**

Bacon Processors Ltd has 1,000 shares in issue. It is owned equally by Tom and Joe Ryan. These shares were acquired for €2 each in 1981. The profit reserves of the company are €1 million. It issues 500 bonus shares to its shareholders (i.e. Tom Ryan and Joe Ryan) and the €1 million reserves are capitalised in full. After the bonus issue, the issued share capital of the company is 1,500 shares.

Tom and Joe Ryan each still hold 50% of the company, but each now holds 750 shares (as opposed to 500 shares).

The distributable reserves of the company are €Nil, as they have been fully capitalised into share capital on the issue of the bonus shares.

Essentially, the split between the share capital and reserves has changed, but the ownership structure has not.

Tom and Joe, for CGT purposes, are not deemed to have acquired the new shares. The 750 shares Tom and Joe hold each are deemed to be the same 500 shareholding that was originally owned (with original base cost and date of acquisition still applying). For example, Tom's base cost of his 750 shares for CGT purposes will remain at €1,000 (i.e. €2 per share × 500 shares); Joe will be in the same position for CGT purposes.

---

## 8.10  Rights Issue

A rights issue is considered a reorganisation of share capital with no CGT implications. A rights issue involves an allotment of shares to the existing shareholders of the company. While a bonus issue consists of the capitalisation of a company's distributable reserves, a rights issue involves an invitation to shareholders to accept a right to subscribe for new shares. These shares will typically be offered at an attractive price to the shareholders.

Shareholders are not obliged to take up the offer to purchase the new shares in the company and may indeed not do so if they feel the offer is not of value to them.

A rights issue will involve a shareholder paying consideration to the company in return for the issue of new shares. The amount paid by the shareholder will be considered as enhancement expenditure for CGT purposes on a future disposal of those shares.

---

**Example 8.11**

Steven Swenson purchased 1,000 ordinary shares in Baca Plastics Ltd in 2007 for €25,000. In January 2016, the company offered a rights issue on the basis of two shares for each share held by the shareholder at €20 per share.

Steven took up the option to purchase 2,000 shares at a cost of €40,000.

Assume Steven sells his full shareholding in January 2017 for €200,000. His CGT will be computed as follows:

|                          | €        |
|--------------------------|----------|
| Proceeds                 | 200,000  |
| Less: base cost          |          |
| Cost – original holding  | (25,000) |
| Enhancement expenditure  | (40,000) |
| Chargeable gain          | 135,000  |

The additional expenditure incurred in respect of the rights issue is treated as being an enhancement cost of his original 1,000 shareholding.

---

## 8.11 Sample Case

Irish Locomotive Group is structured as follows at 1 February 2016:

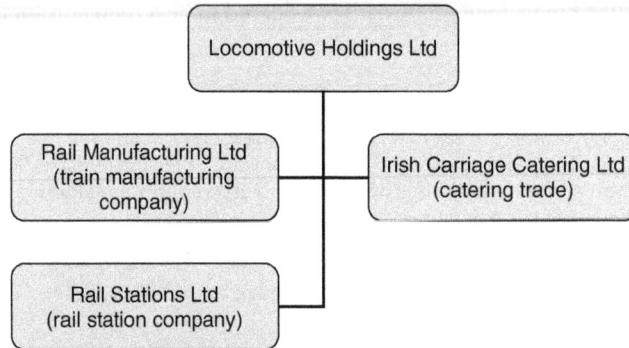

The group is owned by the Kiernan family, a wealthy family whose involvement in the Irish rail industry goes back over four generations.

The management of the group structure has become difficult and inefficient. The shareholders have decided to restructure the group's affairs and create a single trading entity in the top company, Locomotive Holdings Ltd. They see no benefit in the companies' current separate structure. The shareholders are also looking for ways to expand the business as they feel that the current business lines have reached their maximum potential.

**Tax Project Group Restructuring – Step Analysis**

The shareholders wish to restructure the business in the most tax-efficient manner. The shareholders decide to conduct the reorganisation of the group on 1 March 2016.

To transfer the three businesses to Locomotive Holdings Ltd, the following will have to happen on 1 March 2016:

***Step 1 – Rail Manufacturing Ltd***

Transfer the trade (i.e. assets and liabilities) of Rail Manufacturing Ltd to Locomotive Holdings Ltd.

*Tax Issue at Hand*

Disposal of chargeable assets by Rail Manufacturing Ltd
   Section 617 TCA 1997 group relief can be claimed by Rail Manufacturing Ltd and no CGT will therefore arise. While a 10-year clawback period will exist in respect of this transfer, at a practical level it is irrelevant. The clawback would arise if Locomotive Holdings Ltd left the group. As it is the parent, it is difficult to see this happening.

Acquisition of trade/assets by Locomotive Holdings Ltd
   Section 79 SDCA associated companies relief can be claimed in respect of stamp duty and no stamp duty will therefore arise. A two-year clawback period will exist in respect of this transfer.

***Step 2 – Irish Carriage Catering Ltd***

Transfer the trade (i.e. assets and liabilities) of Irish Carriage Catering Ltd to Locomotive Holdings Ltd.

*Tax Issue at Hand*

Disposal of chargeable assets by Irish Carriage Catering Ltd
   Section 617 TCA 1997 group relief can be claimed by Irish Carriage Catering Ltd and no CGT will therefore arise.

While a 10-year clawback period will exist in respect of this transfer, at a practical level it is irrelevant. The clawback would arise if Locomotive Holdings Ltd left the group. As it is the parent, it is difficult to see this happening.

Acquisition of trade/assets by Locomotive Holdings Ltd

Section 79 1999 associated companies relief can be claimed in respect of stamp duty and no stamp duty will therefore arise. A two-year clawback period will exist in respect of this transfer.

### Step 3 – Rail Stations Ltd

Transfer the trade (i.e. assets and liabilities) of Rail Stations Ltd to Locomotive Holdings Ltd.

*Tax Issue at Hand*

Disposal of chargeable assets by Rail Stations Ltd

Section 617 TCA 1997 group relief can be claimed by Rail Stations Ltd and no CGT will therefore arise. While a 10-year clawback period will exist in respect of this transfer, at a practical level it is irrelevant. The clawback would arise if Locomotive Holdings Ltd left the group. As it is the parent, it is difficult to see this happening.

Acquisition of assets by Locomotive Holdings Ltd

Section 79 SDCA associated companies relief can be claimed in respect of stamp duty and no stamp duty will therefore arise. A two-year clawback period will exist in respect of this transfer.

---

**Key Issue**
CGT and stamp duty group relief is based on company relationships remaining intact.

---

Steps 1 to 3 have achieved the desired result of all the group trades, assets and liabilities being within Locomotive Holdings Ltd, which now holds:

1   Trade and assets of Rail Manufacturing Ltd.
2   Trade and assets of Irish Carriage Catering Ltd.
3   Trade and assets of Rail Stations Ltd.

The new group structure on 1 March 2016 is as follows:

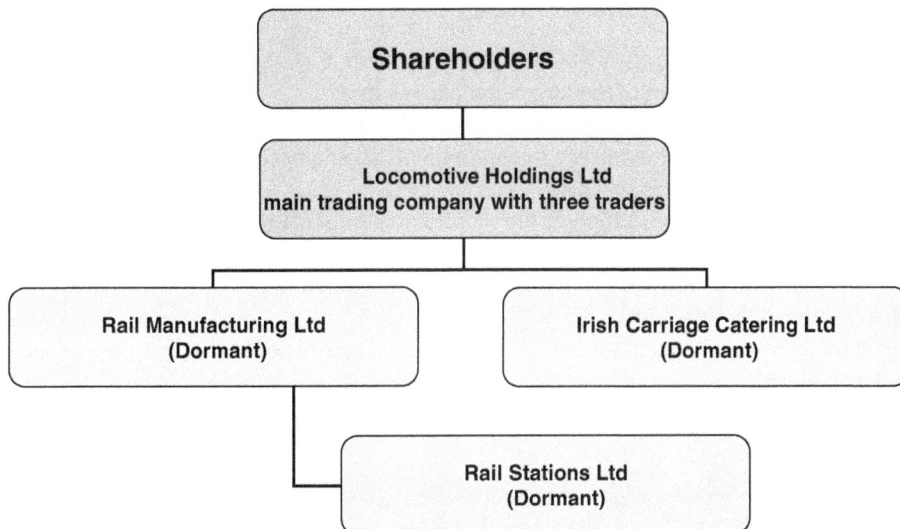

**Future Business Expansion Opportunity – 1 October 2016**

On 1 October 2016, the shareholders of Locomotive Holdings Ltd are presented with the opportunity to acquire an interest in a third-party car park business. The shareholders have known about this business for a number of years, as the target company in question owns private car parks beside all of the train stations run by the Locomotive Holdings Group. The shareholders see the ownership of the private car parks as a very attractive means to expand their business.

The car park owners, however, are not interested in a disposal of their shares for cash consideration, and are interested in a merger of sorts. In order to acquire the car park business, the Kiernan family will have to admit new shareholders to their family business.

The proposal is as follows:

The Target Company is Irish Car Parks Ltd. The company is 100% owned by five individual shareholders equally. Locomotive Holdings Ltd will acquire 100% of the shares in Irish Car Parks Ltd in exchange for the issue of shares in Locomotive Holdings Ltd to the five individuals. The shares issued to the five individuals will reflect the value of Irish Car Parks Ltd. The five shareholders are only interested in conducting the transaction if it can be done at a minimum tax cost.

**Tax Analysis – Amalgamation by Exchange of Shares**

Company amalgamations will involve an **acquiring company (Locomotive Holdings Ltd)** and a **target company (Irish Car Parks Ltd)**.

Section 586 TCA 1997 company amalgamations by exchange of shares states that:

> "…where a company issues shares or debentures to a person in exchange for shares in or debentures of another company, section 584 shall apply with any necessary modifications as if the two companies were the same company and the exchange were a reorganisation of its share capital."

Section 584 TCA 1997 reorganisation relief states that:

> "...a reorganisation or reduction of a company's share capital shall not be treated as involving any disposal of the original shares or any acquisition of the new holding or any part of it, but the original shares (taken as a single asset) and the new holding (taken as a single asset) shall be treated as the same asset acquired as the original shares were acquired."

As Locomotive Holdings is taking a 100% interest in Irish Car Parks Ltd, the requirement under amalgamation relief to gain control of the target company is met.

Amalgamation reorganisation relief provides that the disposal of shares in Irish Car Parks Ltd does not constitute a disposal for CGT purposes. The five individuals should not have a CGT liability as a result of the amalgamation.

Equally, stamp duty relief should apply to the share acquisition by Locomotive Holdings Ltd. Normally 1% stamp duty applies to the acquisition of shares unless stamp duty relief is applied. However, if Locomotive Holdings Ltd, as the acquiring company, ceases to be the owner of the shares within a two-year period, the stamp duty relief will be clawed back.

The amalgamation is undertaken for bona fide commercial purposes and the purpose of the scheme is not the avoidance of tax.

The following corporate structure is achieved following the exchange of shares:

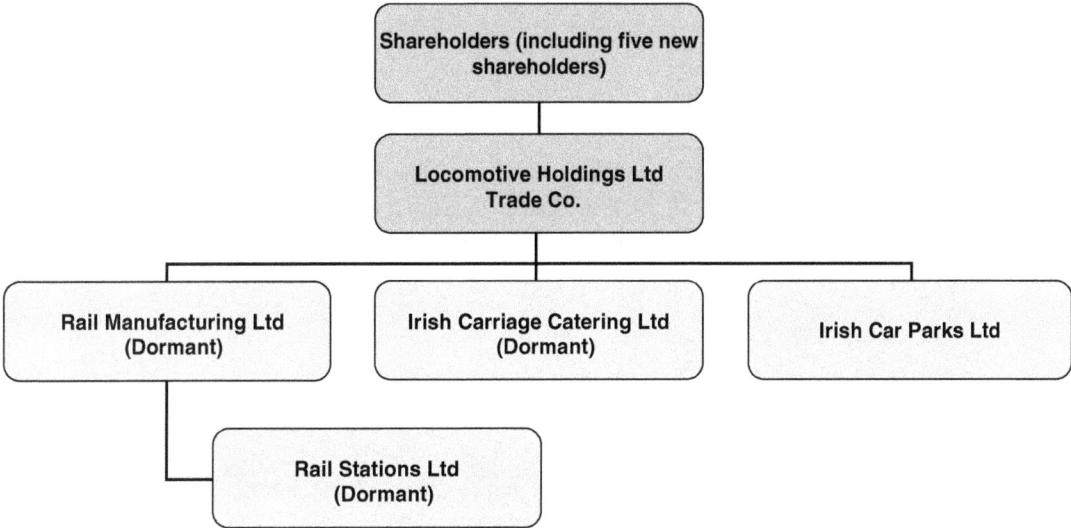

Shareholders (including five new shareholders)

Locomotive Holdings Ltd
Trade Co.

Rail Manufacturing Ltd
(Dormant)

Irish Carriage Catering Ltd
(Dormant)

Irish Car Parks Ltd

Rail Stations Ltd
(Dormant)

## Chapter 8 Summary

| Reorganisation without a change in ownership | • Many reasons for reorganisation<br>• Tax consequences to consider<br>• Relief from CGT and stamp duty available |
|---|---|
| **Reorganisations** | • Many tax and commercial reasons for reorganisations<br>• Close company implications<br>• Share-for-share transactions (with or without consideration passing)<br>• Bonus issue of shares<br>• Rights issue of shares<br>• Relief from CGT and stamp duty |
| **Reconstruction/ Amalgamation** | • Reconstruction/amalgamation relief available<br>• Can take the form of "two-party share for undertaking swap" or "three-party share for undertaking swap"<br>• Interaction of reconstruction relief with group relief |

# Questions

## Review Questions
(See Suggested Solutions to Review Questions at the end of this textbook.)

### Question 8.1

Patrick Ryan acquired 200 ordinary shares in Worldscape Software Ltd. These shares were acquired for €250,000 in June 2007. The share structure of Worldscape was reconstructed in June 2016. Patrick, in exchange for his 200 ordinary shares, received 20,000 non-voting preference shares for €10 each (which was the market value price), plus €200,000 in cash.

**Requirement**
Calculate Patrick's CGT position for June 2016.

### Question 8.2

Joe Flynn owns 100 ordinary shares in Flynn Oil Ltd, acquired in January 2006 for €20,000. It is now 1 July 2016. The current market value of those shares is €250,000. In a reorganisation of the company, Joe is issued with 2,000 "A" ordinary shares in exchange for his existing 100 shares and Joe must also pay €100,000 consideration to the company.

Joe sold his 2,000 shareholding in December 2016 for €1 million.

**Requirement**
Calculate Joe's CGT liability for December 2016.

## Challenging Questions
(Suggested Solutions to Challenging Questions are available through your lecturer.)

### Question 8.1

Ferguson Ltd is an Irish resident company currently involved in the production of football programmes for match day games, which are sold at football grounds around the north of England in Yorkshire and Lancashire.

The company has a number of trading subsidiaries, one of which, Rooney Ltd, was established a few years ago to facilitate the production of Braille programmes for blind football fans. It was not anticipated how successful this venture would be and, as a result, the company has expanded its activities to produce CD versions of the programmes for visually impaired football fans. This activity, unfortunately, has not taken off to the same extent and the programmes are being produced online to try and reach a wider customer base.

Ferguson Ltd has been approached by SeeOnline Ltd, a company that specialises in producing online materials for the visually impaired. SeeOnline is interested in the CD programme trade of Rooney Ltd, but not the Braille programmes.

In addition, Rooney Ltd has a number of Irish investment properties that are surplus to requirements and will be sold prior to any potential reorganisation. Ferguson Ltd had transferred a small property to Rooney Ltd when the company started to trade. The property is now too small and Rooney Ltd has received an offer of €780,000 for it. The property was worth €650,000 when it was transferred to Rooney Ltd in June 2008 and originally cost Ferguson Ltd €260,000 in January 1990.

The production of the CDs is carried out by another wholly owned subsidiary, Scholes Ltd. Once the CD trade is transferred to New Co., Ferguson Ltd would like to package Scholes Ltd and Rooney Ltd together, to facilitate any future potential sale.

Ferguson Ltd has contacted your firm to provide it with tax advice on how best to structure any potential sale. It advises you that Rooney Ltd has trading losses from the start-up periods and the current year totalling €100,000 which remain unutilised. SeeOnline Ltd is keen to use these losses if possible. Indexation from 1990 to 2002 is 1.503.

**Requirement**
(a) Advise Ferguson Ltd on the relief available for the losses arising in Rooney Ltd, both for the Ferguson group and SeeOnline Ltd.
(b) Advise Ferguson Ltd on how to minimise any tax liability arising on the disposal of the investment properties from Rooney Ltd
(c) Advise Ferguson Ltd on the steps required to achieve the sale of Rooney Ltd without the Braille trade being disposed of.
(d) Advise Ferguson Ltd on how to achieve its objective of combining Scholes Ltd and Rooney Ltd.
(e) Explain the tax issues to be considered regarding the transfer of the shares in Scholes Ltd to Rooney Ltd.

# Summary of Tax Planning and Other Issues

**Learning Objectives**

By the end of this chapter you will be able to:

- Consider the tax implications of business decisions for both sole traders and corporate entities.
- Assess the taxation implications of business decisions, including:
  - fiduciary taxes and PAYE/PRSI; and
  - VAT, PAYE and RCT.

## 9.1 Introduction

The purpose of this chapter is to provide a high-level review of key tax issues that may require consideration in the various business circumstances that can arise. This summary document will be helpful in identifying the key tax issues that will require consideration in any practical situation presented.

This chapter does not, however, review and summarise the various technical aspects of each tax matter. These should be reviewed separately, either within this manual or from previous study materials.

## 9.2 Sole Trader: Commencement and Operation of a Sole Trade

- Commencement to trade rules – assessment rules for new trades.
- Liability to income tax as a sole trader – consider the general exposure to income tax and at what rate (i.e. standard rate or higher rate).
- Case I/II sole trade losses – surrender tax losses against other income (aim to maximise loss relief at the highest rate of tax).
- Projected sole trader losses? It may be beneficial to continue to operate as a sole trader if losses are expected in the foreseeable future (i.e. surrender loss relief against other income).
- Computation of taxable profits – disallowed expenditure.
- Pension planning requirements and maximising tax relief.
- Will VAT registration be required?
- What rate of VAT will apply to supplies made in the course of the sole trade?
- What will the rate of VAT recovery be (i.e. 100% recovery or partial recovery)?
- Will staff be required? If so, there will be a need to register for PAYE/PRSI and operate PAYE/PRSI on all payments/benefits to staff.

## 9.3 The Incorporation Decision

- Will the company qualify for the start-up exemption?
- Are significant profits anticipated? The 12.5% rate of corporation tax may be attractive from a business perspective.
- Is limited liability a commercial requirement for the business?
- Transfer of a sole trade business to a limited company – transfer of a business relief is available from a CGT and a VAT perspective.
- Will property used by the business be held by a company or continue to be held personally?
- If funding is required, EIIS relief may be an option.
- Is a holding company structure required? You may wish to consider reorganisation reliefs or group relief if such a structure is required.
- Company will have to register for VAT, PAYE/PRSI and corporation tax.
- Various rates of corporation tax depending on the source of the company's income.
- Close company legislation must be considered carefully.
- Scope for additional pension planning in a new company – director's pension scheme.
- Loss relief rules in a company.
- Cash extraction.
- Is there a future exit strategy from the business? Consider the implications of an asset sale versus a share sale (on exit from a business).

## 9.4 Funding a New Company

- Could the company qualify for EIIS investment?
- Should the company take a bank loan and repay the bank loan from after-tax profits?
- Should the company seek outside investors?
- Plan for regular tax outflows – VAT, PAYE and corporation tax payment requirements/deadlines.
- R&D tax credits – maximise tax relief and/or seek a cash refund.

## 9.5 Cash Extraction from a Company

- Establish the extent to which shareholders will require cash from the business – if significant cash is not needed by shareholders, the balance of cash can remain within the company.
- Maximise cash extraction at a low rate of tax.
- Salary option.
- Dividends (and deemed dividends to shareholders).
- Redundancy, if certain shareholders/employees leave the business. Termination payments could be relevant.
- Pension planning for key executives/working shareholders.
- Loans to shareholders and close company rules.
- Liquidation of the company.
- Consider the close company legislation when extracting cash/assets from a company.

## 9.6 Close Company Issues

- Establish if a company is a close company.
- Identify any close company surcharge issues (i.e. surcharge arising on undistributed estate and investment income within a close company).

- Election to make a dividend "non-surchargeable".
- Payments made out of the company could be deemed to be distributions in the hands of the recipients.
- Transfer of value out of a close company to its participators could also be deemed to be an income distribution.
- Loans to shareholders/participators – obligation to withhold tax on such loans and pay it over to Revenue.

## 9.7    Buying the Assets of a Business: Purchaser Issues

- Consider an apportionment of the purchase price between various asset classes. It may be possible to maximise the value of assets that will qualify for capital allowances (e.g. plant and machinery). The asset purchase agreement could specify the apportionment of the purchase price.
- It is not possible to purchase tax losses when the assets of a business are being acquired (as opposed to a share purchase).
- Consider the stamp duty that will arise on the purchase of assets. If the value is significant, there could be a significant stamp duty cost (2% of asset value).
- Consider the base cost of chargeable assets for future disposal purposes.
- VAT is likely to arise on the purchase of assets (unless transfer of a business as a going concern relief can apply). If a property is being acquired and this relief applies the VAT history of the property will be required as the purchaser will take on the VAT history of the property.

## 9.8    Buying the Shares of a Company: Purchaser Issues

- A due diligence review of the company will be required.
- Warranties may be put in place in respect of historical tax issues.
- Is the share purchase of a single company or a holding company with more than one subsidiary?
- Has group relief been claimed in respect of assets transfer inter-group (i.e. CGT and stamp duty relief)?
- Consider the issue of latent gains within the company.
- Is there a future exit strategy from the company (or the company's assets)? Is the purchase of shares the optimal purchase option?
- Does the company have tax losses? Can these losses be claimed by the new company owner following the sale? Consider the "loss-buying" provisions and restrictions thereon.
- The 1% stamp duty rate will apply to the purchase of shares, which is often more attractive to the purchaser than the 2% rate on the purchase of a business/assets.
- Has the purchase price been discounted for issues within the company (i.e. tax risks, latent gains, etc.)?

## 9.9    Selling the Assets of a Business: Seller Issues

- Tax implications of making the sale.
- Valuation of the assets/business – how is this to be done?
- Apportionment of total consideration between various asset classifications.
- Balancing charges on the sale of assets that qualified for capital allowances – if a charge arises, this could be a significant tax cost for the seller.
- If the sale is made by a company, does the company have tax loss relief to shelter any profit/gain arising on the disposal of assets?

- Does the sale of assets/business constitute a cessation of the trade in the company?
- If the sale is made by a company, how will cash be extracted from the company?
- Could the purchaser be persuaded to purchase the shares in the company if it were a better option for the seller?

## 9.10 Selling the Shares of a Company: Seller Issues

- Tax implications of making the sale – most likely CGT treatment on the disposal of shares.
- Is the seller a company or an individual?
- Retirement relief might be available if shares are sold by an individual.
- Are all business assets held within the company? Are any assets (e.g. property used by the company) held personally?
- A due diligence review may be undertaken.
- Warranties may be provided in the share purchase agreement or a similar legal document.
- Full exit from the business?
- If a share sale is by a company, participation exemption may be available (section 626B TCA 1997).

## 9.11 Reorganisation of a Business: Company Amalgamations

- Identify situations whereby company amalgamations need to take place.
- Amalgamation could happen when a holding company structure is being put in place (perhaps to replace a cluster of personally held companies).
- Amalgamation could occur on a merger of two third-party companies/groups.
- Amalgamation could be a restructuring opportunity to tidy up a complex corporate group.
- Key CGT issue – the transfer of shares will constitute a disposal of a chargeable asset for CGT purposes – amalgamation relief is available so that the transfer does not trigger CGT on the disposal of the shares.
- Stamp duty should arise on the acquisition of shares – amalgamation relief allows an exemption from stamp duty on foot of a bona fide amalgamation.
- Note that the acquiring company must obtain control of the target company, the restructuring must be undertaken for bona fide commercial reasons and that the stamp duty relief requires that shares being issued in the acquiring company must represent at least 90% of the value of the target company.

## 9.12 Reorganisation of a Business: Transfer of a Business

- Identify situations where a transfer of an undertaking could take place.
- The transfer involves the transfer of a business to a new company in exchange for the issue of shares in the new company to the transferor (or the holder of shares in the transferring company).
- While group relief could be claimed to facilitate the same transfer, there is however a 10-year clawback period. There is no clawback period associated with the transfer of an undertaking relief, provided there is a reorganisation that satisfies the conditions in section 615 TCA 1997. If so, the undertaking can be transferred to the new company (at which time it is not in the group) in return for shares in the new company, and no CGT will arise as the assets transfer at no gain/no loss.

## 9.13 VAT: General Business Issues

- Is VAT registration required?
- What rate of VAT will apply to supplies?
- Does the company/trader have full VAT recovery? If not, are they appropriately computing the level of VAT that is not recoverable?
- Is the company's VAT history in order (e.g. outstanding/late returns, etc.)?
- Does the company incorrectly claim back VAT on non-allowable items (e.g. petrol, hotel costs, entertainment, purchase/hire of passenger cars, etc.)?
- When was the company's last VAT audit? This could be an indicator of possible VAT issues.
- How does the company treat items for which they have to self-account for VAT?
- If the company is in the telecommunications, broadcasting or e-services sector, is it availing of the MOSS scheme to register for VAT?*

* A new special scheme known as the Mini One Stop Shop (MOSS) came into operation on 1st January 2015 in Ireland. While MOSS has limited relevance in the context of business planning decisions, students should nevertheless have an understanding of the scheme given its recent introduction. MOSS has been introduced via an EU Council Directive and applies to supplies of telecommunications, broadcasting and e-services to consumers (B2C).

Previously, if the services were supplied by a business established in the EU to a non-taxable person in the EU, the place of supply was where that supplier was located; or, if supplied by a business established outside the EU to a non-taxable person in the EU, the place of supply was where the customer was located.

In order to simplify the obligations of suppliers of telecommunications, broadcasting and e-services, instead of registering for VAT in several Member States, suppliers may opt to declare and pay the relevant VAT due to Member States through the MOSS in the Member State where the supplier has its place of establishment.

## 9.14 PAYE: General Business Issues

- Is the operation of PAYE by the employer correct?
- Does the company have a good compliance history (e.g. no late returns, etc.)?
- Does the company pay cash to employees?
- Is PAYE operated on all payments to shareholders/directors? If not, are all other payments treated as distributions to shareholders? The close company rules are also relevant here if the company is a close company.
- Does the employer retain all required records in respect of expense payments made to staff?
- Does the employer pay unvouched expenses to staff members?
- Does the employer have payroll/BIK/redundancy policies?
- Have redundancy payments been computed correctly?

## 9.15 Corporation Tax: General Business Issues

- Has the company met its preliminary tax requirements?
- Does the company have expense items which must be added back for computational purposes?

- Does the company intend to sell valuable assets? Exposure to a balancing charge may apply if capital allowances have been claimed.
- Is loss relief available?
- Consider the order of loss relief.
- Is group relief available for surrender/claim?
- Is there a close company surcharge exposure?

## 9.16 Investor Wishing to Enter a Business: Typical Tax Considerations

- How will the investor take a holding in the company?
- Issue of new share capital by company to investor.
- Loan notes (with or without interest applying) and small shareholding.
- Loan notes only (with interest applying).
- Purchase of shares from existing shareholder.
- Repayment of an interest-free loan note can be received tax free by the investor.
- If shares are purchased, the base cost on a future disposal of shares will be the purchase price.
- If a nominal shareholding is taken (e.g. 100 shares for €100 which will equal a % shareholding in the business), the base cost on the future disposal of shares is nominal (i.e. full exposure to a gain).
- Could the investor use a holding company to purchase shares in a target company? If so, there could be potential to make use of section 626B TCA 1997 participation exemption on a future disposal.
- Will a due diligence review be required?
- Can the shareholder take a small holding now with an option to purchase a further interest at a later date?
- Importance of the investors establishing a future exit strategy from the business (including their intended term of holding the investment).
- Is a restructuring of the business required prior to the investor investing funds? (For example, a holding company may be put in place to take ownership of a group of companies, so that the investor can take an interest in the whole group.)

## 9.17 Investor/Shareholder Wishing to Exit a Business: Typical Tax Considerations

- Are there any loans owing by the company to the shareholder due for repayment? The repayment of these loans is likely to involve a tax-free reimbursement of funds.
- If a share sale is planned, will retirement relief be available?
- Is a restructuring or a reorganisation of the business required prior to exit of the shareholder?
- What is the base cost of the shares held for CGT purposes?
- Will the shares be sold to a connected party? If sold at an undervalue, the market value will be deemed to be the sale price.
- Will the timing of the share sale be relevant? It may be required to take into account the CGT payment deadlines prior to completing the share sale.
- If a company is making the share disposal, will the participation exemption be available?
- If a full exit from a business is planned by way of company asset/trade sale, how will the shareholder extract the post-sale funds from the company? An exposure to double taxation must be considered in this scenario.

## Chapter 9 Summary

**General considerations**

- Review commerciality of the deal in question – is it best for purchaser/seller?
- Where can savings be made?
- What is the worst case scenario of the deal?
- Have legal aspects been fully covered?

**Tax considerations**

- Disposal by a company will lead to a double tax charge to extract cash
- Tax-efficient ways of extracting cash should be considered
- What rate of income tax is anticipated in the future?
- Losses for self-employed are more useful than losses for companies
- Consider best exit strategy for personal circumstances
- Self-assessment tax return deadlines

**Other considerations**

- A business decision may not be led by the optimum tax treatment
- Must consider commercial reasons for undertaking a transaction
- Could have adverse tax effects, but need to weigh-up against the bigger picture
- VAT, stamp duty and CGT implications of a transaction need to be considered

# Revenue Penalties and Audits

**Learning Objectives**

By the end of this chapter you will have considered:

- The duties and obligations of the client in relation to Revenue audits and investigations, to include:
  - different types of audits;
  - self-correction;
  - importance of qualifying disclosure and its significance for penalties and publication; and
  - right to review for aggrieved client.

## 10.1 Revenue Audits and Penalties

Before reading this chapter, it is recommended that students obtain a copy of the Revenue Commissioners' *Code of Practice for Revenue Audits and other Compliance Interventions* as updated in 2015 (effective from 20 November 2015), available at www.revenue.ie. The *Code of Practice* contains the basis by which Revenue audits and compliance interventions take place and explains the obligations for both the taxpayer and the Revenue official in respect of this process.

Failure by a company* to operate all applicable taxes can lead to:

- tax penalties;
- publication; and
- prosecution.

**\*Note:** Revenue audits and compliance interventions apply to individuals, companies and all other chargeable entities, for ease of reference, some parts of the following text will only refer to companies.

The Revenue Commissioners' audit selection process can be based on a number of criteria. These include:

**Random Selection**
A small number of compliance interventions conducted by the Revenue Commissioners are purely on a random basis. The taxpayer will not be informed that they are subject to a random selection. The objectives of the Random Audit Programme are to measure and track compliance with tax legislation.

**Revenue's Predetermined Criteria**

The Revenue Commissioners operate a system known as REAP (risk, evaluation, analysis and profiling), which is their knowledge-based expert software system of risk analysis. This involves the use of sophisticated software tools that analyse the taxpayer's information. The tax paid/refunded to/by the taxpayer is monitored, along with compliance history, backup lifestyle information, asset portfolios, residence issues, etc. The use of advanced analytics supports real-time risk models for VAT and PAYE. The VAT Real Time Risk Framework (VAT RTRF) identifies potential VAT fraud at the earliest opportunity. VAT RTRF applies to VAT returns that are VAT-payable and VAT-refundable.

The PAYE Real Time Risk Framework (PAYE RTRF) assists in the prevention of incorrect claims (when they are made) and the detection of under-declared income.

**Regional Structure**

The Revenue's current structure involves the establishment of the Large Cases Division, which manages individual entities/groups/persons with each regional tax office throughout Ireland.

**Sector/Industry Audits**

In some cases, the Revenue Commissioners will announce their intention to focus on specific economic sectors or industry-wide audits. The selection of particular projects arise from intelligence gathered by Revenue, based on:

- the use of the REAP system;
- results from other enquiries and audits in the sector;
- local knowledge; or
- information from third parties (including suppliers).

## 10.2 Types of Revenue Audit and Revenue Interventions

Revenue audits can include:

- Desk checks.
- On-site ("field") audits.
- Transaction audits (e.g. one particular property sale).
- Computer audits.
- National investigations.

Desk audits are typically verification checks. This, for example, could include a request for supporting invoices to a VAT 3 return on which a refund of VAT is claimed by the taxpayer. The taxpayer might be contacted by letter or phone from the local tax district. These desk checks do not constitute an audit for the purposes of the *Code of Practice*.

A field audit will constitute an audit for the purposes of the *Code of Practice* and, as such, all disclosure rules will apply if the taxpayer receives an audit notification from the Revenue Commissioners.

A transaction audit will apply to a particular transaction, for example this could include a property transaction or a share sale. The Revenue Commissioners will clearly indicate that their inquiry relates to that transaction (i.e. and not to other taxes or other periods). The disclosure procedures as outlined in the *Code of Practice* will apply and, as such, the taxpayer should consider if there are any issues that will require disclosure before corresponding with the Revenue Commissioners. This could impact on the level of penalties that could apply if a tax default/issue exists.

Computer audits are becoming a more frequent means of auditing a taxpayer's tax records. This reflects the significant investment by the Revenue Commissioners in software technology and the efficiency of conducting the audit in this manner. Revenue's audit notification will include a line stating that the audit will involve an investigation of the company/taxpayer's computer records. The audit will review the data being entered and processed and that controls are in place to ensure the accurate and correct computation of tax.

### 10.2.1 Definition of a Revenue Audit

A Revenue spokesperson has provided a definition of Revenue audit as follows:

> "A Revenue Audit may be defined as a review, either partial or total, of a company's corporation tax return or declaration of liability, books and records normally for one year to ensure that the major areas of income, deductions and reliefs are correct. It is essentially a check on the accuracy of the corporation tax return or declaration and on the validity of the allowances, etc. claimed."

The *Code of Practice* states that the primary objective is to "promote voluntary compliance with tax and duty obligations" and that the "interventions programme are mainly concerned with detecting and deterring non-compliance".

A Revenue audit is an **examination** of:

- a return for income tax (including DIRT and other fiduciary taxes), corporation tax, capital gains tax, stamp duties or capital acquisitions tax (either in whole or in part); or
- a declaration of liability, or a repayment claim, for VAT, PAYE/PRSI or relevant contracts tax (RCT); or
- a statement of liability to stamp duties.

### 10.2.2 Field Audit

Where a business is involved, most audits, whether comprehensive or single tax head, include **visits** to the business premises. The length of such visits depends on the number and complexity of the points at issue. **Twenty-one days' notice** is generally given in such cases to both the company and its agent. In certain exceptional circumstances (e.g. where it is suspected that records are likely to be removed or altered), a visit may take place unannounced.

### 10.2.3 Desk Audit

Certain audits (mainly verification of specific claims to expenses, allowances or reliefs) are conducted by letter (post, fax or e-mail), or by telephone, where straightforward issues are involved. This type of audit, known as a desk audit, may also arise in a review of a director's tax affairs or where a company has unearned income. Similarly, CAT and stamp duty audits are normally desk audits. Taxpayers will be informed of the issues being examined in the course of a desk audit.

It should be noted that a desk audit may subsequently involve field work, if this is deemed necessary, including visits to the company's premises to examine records.

### 10.2.4 Audit Notification

The company will receive notification in writing:

- notifying them of a Revenue audit; **or**
- raising a query.

Revenue will specify a date at which it wishes to visit the company's premises to examine the books and records of the business. Almost all audits are carried out for a reason, e.g. Revenue will have information or indications that the company may have underpaid tax. Though some audits are carried out on a random basis, Revenue frequently targets specific trades or industries.

The Audit Notification will specify the tax head or heads (corporation tax, VAT, etc.) and the year of assessment or period in question. The Revenue auditor is confined to examining the issues **as notified** and cannot extend the audit without good reason at the time of the visit.

## 10.3 Tax, Interest and Penalties

**Tax**
Any tax due as a result of the Revenue audit must be paid.

**Interest**
Interest is always charged if a failure to pay is identified. Interest **cannot** be mitigated.

**Application of Penalties**
Penalties will apply if, in the course of the audit, tax defaults are identified. Penalties are "tax-geared", which means that the penalty is expressed as a **percentage of the tax** (but not the interest) in question. Penalties will apply in circumstances where there has been:

- careless behaviour;
- careless behaviour with significant consequences; **or**
- deliberate behaviour.

*Careless behaviour*
Careless behaviour will arise if a company of ordinary skill and knowledge, properly advised, would have foreseen as a reasonable probability or likelihood the prospect that an act (or omission) would cause a tax underpayment, having regard to all the circumstances but, nevertheless, the act or omission occurred. There is also a **materiality test**. The tax shortfall must be **less than 15%** of the tax liability ultimately due in respect of the particular tax.

*Careless behaviour with significant consequences*
Careless behaviour with significant consequences is the lack of **due care**, with the result that tax liabilities or repayment claims are **substantially incorrect** and do not pass the 15% test described above. Careless behaviour with significant consequences is distinguished from "deliberate behaviour" by the **absence** of indicators consistent with intent on the part of the company.

*Deliberate behaviour*
Deliberate behaviour has indicators consistent with **intent** and includes tax evasion and the non-operation of fiduciary taxes such as PAYE.

### 10.3.1 Self-correction

This category arises outside of the audit or enquiry process. A return may be self-corrected **without** penalty where:

- Revenue is notified in writing of the adjustments to be made, and the circumstances under which the errors arose.
- A computation of the correct tax and statutory interest payable is provided, along with payment in settlement (the errors must not be in the 'deliberate behaviour' category).

**Time Limits for Self-correction**

| | |
|---|---|
| **Income Tax** | Within 12 months of the due date for filing the return. |
| **Corporation Tax** | Within 12 months of the due date for filing the return. |
| **Capital Gains Tax** | Within 12 months of the due date for filing the return. |
| **VAT** | Before the due date of the income tax or corporation tax return for the period in which the VAT period ends, e.g. a self-correction of the Jan–Feb 2015 VAT3 for a company with a December year end must occur before 21–23 September 2016. Where the net underpayment of VAT for the period being corrected is less than €6,000, the amount of tax can be included (without interest) as an adjustment on the next corresponding VAT return following that in which the error was made. |
| **PAYE/PRSI** | Within 12 months of the due date for filing the annual return. |
| **Relevant Contracts Tax** | Within 12 months of the due date for filing the annual return. |

### 10.3.2   Reduction of Penalties

Under the Taxes Consolidation Act 1997, reduced penalties may apply in the following circumstances:

- Cooperation by the company.
- Qualifying disclosures made by the company.

**Cooperation**
Cooperation includes the following:

- Having all books, records, and linking papers available for the auditor at the commencement of the audit.
- Responding promptly to all requests for information and explanations.
- Responding promptly to all correspondence.
- Prompt payment of the audit settlement liability.

**Penalties in Death Cases**
Previous Revenue practice regarding the recovery of penalties from the estate of a taxpayer after death has been placed on a statutory footing. Penalties will only be recovered from the estate where the taxpayer either agreed in writing to pay the penalty or a court has determined, before the taxpayer's death, that the taxpayer was liable to the penalties.

### 10.3.3   Qualifying Disclosures

The company may elect to carry out a review of its own tax affairs and identify where mistakes were made **prior** to their discovery by the Revenue auditor. This type of review is called a "qualifying disclosure", and Revenue has in place special incentives for companies that wish to make qualifying disclosures. A qualifying disclosure results in the following:

- Further mitigation of penalties.
- Non-publication under section 1086 TCA 1997.
- No prosecution.

Qualifying disclosures can be either "unprompted" or "prompted":

- An unprompted disclosure is a disclosure that is made before the company is either notified of an audit or contacted by Revenue regarding an enquiry or investigation relating to its tax affairs.
- A prompted disclosure is a disclosure made after an audit notice has issued but before an examination of the books and records or other documentation has begun.

### Format of the Qualifying Disclosure
The following conditions must be satisfied for a disclosure to be a **qualifying disclosure** for the purpose of mitigation of penalties:

- The disclosure must be made in writing and signed by or on behalf of the company.
- The disclosure must:
  - in the case of **all** disclosures, whether prompted or unprompted, state the amounts of all liabilities to tax, interest and penalties, as respects all tax heads and periods, which were liabilities previously undisclosed by reason of **deliberate behaviour** by the company; **and**
  - in the case of a **prompted** disclosure, must also state the amounts of any liabilities previously undisclosed, for any reason other than **deliberate behaviour**, which are liabilities to tax, interest and penalties within the scope of the proposed audit or audit enquiry (including related liabilities for tax heads or periods that are not within the initial scope of the audit or audit enquiry).
- The disclosure must be accompanied by a payment of the total liability arising in respect of the tax, interest and penalties.

### Preparation of a Qualifying Disclosure
In order for the company to secure an agreed period of time in which to prepare and make a qualifying disclosure, **notice of the intention** to make a disclosure must be given.

In the case of an **unprompted disclosure**, the notice of the intention to make a disclosure must be given **before:**

- a notice of audit is issued; **or**
- the company has been contacted by Revenue regarding an enquiry or investigation relating to its tax affairs.

In the case of a **prompted disclosure**, the notice of intention to make a disclosure must be given **within 14 days** of:

- the day of issue of the notification of audit; **or**
- in the case of an enquiry or "desk audit", the date the enquiry is made.

A person who has given notice within the time allowed of his intention to make a **qualifying disclosure** will be given **60 days** in which to quantify the shortfall and to make the relevant payment. This period of 60 days will begin from the day on which the notice of intention to make a disclosure was given and will be communicated to the company in writing by Revenue. The 60-day period allows the company or its agent to contact Revenue to discuss any matters arising, including the category of default on which the mitigated penalty is to be based.

### Penalty Tables for Prompted and Unprompted Disclosures
The amount of the reduction available is determined by whether a qualifying disclosure is unprompted or prompted, and whether the disclosure is for the first time or otherwise. The tables below set out the level of penalty mitigation, which are self-explanatory.

| PENALTY TABLE A | UNPROMPTED QUALIFYING DISCLOSURE MADE | | |
|---|---|---|---|
| Disclosure | Category of Behaviour | Penalty % | Full cooperation penalty reduced to |
| All unprompted qualifying disclosures in this category | Careless behaviour without significant consequences | 20% | 3% of tax/duty default |
| First unprompted qualifying disclosure in this category | Careless behaviour with significant consequences | 40% | 5% of tax/duty default |
| | Deliberate behaviour | 100% | 10% of tax/duty default |
| Second unprompted qualifying disclosure in this category | Careless behaviour with significant consequences | 40% | 20% of tax/duty default |
| | Deliberate behaviour | 100% | 55% of tax/duty default |
| Third or subsequent unprompted qualifying disclosure in this category | Careless behaviour with significant consequences | 40% | 40% of tax/duty default |
| | Deliberate behaviour | 100% | 100% of tax/duty default |

| PENALTY TABLE B | PROMPTED QUALIFYING DISCLOSURE MADE | | |
|---|---|---|---|
| Disclosure | Category of Behaviour | Penalty % | Full cooperation penalty reduced to |
| All prompted qualifying disclosures in this category | Careless behaviour without significant consequences | 20% | 10% of tax/duty default |
| First prompted qualifying disclosure in this category | Careless behaviour with significant consequences | 40% | 20% of tax/duty default |
| | Deliberate behaviour | 100% | 50% of tax/duty default |
| Second prompted qualifying disclosure in this category | Careless behaviour with significant consequences | 40% | 30% of tax/duty default |
| | Deliberate behaviour | 100% | 75% of tax/duty default |
| Third or subsequent prompted qualifying disclosure in this category | Careless behaviour with significant consequences | 40% | 40% of tax/duty default |
| | Deliberate behaviour | 100% | 100% of tax/duty default |

## 10.4  Conduct of a Revenue Audit

At the commencement of any **field audit**, the auditor identifies himself, shows his authorisation and explains to the company the purpose of the audit. The auditor will outline the authority that is vested in him under the various Finance Acts in relation to inspection of records, documents, etc. The company is **informed** about the Revenue practice on charging interest and penalties. In addition, the auditor advises the company of the **effects** of a **disclosure** regarding penalties and publication.

Having explained his authority, the auditor will normally proceed to point out that, in the event of any irregularities being found which have led to an apparent underpayment in tax, he will request a **final meeting** with the company and its agent to:

- Discuss and present a report on the results of his audit.
- Ask for comments and responses from the company and its agent.

▦ If possible, reach agreement on the undercharges (if any) under each tax heading, i.e. corporation tax, levies/USC, VAT, PAYE, PRSI, surcharges, interest and penalties.

▦ Invite the company/agent to make a formal settlement offer in writing in the event of discrepancies not being fully explained.

Following the final interview, a **written report** will be sent to the company or its agent setting out the main points arising from the audit. The auditor will also normally indicate at the interview the **approximate duration** of the audit, where it will be carried out, and will invite questions from the company and his agent in relation to the audit.

A **written record** of all requests, replies and other requirements, whether raised at the initial interview or subsequently, should be kept by the company to ensure that the audit is conducted in an orderly way. If some questions raised by the audit are complex, it may be preferable to request the auditor to submit them **in writing**.

In the case of a **desk audit**, the auditor will request records to be submitted to him for examination and, other than in exceptional circumstances, an auditor will **not retain** records for **longer than 30 days**. If more time is required, the auditor will negotiate this with the taxpayer or his agent. The 30-day period can commence only **from the date** on which the auditor has received **all** of the records requested. If items are omitted, then clearly the auditor cannot commence his audit until he has all relevant documentation.

As a matter of normal practice, Revenue **does not issue assessments** where a settlement is reached and agreed with the company and/or his agent. An assessment is normally only issued where it is **requested** by the company to enable it to take the matter before the Appeal Commissioners.

## 10.5 Review Procedures

The company, acting through its directors, has the right to request a **second opinion** in relation to the conduct of an audit in particular in relation to the following:

▦ Proposed adjustments to receipts or profits figures, claims for reliefs or allowances, other adjustments to tax computations.

▦ Penalties to be imposed.

▦ Publication of the settlement.

The request for a second opinion should be submitted in writing to the **Internal Review Unit in the Office of the Chief Inspector of Taxes**. The request should state the reasons why a review is requested and whether the company wishes the review to be carried out solely by the Inspector in charge of the Review Unit or jointly with an external reviewer.

The entitlement of the company to request a review is **separate** from the right to **appeal** any assessment raised as a result of the audit. Accordingly, if the company is not happy with the findings of the reviewer, a **statutory right** to appeal any assessment raised still exists. A review will not be granted once notification of the time and place for the hearing of an appeal has been issued to the company.

---

**Example 10.1**

It is May 2016. You are a tax senior with a mid-sized accountancy practice. You have been asked to talk to a client who has been selected for a Revenue audit next month. The audit is an "all tax heads" Revenue audit and it is for the 2015 year. The client is very concerned as to what the Revenue auditor might uncover and you have also been asked to review the books and records for the year under audit. The company has never had a Revenue audit before and therefore does not know what to expect.

*continued overleaf*

The following facts are relevant. The company, Squareball Ltd, makes GAA jerseys in a factory it owns in Mayo and has been in operation for three years. It has a sales force of four, all of whom have company cars. It supplies both the domestic and international markets, with a big demand among the Irish expat community in the UK for their replica jerseys. In 2015, the company made a loss for corporation tax purposes of €20,000.

You identified the following during your review of the books and records:

1. In early 2015, invoices were received from a solicitor's firm in London for professional advice regarding an expansion of their sales activities into the UK. The invoices, for £50,000 (say €60,000) had VAT of £8,750 (say €10,500) on them and were reclaimed through the March/April 2015 VAT. The net VAT liability for that period was €30,000.

2. The company has reclaimed all VAT on fuel costs since it started trading. On average, the VAT was €4,000 per annum. 50% relates to petrol for cars and 50% to diesel for vans.

3. They were not aware that there are Civil Service rates for subsistence and paid a flat rate to the sales reps. For 2015, you estimate that each employee was paid €1,000 in excess of the allowed rates.

4. No element of client entertainment has been disallowed. You estimate that €5,000 should be added back.

Based on your findings, you advise the client as follows:

The errors discovered will mean a settlement should be made with Revenue. To mitigate the level of Revenue penalty likely to apply, a "qualifying disclosure" should be made in writing prior to the Revenue audit commencing. As notification of a Revenue audit has been received, it is not possible to make an "unprompted qualifying disclosure", which impacts on the level of penalty. As this is the first Revenue audit and the first qualifying disclosure, mitigation of penalties should be possible if the client follows your advice on how to make the disclosure to Revenue.

Turning to the specific errors discovered:

1. This is incorrect and the VAT reclaimed needs to be disallowed. As this is quite a significant figure, Revenue may not be happy with the quantum of the error. Based on the figures for the March/April 2015 VAT 3, Revenue may regard this error as "careless behaviour with significant consequences" as the error is greater than 15% of the tax due. This has an impact on the level of penalty Revenue could seek, which in this case may be 20% of the tax assuming a prompted qualifying disclosure is made. The good news is that the UK solicitor should not have charged UK VAT on this invoice and it may be possible to seek a refund of the UK VAT paid over to them.

2. For 2015, there is a VAT over-claim of €2,000 as VAT on petrol cannot be reclaimed. It seems likely that this error has been repeated in prior years and it should be corrected. For a disclosure to be a qualifying disclosure, it must be a full disclosure, which normally would involve going back four years from the year of the Revenue audit. In this case, all the VAT on petrol over-claimed since the company started business three years ago should be worked out. The interest and the penalty should then be applied to the figures. This error would seem to be in the category of "careless behaviour without significant consequences", which means a 10% penalty for a prompted qualifying disclosure.

3. Essentially, each employee has been paid an additional salary of €1,000. As an employer, a settlement needs to be made for the PAYE/PRSI/USC that has not been paid over to Revenue. The rate of income tax and USC will depend on each employee's salary level/marginal rate. The interest and the penalty should then be applied to these figures. This error would again seem to be in the careless behaviour without significant consequences category, which means a 10% penalty for a prompted qualifying disclosure. As with the VAT error on the petrol, it should be verified as to whether this error was also made in prior years, with a settlement being made now on that. Furthermore, the correct procedures on subsistence should be put in place with immediate effect.

4. For the client entertainment, there should be no tax impact as the trading loss will simply be adjusted downwards to €15,000. It is unlikely to attract any interest or penalty, though it should be disclosed to Revenue prior to the audit commencing to ensure it is a qualifying disclosure.

## Chapter 10 Summary

**Self-assessment regime**

- Under the self-assessment regime, taxpayers have an obligation to "pay and file" by a deadline
- Revenue has the power to audit taxpayers in the self-assessment system
- Taxpayers can self-correct tax returns in certain circumstances

**Types of audit and process**

- Audit can be on a taxpayer's site or offsite
- Revenue operates within legislation and a "code of practice"
- Revenue must notify a taxpayer in writing for an on-site audit

**Consequences of audits**

- Prior to the commencement of an audit, the taxpayer has an opportunity to make a qualifying disclosure
- A qualifying disclosure must be in writing and include tax underpaid and interest thereon
- The benefits of a qualifying disclosure include the avoidance of higher penalties and publication
- The absence of a qualifying disclosure and cooperation may result in tax geared penalties of 100% on top of publication
- A taxpayer may seek a second opinion using internal review process

# Suggested Solutions to Review Questions

## Chapter 1

### Question 1.1

Terminal loss relief calculation for last 12 months of trading:

|                                                        | €        |
|--------------------------------------------------------|----------|
| Case I loss for 6 m/e 30 June 2017                     | 55,000   |
| Case I loss for 6 m/e 30 June 2016 (€5,000 × 6/12)     | (2,500)  |
| Terminal loss relief available                         | 57,500   |

Application of terminal loss relief:

|                        | 2016 | 2015      | 2014      |
|------------------------|------|-----------|-----------|
| Case 1                 | 0    | €25,000   | €22,000   |
| Sec 385 relief         | 0    | (€25,000) | (€22,000) |
| Net assessable Case I  | 0    | 0         |           |

Unutilised loss is €10,500 (€57,500 − €25,000 − €22,000).

## Chapter 6

### Question 6.1

(a)  Group relief available to GAS Limited.

OIL Limited's excess of management expenses over the total profits for the accounting period is €11,800. Management expenses do not include any amounts carried forward from earlier periods. So, in this case, the €2,500 management expenses brought forward from the previous accounting period are disregarded.

Calculation of OIL Limited's excess management expenses for the purposes of group relief.

|                                   | €       |
|-----------------------------------|---------|
| Current year management expenses  | 15,000  |
| Case III income                   | 3,200   |
| Excess management expenses        | 11,800  |

GAS Limited's total profit, as reduced by other reliefs, is €9,400, calculated as follows:

|                                        | €       |
|----------------------------------------|---------|
| Trading profits                        | 10,000  |
| Less: charges paid                     | 600     |
| Total profits as reduced by other reliefs | 9,400 |

The group relief is limited to the smaller of €11,800 and €9,400, i.e. €9,400.

(b)  Revised profits chargeable to corporation tax for the group for the year ended 31 March 2016.

OIL Limited's CT computation for the accounting period to 31 March 2016 is as follows:

|  | € |
|---|---|
| Case III income | 3,200 |
| Less: management expenses | 3,200 |
| Corporation tax profits | Nil |

OIL Limited's carry forward position as at 31 March 2016 is as follows:

|  | € | € |
|---|---|---|
| Management expenses (including amounts brought forward from earlier periods) |  | 17,500 |
| Less: allowed in computation | 3,200 |  |
| Surrendered as group relief | 9,400 | 12,600 |
| Excess management expenses available to carry forward |  | 4,900 |

GAS Limited's revised profits chargeable to corporation tax for the accounting period to 31 March 2016 are as follows:

|  | € | € |
|---|---|---|
| Case I income |  | 10,000 |
| Less: charges | 600 |  |
| Less: group relief claimed | 9,400 | 10,000 |
| Revised corporation tax profits |  | Nil |

## Question 6.2

First, we compute Company B's excess of charges over the gross profits for the accounting period.

The total profits are calculated without taking into account losses of any other period. However, chargeable gains are calculated according to CGT principles prior to being brought into the company's total profits. Thus, the allowable losses carried forward reduce the current year gains to give a net figure. This capital gain is what is recomputed as the chargeable gain for inclusion in the company's total profits, i.e. the capital gain of €3,200 is reduced by the €1,800 capital losses brought forward and then the factor of 33/12.5 is applied to give a chargeable gain of €3,696.

Calculation of Company B's excess non-trade charges:

|  |  |  |
|---|---|---|
| Charges |  | €5,500 |
| Chargeable gains as recomputed | €3,696 |  |
| Case III | €1,000 |  |
| Management expenses | (€2,000) |  |
|  |  | €2,696 |
| Excess charges |  | €2,804 |

*(continued overleaf)*

Company A's total profit as reduced by other reliefs is €1,300, calculated as follows:

| | | |
|---|---:|---:|
| Trading profits | | €1,000 |
| Case III income | €500 | |
| Less: charges paid (used to offset higher rate income first) | €200 | €300 |
| Total profits as reduced by other reliefs | | €1,300 |

The group relief is limited to the lesser of €2,804 and €1,300. Therefore, Company A can claim a maximum amount of €1,300.

## Question 6.3

1. Calculate the maximum amount of losses available for consortium relief:

   ▨ Tree Limited has losses of €400,000 available. This must first be offset against other relevant trading income under section 420A TCA 1997 before it can be used in any value-based claim. €90,000 of the losses can be used in a value-based claim under section 420B TCA 1997 to offset the Case III income.

   ▨ As Garden Limited and Tree Limited have an overlapping period of nine months, the maximum losses available are:
   9 months × €290,000 = €217,500; or
   9 months × €400,000 × 40% = €120,000.

   ▨ Maximum loss available under section 420A TCA 1997 is €120,000.

   ▨ Park Limited − €200,000 or €400,000 × 10% = €40,000. Maximum loss available under section 420A TCA 1997 is €40,000.

   ▨ Pitch Limited − €160,000 or €400,000 × 30% = €120,000. Maximum loss is €120,000 under section 420A TCA 1997. A claim under section 420B TCA 1997 is also possible and the maximum loss is the loss available for surrender (i.e. 400k − 120k − 40k − 120k − 90k = €30,000) or (€40,000 × 30%) @ 25%/12.5% (i.e. the amount of loss which needs to be claimed to reduce CT on 30% of Case III to €Nil) = €24,000. Maximum claim under section 420B TCA 1997 is €24,000.

   ▨ This ensures all of Tree's loss is used to the maximum extent possible and €6,000 is available for carry forward:

   | | |
   |---|---|
   | under section 396B TCA 1997 | €90,000 |
   | under section 420A TCA 1997 | €280,000 |
   | under section 420B TCA 1997 | €24,000 |
   | carry forward | €6,000 |

2. Calculate the corporation tax liabilities for the companies:

| | Tree Limited | Garden Limited | Park Limited | Pitch Limited |
|---|---:|---:|---:|---:|
| | € | € | € | € |
| Case I | | 290,000 | 200,000 | 160,000 |
| Less: section 420A TCA 1997 claim | | (120,000) | (40,000) | (120,000) |
| Revised Case I, taxable at 12.5% | Nil | 170,000 | 160,000 | 40,000 |
| Case III, taxable at 25% | 45,000 | Nil | Nil | 40,000 |
| Less: non-trade charge | | | (75,000) | |
| Total income | 45,000 | 170,000 | 85,000 | 80,000 |

Corporation tax payable:

| | | | | |
|---|---|---|---|---|
| @ 12.5% | Nil | 21,250 | 10,625 | 5,000 |
| @ 25% | 11,250 | Nil | Nil | 10,000 |

Less: value-based claim under
   section 420B TCA 1997
  – Tree €90,000
  – Pitch €24,000 | (11,250) | | | (3,000) |

| | | | | |
|---|---|---|---|---|
| **Final liability** | Nil | 21,250 | 10,625 | 12,000 |

# Chapter 7

## Question 7.1

The carry forward of trading losses incurred before a substantial change in ownership of a company is not allowed where, in a three-year period, there is:

(a) a change in ownership and either (b) or (c) occur;
(b) a major change in the nature or conduct of the company's trade; or
(c) the activities of the loss-making trade had become small and negligible and there is a change in ownership before any considerable revival of the trade.

A change in the machinery used might appear to be a major change. However, Revenue has said it may not consider changes made to keep pace with technology to be a major change in the nature or conduct of a trade.

   If McIlroy Limited closes the Spanish division, this might be seen as a major change in the services provided. However, as this division has been performing poorly for a number of years, it might be considered to be part of a rationalisation process and Revenue could consider the company's overall trade rather than just the Spanish division.

   Finally, the opening of a German division might be considered to be a major change in markets and customers, and therefore the losses might be not be available to carry forward against the profits of this division.

   Revenue will look at all the factors. Any change will have to be a significant one, but not necessarily a fundamental one. Qualitative and quantitative factors will be considered in reaching the decision.

## Question 7.2

(a) Rover Limited owns 12% of Ford Limited, i.e. the 8% direct holding and the 4% indirect holding through Porsche Limited. As Rover Limited controls Porsche Limited, the shares in Ford Limited are treated as being owned by Rover Limited as both companies are members of a 51% group. Thus the sale of the shares would qualify for the participation exemption.
(b) On their own, the remaining shares in Ford Limited would not qualify for the participation exemption. However, under the group provisions noted above, the exemption is still available for disposals in the 12 months following 1 July 2016. Therefore, any potential sale should be carried out before 1 July 2017.

## Chapter 8

### Question 8.1

Patrick's CGT liability would be as follows:

|  | € |
|---|---|
| Cash consideration received | 200,000 |
| Attributable base cost: | |
| $250{,}000 \times \left(\dfrac{200{,}000}{200{,}000 + 200{,}000}\right)$ | (125,000) |
| Chargeable gain | 75,000 |

Patrick will be liable to CGT on a €75,000 gain arising by virtue of cash received on foot of the reconstruction of Worldscape, subject to any available CGT reliefs that would reduce his gain.

### Question 8.2

Joe's CGT will be computed as follows:

|  | € |
|---|---|
| Consideration | 1,000,000 |
| Less: cost | |
| Original shares | (20,000) |
| Enhancement expenditure | (100,000) |
| Chargeable gain | 880,000 |

Joe is liable to 33% CGT on the above chargeable gain, subject to any available reliefs that would reduce his gain.

# CHARTERED TAX CONSULTANT